WALKING IN FRANCE

GILLIAN AND JOHN SOUTER

Interlink Books

An imprint of Interlink Publishing Group, Inc.
Northampton, Massachusetts

First American edition published 2006 by

Interlink Books
An imprint of Interlink Publishing Group, Inc.
46 Crosby Street, Northampton, Massachusetts 01060
www.interlinkbooks.com

Library of Congress Cataloging-in-Publication Data

Souter, Gillian.
Walking in France : exploring France's great towns and finest landscapes on foot / by Gillian and John Souter.— 1st American ed.
p. cm.
Includes bibliographical references and index.
ISBN 1-56656-619-3 (pbk. : alk. paper)
1. Walking—France—Guidebooks.
2. France—Guidebooks. I. Souter, John.
II. Title.
DC16.S67 2006
914.404'84—dc22

2005021183

Cover Images: Top: Country road in France; Authors Image / Alamy
Bottom: Lavender in Provence; Dynamic Graphics Group / IT Stock

Printed and bound in China

To request our complete 40-page full-color catalog, please call us toll-free at 1-800-238-LINK, visit our website at www.interlinkbooks.com, or send us an e-mail: info@interlinkbooks.com.

CONTENTS

INTRODUCTION

The French have made an artform of walking: every shade of variation has been named. The philosophical stroll – when one ambles with no destination but an open mind – is a *flânerie* and one who indulges in this is a *flâneur*. A *balade* is a walk with more direction but little serious purpose; a *promenade* has more of a social function. Then there is the *marche*, the *petite randonnée*, the *tour* and, of course, the *grande randonnée*, outings of increasing length and with a specified route.

True, we have many synonyms for 'a walk' in English, but the French seem to infuse theirs with far greater meaning and then make full use of them. Walking, as a pastime, is a popular activity in France and the rigour with which the French mark and record their walking routes is remarkable. This, of course, is a great boon to those of us who wish to see their country at walking pace.

For France is a country that repays close inspection. It boasts a vast array of diverse and beautiful landscapes: vine-covered hills, deep gorges, jagged coastline, snow-capped peaks, to name a few. Its regions have a distinct cultural identity, visible in local costume and architecture, audible in its many dialects and edible in local cuisine. The French are particularly proud of their local *patrimonie* or heritage; major historical events took place right across the country. There are signs of Celtic settlement, Roman occupation, the monastic movement, Wars of Religion, Anglo-French conflict, the Renaissance, Revolutionary and Napoleonic forces in the most surprising places. The effect of encountering these sites on foot is far more profound than that created when alighting from a bus and joining a tour group. The same holds true in cities: the view from the ground has more immediacy and permanence than through the coach window. This book is designed for people who have a love of landscapes and an interest in historic and cultural aspects of the cityscape. It's for those who like to travel slowly, getting a sense of a region as somewhere people live and have lived.

Walking holidays are becoming a more popular travel option with each year and an array of tour companies provide packaged walking trips, guided or self-guided, to the better-known destinations in France. Such tours have their place, but they can be inflexible and expensive and France's well marked network of footpaths makes such restrictions unnecessary. The prospect of walking independently in a foreign country poses a few challenges: where and when to walk; which villages to stop at; which walks to try; how to get to the trail head; what map to buy... Our aim is to ease you into the great delights of independent walking by providing answers to such questions and to offer plenty of inspirational walking ideas. We've personally 'road-tested' all the main walks and most of the supplementary ones at the end of each chapter. One of us took the photographs en route, so they're a real reflection of what there is to see when you head off along the path. We hope you have as much fun as we did!

< On foot in France

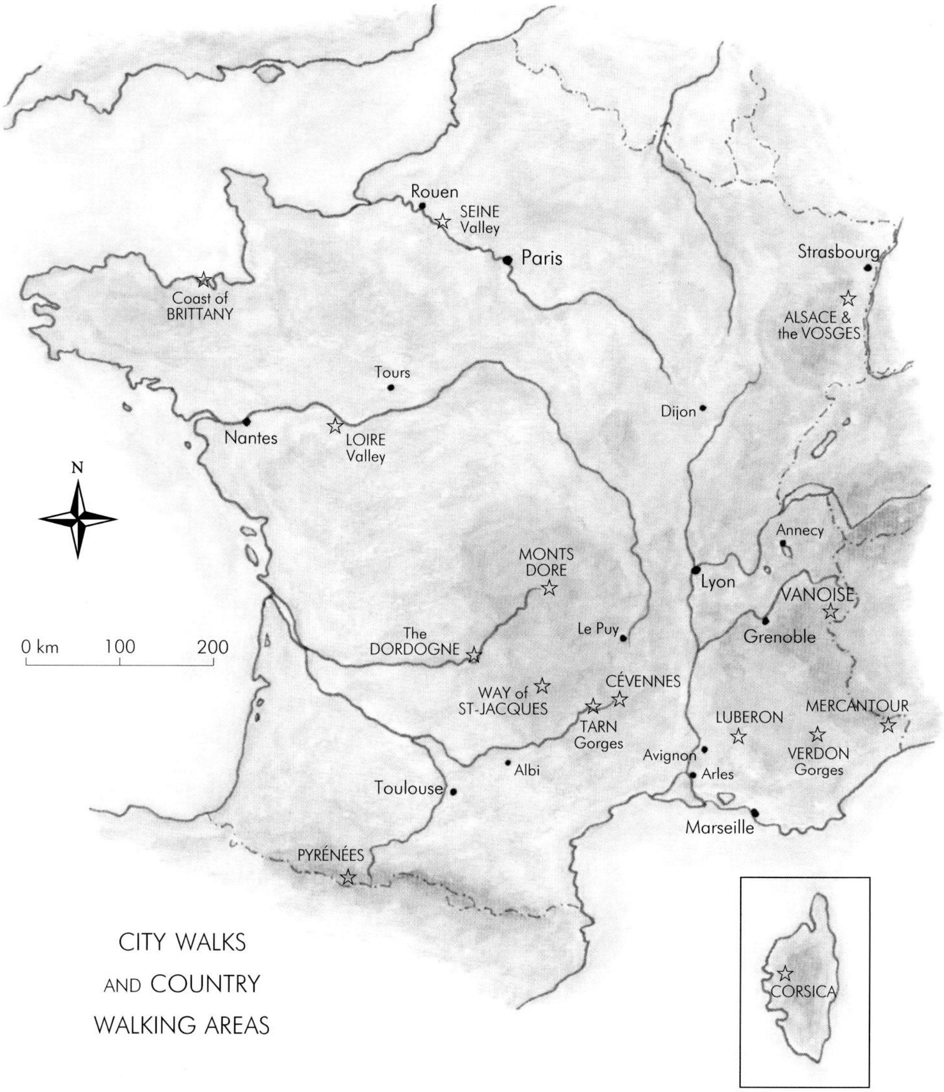

Rouen
SEINE Valley
Paris
Strasbourg
ALSACE & the VOSGES
Coast of BRITTANY
Tours
Dijon
Nantes
LOIRE Valley
N
Annecy
MONTS DORE
Lyon
VANOISE
Grenoble
Le Puy
0 km 100 200
The DORDOGNE
CÉVENNES
WAY of ST-JACQUES
TARN Gorges
LUBERON
MERCANTOUR
VERDON Gorges
Avignon
Arles
Albi
Toulouse
Marseille
PYRÉNÉES
CORSICA

CITY WALKS AND COUNTRY WALKING AREAS

KEY TO MAPS
starting point
walking route
walk extension
road
river / waterfall
fortified walls
rail station
M
metro / bus station
tourist office
viewpoint
settled area
church / ruin
steps
château
refuge / cave
natural feature
mountain pass
mountain peak
glacier
lake

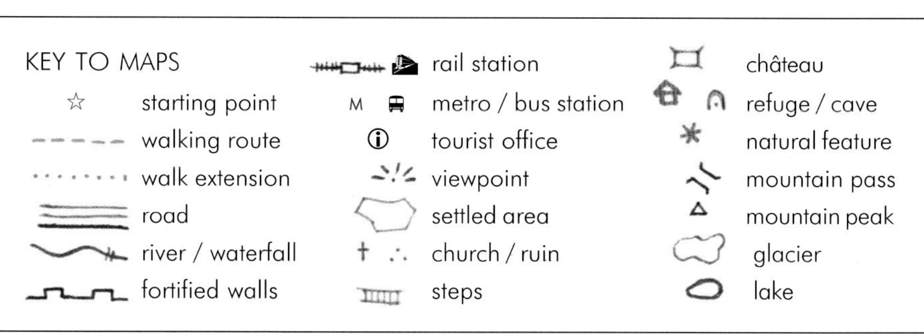

A *balise* in Brittany >

THE FRENCH PATH SYSTEM

Walking clubs first developed in mountain regions such as the Vosges and, in 1874, the *Club Alpin Français* (CAF) was formed for mountaineers. France's popular cycling club added an arm specifically for walkers in 1904. These fragmented groups worked together to create, in 1947, a national body to promote walking: today it is known as the *Fédération Française de la Randonnée Pédestre* or FFRP. Its volunteers have waymarked over 60,000 km of long distance paths – old mule paths, drove tracks or pilgrimage routes – as *grandes randonnées* or GRs. The standard waymark for these is a red-and-white stripe, usually painted on a tree or boulder. Some of the walks in this book are sections of a longer GR; others make use of various GRs to create a unique route.

There are even more kilometres of shorter routes called PRs (*promenades et randonnées*), waymarked with a single stripe in either blue, yellow, green or black. National parks tend to mark walking tracks using their own system, often with a yellow signpost or *balisé*. A variation on the linear long-distance path is the GR de Pays: a loop that explores a region, marked with red-and-yellow stripes. Horse-riding trails are marked in orange.

< Path waymarking

OUR WALKS

There is something extremely satisfying in a long-distance walk, especially when you get a comfortable bed and a good meal each night. We've made full use of the GR system and many of the chapters that follow outline multi-day walks. In these cases, we've included a boxed breakdown of the itinerary, listing any location en route offering accommodation. If our staging of the walk doesn't suit you, use this to plot an itinerary that suits you better.

In mountain areas, where the weather is more changeable, we've usually suggested day walks from a base. Almost all the country walks, whether in mountains or not, will involve ascents and descents! Needless to say, the fitter you are, the more you'll enjoy it, so do some walking beforehand. We're assuming a reasonable level of fitness and stamina to walk for some hours though we've allocated each walk a grading. Our estimate of walking times excludes lunch breaks. We haven't given times for the city walks as these will depend greatly on how long you spend at each point of interest.

Our grading scheme is necessarily

subjective and gradings assume decent weather and that the path remains in its current condition. Our gradings take into account the route length and distance, height gained and lost, navigational difficulty and the roughness of the path.

WHERE TO GO

This book offers a selection of places that are ideal for walking, organised roughly down the west coast and then down the eastern half. If you think this is your one and only chance to visit France, you'll no doubt want to visit Paris, a city that bears revisiting many times.

Our ideal holiday would combine a few towns interspersed with nearby country areas. Some of the walks start in or near interesting cities: the Seine valley south of Rouen, the Vosges not far from Strasbourg, the Vercors southwest of Grenoble and the Calanques on the outskirts of Marseilles. In the case of Le Puy where the St Jacques pilgrimage commences, the one is a logical precursor to the other. With France's excellent rail system and fast TGV service, nothing is very far from anything else.

THE TOWNS

Paris is a city that rewards many return visits. We have included four walks that take in its major sights, but it's a paradise for *flâneurs*. Our selection of other city and town walks is unashamedly subjective and necessarily incomplete. Some cities are industrialised or have lost their old core to bombing. Some, such as Nice and Aix-en-Provence are popular with tourists but didn't greatly appeal to us. We've included some, such as Nantes and Toulouse, because they make good stops in a journey. Others – Annecy, Arles, Albi, Le Puy – are gems that shouldn't be overlooked by anyone.

THE COUNTRY

Our most difficult decisions revolved around which parts of France's wonderfully varied

You'll need a break from town walking

back country or *arrière-pays* to include. The renown of the Loire valley and that of the Dordogne made them automatic inclusions. France has some wonderful coastline and it was difficult to select only a section of the rugged Brittany and Côte d'Azur coasts to walk. Most of the best walking, though, is to be had in the southern half of France, and much of this book is centred here. There you are spoiled for choice, regardless of whether you prefer farmland (the Dordogne), river gorges (the Verdon and Tarn) or more mountainous terrain (the Pyrénées, Vanoise or Mercantour). France's islands are represented here by the largest, Corsica. There are countless other areas that offer excellent walking; some have been mentioned briefly in the back of the book.

One of the bonuses of country walking is the opportunity to see wildlife, though sadly, French hunters have seen to it that there's not too much left, outside of national parks. Most likely, you'll spy some soaring birds of prey, present both in wild and farmed countryside. Wild boars are quite common in woodland, though you're more likely to hear them or to see only the signs of their

A shy marmot

scrabbling in the earth. In high regions above the treeline, you may be fortunate enough to witness marmots, chamois and ibex; your chances are increased in national parks.

Wildflowers are much thicker on the ground and spring and early summer are the best times to see them. The vegetation of the Mediterranean areas is quite different to the Alpine flora. The meadows and gardens of the north – Normandy, Brittany, Alsace and the Loire valley – are ablaze with flowers in summer.

WHEN TO GO WHERE

France is affected by three major climatic influences: the Atlantic, the Continental and the Mediterranean. The first gives Brittany and Normandy frequent but light rainfall. Alsace gets more rain and is cooler. The Massif Central has cold and wet winters but warm and dry summers. Further south, including in Corsica, the Mediterranean leads to hot, dry summers and heavy thunderstorms in spring and autumn. This is an over-simplification, but it offers a rough guide for your travel plans.

Country walking is more constrained by season and climate than is walking in towns and cities but, whatever the time of year, you can find walks in this book to suit.

July and August, the hottest months, are also the most touristed. The French take their holidays *en masse* from mid-July to the end of August; stay well clear of the coast at this time.

June to September is the best time for walking in mountain areas. Here, wild-flowers are at their best in June and early July. Services – buses, *refuges*, chairlifts, etc. – can be severely reduced either side of mid-June and mid-September. Adjusted summer time (which runs to late October) gives you an extra hour for walking. Avoid low-altitude walks during summer, especially in Provence or Corsica.

Away from the mountains, spring and autumn are ideal walking seasons. Winter is no barrier to city walking, but be prepared for near-freezing temperatures in the north.

HOW TO TRAVEL

We confess to a strong public transport bias. France has an excellent and inexpensive rail system that, in combination with local bus services, will take you almost everywhere. Using public transport is environmentally-

The Paris métro

friendly, less stressful and means that you don't have a rental car sitting idly while you walk. However, you do need to read any timetables carefully.

The state rail system is known as SNCF and their website (www.sncf.fr) can be extremely useful for planning your itinerary. Note that buses replace trains on some rural lines. The local tourist websites given at the start of each chapter may provide some bus information, and you could email them if you have a particular transport query.

WHERE TO STAY

Most French cities and towns offer a good range of accommodation, from small, family-run hotels to more opulent affairs. You might also consider an *auberge de jeunesse* or hostel in towns. Information on hotels is available in the countless guide books currently published; select a guide pitched at your comfort level and budget. Alternatively, some tourist office websites list hotels and prices, particularly in rural regions. Avoid the sites of commercial agencies, as these tend to list only the more expensive hotels.

In the countryside, hotels will be fewer and simpler, but you might have other options. These include *chambres d'hôtes* offering a room in a home, breakfast and sometimes dinner, and *gîtes d'étape* (not to be confused with plain *gîtes* or self-contained cottages). A *gîte d'étape* is like a small hostel for walkers (usually on or near GR paths), offering a cheap bunk for a night or two. If privately operated, the owner will probably be on hand to cook a hearty dinner and a simple breakfast. A *gîte communale* is an unmanned *gîte d'étape* that is run by the village; you'll need to collect the key and cater for yourself (or find a restaurant). Mountain routes above villages are well supplied with *refuges*, operated by the CAF or the national park. There's a great sense of camaraderie to be had at *gîtes d'étape* and *refuges*, where you're among fellow walkers. Both types of accommodation are marked on 1:25,000 maps and the site www.gites-refuges.com has a comprehensive listing.

A gîte d'étape in the Pyrénées

A mountain refuge

Available options along a long-distance walk are summarised in a box at the end of the walk notes, under 'acc': H for hotel, C for *chambre d'hôte*, G for *gîte d'étape*, A for *auberge de jeunesse*, F for *ferme-auberge* and R for *refuge*.

Whether or not you book ahead should depend on the season, your itinerary and level of flexibility. At the least, you might want to phone each morning to ensure you have a bed that night. The local tourist office will also be able to assist and may find you a bed if you arrive with nothing reserved.

WHAT TO TAKE

We pack lightly and wash clothes often. Modern fabrics that dry quickly are a great boon to the walker-traveller. Trousers with zip-off legs are versatile in changeable weather. Take a good pair of walking boots that you have already worn in, plus a light pair of comfortable shoes for night or city. Thin lining socks, worn in conjunction with a pair of thick socks, can increase comfort and reduce washing. You'll also need a good waterproof jacket, sunscreen and sunglasses.

Aluminium or nalgene water bottles are lightweight but much more sturdy than a supermarket plastic bottle. A penknife is indispensable for picnics; pack it in your main luggage on flights. A torch can be quite useful for investigating caves and unlit churches and for the occasional tunnel. A compass is handy, not only if you lose your way, but for identifying major landmarks. A compact pair of binoculars is good both for watching distant wildlife and for inspecting high architectural detail. Pack a lightweight towel and some soap if you plan to stay in *gîtes d'étape* or *refuges*. We carry several things that we hope not to use: a basic first-aid kit, whistle and blister plasters.

Depending on the season and your destination, you might need gloves, a warm hat, warm polypropolene garments (thermals), or conversely, shorts and swimwear. A sunhat is essential year round. Collapsible walking poles are a good investment if, like us, you plan to keep walking into old age. They are particularly useful for saving your knees on steep descents and ascents, and for crossing streams, loose scree or muddy patches.

We each take a lightweight day-pack as our hand luggage on flights and then carry these on day walks or in cities. We each use a 65-litre backpack as our main luggage and leave space in it for lunch provisions and the daypack. Combination packs (two different packs that join) are not really suitable for long-distance walking.

Never carry this much!

USING THIS BOOK

This is a walking book, rather than a general guide. It contains few accommodation or dining recommendations, nor does it provide detailed information on transport, entry fees and so on. Most readers will probably want to supplement this book with a general guide book on France or with something more specialised on a particular region or city.

The schematic maps in this book are a good starting point and for city walks could prove sufficient for your needs, but we do recommend buying a good topographical map in country areas. These can sometimes be bought in advance at a map shop in your own country or online. Alternatively, you should be able to buy a map from the local bookshop or newspaper shop when you arrive in a particular region. A key to the maps in this book appears on page 5.

Visit the local market for picnic fare >

OTHER TRAVEL INFORMATION

France is well served with tourist offices. In cities and towns there will be an Office du Tourisme (OT) that can usually provide a free town map and information on local accommodation and transport. Smaller towns and some villages may have a Syndicat d'Initiative (SI), a tourist office that aims to encourage business. Walkers take little account of administrative boundaries so there isn't always a single source of information for our long-distance routes. National park offices are a good source of information on walking paths and walkers' accommodation.

WARNINGS & TIPS

Here are a few suggestions to make your trip safer and more enjoyable.

In cities and towns, opening hours can be a source of frustration. The hours of galleries, museums and other attractions are usually shorter in winter months. Details appear at the chapter's end (in order of appearance in the walk) but they can change.

Shopping for lunch supplies (and then consuming them) is one of the joys of walking in France. An early visit to the *boulangerie* for bread, the *charcuterie* for *saussicon* or *pâte*, the *épicerie* for fruit and, of course, the *pâtisserie* for a little snack, is all part of our walking ritual. On country walks, always pack an emergency food supply – some chocolate at least – even if you expect to buy lunch en route. Take plenty of water and refill bottles at every opportunity.

If you've built up a good appetite by the end of the day, the *menu fixe* – a set number of courses with limited choice of dishes – is usually excellent value and a good way to taste regional dishes.

Watch out for poisonous vipers in summer and for men with guns during the hunting season, particularly in October. Don't start a mountain walk in uncertain weather conditions (ask your host or the tourist office) and don't be too proud to turn back if you're having any difficulty.

On slopes, don't short cut the track as this causes erosion. Where a path passes through farmland, respect the owner's rights by obeying signs, closing gates and not damaging crops. In national parks and reserves, it goes without saying that wildflowers are protected.

Those who live in rural France can seldom speak English but will greatly appreciate any attempts you make at French. While a command of the language is not essential, a smattering of words and phrases is certainly useful and will make your trip more enjoyable.

You can often stay in smaller towns and visit cities on a day trip. Sometimes we'll visit a town or city in transit, leaving our luggage at the rail station and walking around unencumbered, then collecting it and heading on to our night's destination.

Everyone develops his or her own pace and style of travel, the idiosyncrasies of which make it such a fascinating experience. We hope you can adapt the information in this book to your own needs and likes, and enjoy what France has to offer!

Paris

There is a great deal of romance attached to the city of Paris. For some this stems from its famous monuments: Gustave Eiffel's steel tower, the Gothic masterpiece of Notre-Dame, Napoleon's triumphal arch, to name a few. Others find its attraction in smaller things like its streetscapes, cafés, quays and bridges. Part of the adventure is making your own discoveries.

From boulevard to winding alley, this is a city that demands to be explored on foot, although you may want to make use of its excellent métro system to start and finish your wanderings. Paris is a compact city of twenty *arrondissements*, sections that begin at the Louvre and spiral clockwise to end at the easterly Porte de Vincennes. The Seine courses through the middle, dividing Paris into *rive droite* and *rive gauche*, or the Right Bank and Left Bank.

Mid-river are two connected islands, Île de la Cité and Île Saint-Louis, where Paris was first settled well over two thousand years ago. Clovis I, the Frankish king adopted it as capital of his small kingdom of France in 508. French kings endowed the city with palaces and churches, while their courtiers built grand mansions. Emperors continued the tradition and Napoléon III had his city planner Baron Haussmann remodel the city with grand boulevards. Modernisation continues with such buildings as the Pompidou Centre and the Louvre pyramid, both of which were controversial not so long ago.

Despite, or perhaps because of, changes over the centuries, the Seine threads together some very different quarters. The *quartier* Latin, home to Paris students for eight centuries, is a world away from the bustle of the Opéra quarter. This, in turn, has a different atmosphere to the quiet Marais with its 17th-century *hôtels*. Each museum also offers a world in miniature: that of Rodin or Picasso, or the great span of artistic endeavour captured in the Musée d'Orsay or the Louvre. We have one piece of advice: wear comfortable shoes.

NOTES

Getting there: rail from CDG airport (25 km NE); bus-rail from Orly (14 km S)
Tourist Office: 127 Av.des Champs-Élysées ☏ 0836683112 Fax: 0149525300
www.paris-touristoffice.com
Markets: include Rue de Buci 6e and Rue Mouffetard 5e, both Tue-Sun 8-1
Note: a 1-, 3- or 5-day museum and monument pass is available

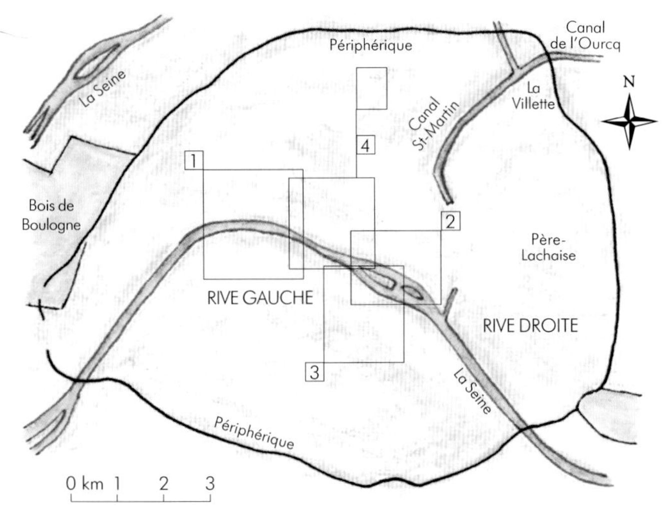

Catching Paris on canvas >

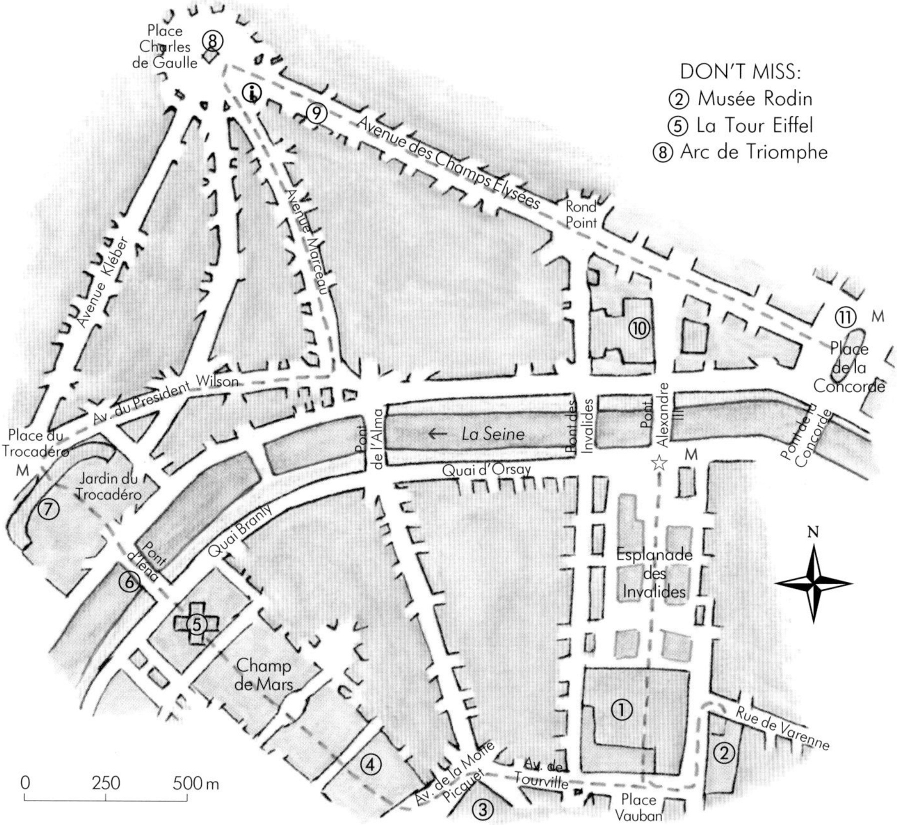

DON'T MISS:
② Musée Rodin
⑤ La Tour Eiffel
⑧ Arc de Triomphe

WALK 1: MONUMENTAL PARIS

This pilgrimage around the larger Paris landmarks can be shortened somewhat with a métro ride midway.

The walk begins by Pont Alexandre III, built for the 1900 exhibition, on the left bank of the Seine (*métro Invalides*). Stroll down the Esplanade, lined with limes, and through the gardens of

① **Les Invalides**, erected in the 1670s by Louis XIV to house some 4000 disabled veterans. The buildings on either side of the main courtyard contain a military museum. Beyond it is the classical Église du Dôme, designed by Hardouin-Mansart and completed in 1735. It holds, in great pomp, the tomb of Napoleon, whose body lies in six coffins, one within another, and then in a red porphyry sarcophagus.

Les Invalides >

Exit at Place Vauban where you should make a detour around the east side of Les Invalides and into Rue de Varenne to visit
② **Musée Rodin**. The 1728 Hôtel Biron and its garden are a beautiful setting for the sculptures of Auguste Rodin, who lived and worked in the mansion before his death in 1917. This lovely museum offers a tranquil space in sharp contrast to the rest of this walk!

Return to Place Vauban and walk west to skirt the corner of the
③ **École Militaire**, built in the 1760s as a military academy, originally for youths 'without means'. The young Napoleon trained here as a lieutenant; it is still a military school and is closed to the public.

Cross Avenue de la Motte Piquet and enter
④ **Champ de Mars**, laid out as the parade ground for the École Militaire, but opened to the public in 1780. The first hydrogen-filled balloon was launched here in 1783. Various World Exhibitions were held here; towards the end of the gardens stands an artefact from the one held in 1889:
⑤ **La Tour Eiffel**. This Paris landmark was, at 300 m, the highest construction in the world. Many artists and writers protested the plan, but Gustave Eiffel's tower proceeded. It was

La Tour Eiffel

Musée Rodin

Arc de Triomphe

almost pulled down in 1909, but its value for modern communications (a television tower has since added a further 20m) saved it and it is now an integral part of the Paris skyline. Visitors can climb steps up to the 1st or 2nd platforms, or catch a lift as high as the 3rd.

Cross Quai Branly, on which you'll find the new museum of ancient civilizations, and then cross over the Seine on the

⑥ **Pont d'Iéna**, built at the command of Napoleon. When the Empire fell, it was almost pulled down since it glorified a Prussian defeat but was saved at the request of Louis XVII.

Now walk up through the formal **Jardin du Trocadéro**, named after the site of an 1823 victory over the Spanish. This brings you to a terrace with a fine view back over the Tour Eiffel. This hill was the site of a country estate for Catherine de Medici in the late 16th century; her mansion later served as a convent. Napoleon razed this, planning to build a palace for his son, but events intruded. The white, two-winged

⑦ **Palais de Chaillot**, was erected for the 1937 World Exhibition. Today it houses theatres and museums of French naval history and of French monuments.

From Place du Trocadéro, dominated by a statue of Marshal Foch, you could catch the *métro* to *Ch.de Gaulle-Etoile*. Alternatively, walk east along Avenue du President Wilson. Past Place d'Iéna, you pass between the 1888 **Palais Galliera** (left, now a costume museum) and the **Palais de Tokyo**, built for the 1937 exhibition and how housing a museum of modern art. Turn left into Avenue Marceau, passing **St Pierre de Chaillot**, built in 1937 in neo-Romanesque style. The area to your right is known as the **Triangle d'Or**, and constitutes an exclusive neighbourhood of fine residences and hotels. Continue north to Place Charles de Gaulle where stands the

⑧ **Arc de Triomphe**. This monument to his own victories was commissioned by Napoleon in 1806. It was completed in 1836 and has since seen various armies march through it in triumph. In 1920 the body of an unknown WWI soldier was interred beneath the arch. Across the road are steps leading underground that allow you access to the arch; from the top there's a marvellous view of the twelve avenues that radiate out, and of the traffic chaos below.

Now make your way along that most famous thoroughfare of Paris, the

⑨ **Champs Élysées.** This fashionable avenue was given its name – the Elysian Fields – in 1709, when it ran through countryside. It's heyday was during the Second Empire (1852-1870) but it is still a rallying point for Parisians. The most attractive section is that beyond the Rond Point, where you pass by the

⑩ **Grand et Petit Palais,** halls built for the 1900 World Exhibition. The Grand Palais now serves as a convention centre; the Petit contains a museum of art, antiques and objets d'art.

Further along, just beyond the replica **Chevaux de Marly** (the originals are in the Louvre) you enter

⑪ **Place de la Concorde.** This immense square was laid out for Louis XV. In 1793, it was the site of the guillotine for the execution of Louis XVI and, from then until 1795, 1343 more victims were beheaded here. It was given its optimistic name shortly after. The pink granite obelisk is some 3300 years old and was a gift from the Viceroy of Egypt to Charles X.

Nearby is the *Concorde métro.*

Pont Neuf

The view from Notre-Dame

WALK 2: ISLANDS & RIGHT BANK

A scenic walk from Paris' birthplace, via its Renaissance centre, to the modern structures of the Centre Pompidou and Les Halles.

From *métro Pont Neuf* cross over to Île de la Cité on the **Pont Neuf,** the city's oldest bridge, completed in 1604 and decorated with grotesques above the arches. The Cité, as the island is known, was the site of the first settlement when, around 250 BC, boatmen of the Parisii tribe made it their home. Behind the statue of Henri IV is a square known as Vert-Galant (Henri's nickname) from where there's a fine view upstream.

Walk through the shaded Place Dauphine, laid out in 1607; the façade of no.14 remains much as it did then. Follow Quai de l'Horloge where you'll find the entrance to the

① **Conciergerie,** built as a royal palace in the 14th century, but later used as a prison and place of torture. During the Revolution, as many as 1200 men and women were held here at any one time, awaiting trial by the Tribunal that met in the Palais des Justice next door. Inside,

The Conciergerie

you can visit various royal chambers and the prison cell of Marie-Antoinette.

Around the corner, passing the Tour de l'Horloge where a public clock has been mounted since 1370, are the massive gates to the **Palais de Justice**, still operating as law courts. Security is tight, but you need to enter the complex to see the Gothic jewel of ② **Sainte Chapelle**. When Louis IX acquired various relics (including a Crown of Thorns) he commissioned a chapel in which to treasure them. Completed in a mere 33 months and consecrated in 1248, it was a great feat of architecture. The lower chapel was for palace servants; the upper chapel is breathtakingly beautiful, a royal blaze of stained glass, seemingly unsupported by walls.

Return through the gates and walk up Rue de Lutece passing, on your left, a flower market. Cross Rue de la Cité and gain the Place du Parvis (a corruption of *paradise*). In the centre is a bronze plaque marking **Point Zéro**, from where all road distances in France are measured. Ahead is the beautifully proportioned west façade of the

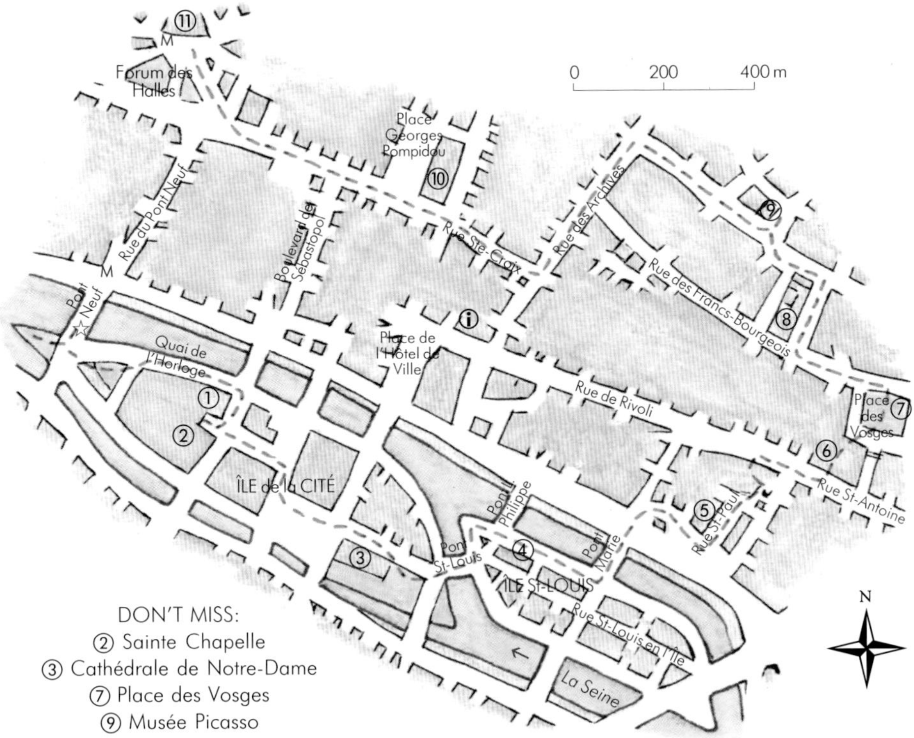

DON'T MISS:
② Sainte Chapelle
③ Cathédrale de Notre-Dame
⑦ Place des Vosges
⑨ Musée Picasso

Detail, Sainte Chapelle

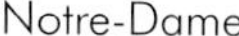

Notre-Dame

③ **Cathédrale de Notre-Dame**, built on the site of a Roman temple. This Gothic masterpiece was begun in 1163 and took almost two centuries to construct, unusually, without any changes to the original plans. Various coronations have taken place here but during the Revolution it was renamed the Temple of Reason and used to store food. Restoration was undertaken in the 19th century under the control of Viollet-le-Duc, who rebuilt the spire.

Inside, the huge rose windows of the west face and transept are mesmerising; the north one, depicting the virgin surrounded by Old Testament figures, has remained virtually intact since the 13th century. An ascent of the north tower gives you a close encounter with the gargoyles, the great bell, and a splendid view over the river and the whole of the city.

Behind the cathedral is a formal garden laid out in 1844, from where you can enjoy its east end, bedecked with flying buttresses. Now take Pont St-Louis to arrive on

④ **Île St-Louis**, which was two islets before they were joined in the early 17th century and the land sold for housing. The consistency of its architecture and the lack of major monuments lends its streets a charming tranquility. Its artery, Rue St Louis en l'Île, is lined with boutique art galleries. Walk around

Place des Vosges

the tip of the island and along Quai de Bourbon, enjoying a view of St-Gervais across the river, to arrive at Pont Marie.

Cross to the Right Bank and soon reach the lovely garden of the **Hôtel de Sens**, one of only three medieval private residences remaining in Paris. Wind around the mansion via Rue du Figuier to enter its courtyard: as well as charming Flamboyant Gothic detail, it contains excellent toilets. Walk along Rue de l'Ave Maria, then turn left along Rue St-Paul, following the

⑤ **defensive wall** built by Philippe August early in the 13th century. This also served as a dyke when the area now known as the Marais was cleared and made habitable.

Cross Rue Charlemagne and follow Passage St-Paul to enter **St-Paul-St-Louis**, a baroque church built by the Jesuits in 1641. Leave the church by its main door and turn right along Rue St-Antoine to reach the

⑥ **Hôtel de Sully**, one of the mansions that were built in the Marais when the district became fashionable in the early 17th century. Walk through the gate and admire its lavishly decorated courtyard before continuing through the *orangerie* to enter the

⑦ **Place des Vosges**, the oldest square in Paris. Henri IV commissioned this architectural beauty; when completed in 1612, it became the playground of the elegant rich. Famous residents of the 36 symmetrical houses have included Richelieu and the writer Victor Hugo, whose home is now a museum. The present name honours the fact that the Vosges department was first to pay its taxes in 1800.

Cross the square to the Pavillon de la Reine and stroll under the arcade, then along Rue des Francs-Bourgeois, named for the *francs* or almshouses at nos.34 & 36. In the 17th-18th centuries the aristocracy relocated to Versailles and then to the 7th arrondissement, and the Marais became less fashionable. After the Revolution it fell into decay; restoration of the district is a relatively recent thing and many old mansions are now small museums. One such is found at no.23 Rue de Sévigné.

⑧ **Musée Carnavalet** covers the entire history of Paris, including an excellent array of items relating to the Revolution. The collection is displayed in two adjoining Renaissance mansions, well worth a look themselves.

At the end of Rue de Sévigné, turn left into Rue du Parc Royal where there is a children's playground; if you need a rest, there's a quieter park around the corner in Rue Payenne. Cross Place de Thorigny to visit the ⑨ **Musée Picasso**, housed in the 1659 Hôtel Salé that was built for a salt-tax collector. It's a delightful setting for an amazing array of Picasso's paintings and sculptures, arranged in chronological order so you gain a sense of the artist's development.

Retrace your steps a short way and turn right along Rue de la Perle. After the next crossroads you pass, on your left, the **Hôtel de Rohan**, once the residence of four successive cardinals. Further on, to the right you pass a screened garden belonging to **Hôtel Guénégaud**, built in 1650. Turn right into Rue des Archives to look into the courtyard of the mansion that now houses a museum of hunting.

Now head south down Rue des Archives, so named because the national archives have their headquarters in the very elegant **Hôtel de Soubise**, entered by its 14th-century gate at 60 Rue des Francs-Bourgeois. Continue along Rue des Archives until, on the left, you reach the **Clôitre Billettes**, the only remaining medieval cloister in Paris. Cross the road and wind around into Rue Ste-Croix de la Bretonnerie that brings you to the infamous ⑩ **Centre Georges Pompidou**. In order to keep the interior spacious for the display of modern art, the architects chose to put all the structural elements on the outside of the building, all colour coded by function.

Musée Picasso

St-Eustache

Continue west along Rue Aubry le Boucher, strolling through the **Square des Innocents**, that stands on the site of a 12th-century cemetery. The Renaissance fountain had only three decorated sides in its original position; when it was moved here in the 18th century, a fourth was added.

Beyond the square is the **Forum des Halles**, a huge underground shopping mall. It replaced the old markets known as Les Halles that operated here until 1969. Cut diagonally across the park to reach the beautiful church of ⑪ **St-Eustache**, erected in Gothic style from 1532 to 1637, with a west façade added later. Inside, the decoration is mostly Renaissance and the gigantic, 8000-pipe organ is often used for concerts; indeed, the church has a long tradition of musical excellence.

Outside, you may be tempted to join children clambering on the giant sculpted *l'Ecoute*. The nearest *métro* is *Les Halles*, just nearby.

WALK 3: THE LEFT BANK

Discover the remains of Roman Paris and visit some haunts of the city's intellectuals and philosophers on this fascinating tour.

Just by the new Pont Solferino, and above a new *métro* station, is an elegant 1900 building designed by Victor Laloux to house the terminus of the Orleans rail line. Its role as a major station ended in 1939 and the iron and glass structure was almost demolished in 1970. Fortunately, it was restored to open in 1986 as ① the **Musée d'Orsay**. Its collection of visual arts range from 1848 to 1914, bridging the gap between the Louvre and the Pompidou Centre, displayed in a wonderfully airy interior. The balcony off the museum café has good views across the Seine to Montmartre.

Walk upstream along Quai Voltaire. Its 18th-century houses have been the residence of many well known names, including Ingres, Corot, Baudelaire, Sibelius, Oscar Wilde and Voltaire, who both lived and died at no.27. On Quai Malaquais you pass the French school of fine arts and then the domed **Institut de France**, home of various organisations including the Académie française, whose 40 members, known as *Immortels*, strive to preserve French culture.

Just before the Pont Neuf is the **Hôtel des Monnaies**, an 18th-century building that houses the mint. Beyond this you pass the quaint Rue de Nevers, a blind medieval alley. Continue along Quai des Grands Augustins, built in 1313, and at Place St-Michel, fork

Musée d'Orsay >

down Rue de la Harpe to reach the beautiful late Gothic church of
② **St Séverin**. Named after a 6th-century hermit who lived hereabouts, the present church was completed in the early 16th century. The attraction inside is its unusual double ambulatory. Outside, peer through the railings at the gable-roofed charnel house or *charniers* where bones were once stacked to make room in the graveyard. The first known operation for gall stones took place here in 1474 on a man condemned to death; the lucky fellow survived and won his freedom.

Head south, cross the Boulevard St-Germain, then take the quiet Rue de Cluny to enter the ③ **Musée du Moyen-Age**, housed in the 16th-century Hôtel de Cluny and in the adjoining remains of Gallo-Roman baths. This stunning collection of medieval art and artefacts has as its highlight the series of late 15th-century tapestries called *La Dame à la Licorne* (the Lady and the Unicorn) that should not be missed.

Wend onto Rue St-Jacques, one of Paris' oldest roads, to skirt France's first university, ④ the **Sorbonne**, founded in 1253 by Robert de Sorbon as a college to train 16 poor students in theology. Communication between students and teachers was in Latin so the area acquired the name of *Quartier Latin*. In 1968 a student uprising led to the decentralisation of the Paris University but some lectures are still held here.

Panthéon

Turn left at Rue Soufflot, named after the architect of the domed building ahead, the ⑤ **Panthéon**. Completed as an abbey church

St-Étienne-du-Mont

in 1789, it was converted two years later by the Revolution into a mausoleum for "great men who died in the period of French liberty". The remains of Voltaire, Rousseau, Zola and Hugo lie in the crypt. In 1849 Leon Foucault used the dome's height to set up an experiment that demonstrated the rotation of the earth; a reconstruction of his pendulum still swings.

Skirt north of the Panthéon to visit the lovely ⑥ **St-Étienne-du-Mont**, built between 1492 and 1626. Inside you'll find Paris' sole rood screen; these architectural features were included in all Renaissance churches but were generally torn down during the Revolution as they concealed the chancel from the people. This one, with its wide arch and clear view, was left untouched.

Follow Rue Clovis and turn right into Rue du Cardinal Lemoine, then turn left into the cobblestone Rue Rollin that leads you via steps to Rue Monge. Go through the porch of no.49 and you will find yourself suddenly in

⑦ **Arènes de Lutèce**, a partly restored amphitheatre that could once seat 10,000 spectators. It dates from the 2nd century and was only rediscovered in 1869.

Take the main passage out to Rue Navarre and zigzag along Rue Lacépède then Rue de la Clef. In Rue du Puits de l'Ermite you'll find the ⑧ **Mosquée de Paris**, a focal point for the Paris Muslim community. Built in the 1920s in ornate Hispano-Moorish style, it has a sunken garden and decorated patios, plus a tearoom.

Tun left out of the mosque and then right along Rue Daubenton. Cross Rue Monge and follow Rue de Mirbel, then turn left into **Rue Mouffetard**, a charming medieval lane, with fruit and vegetable stalls along its lower end. Climb the hill to reach

⑨ **Place de la Contrescarpe**, a pleasant square where Rabelais attended the cabaret over 450 years ago and Hemingway later sat writing at the café La Chope.

Leave the square on Rue Blainville and wend around into Rue de l'Estrapade. Keep on to cross Rue St-Jacques and, after a dogleg, the Boulevard St-Michel to reach a gate into the

⑩ **Jardins du Luxembourg**. In 1615 Marie de Médicis, widow of Henri IV, had a palace built to remind her of Florence's Pitti Palace where she had lived. Today the palace is the seat of the French Senate and the formal gardens, which include the 1624 **Fontaine de Médicis**, are enjoyed by the people of Paris.

Exit the gardens at Place Paul Claudel; turn left along Rue de Vaugirard, Paris' longest street, and then right into Rue Garancière. Turn left into Rue Palatine and reach

⑪ **Place St Sulpice**, where the fountain known as Quatre Points Cardinaux makes a mischievous pun. The four cardinal points of the compass each portray a churchman who achieved greatness but not the rank of cardinal: they are therefore *point* (not at all) cardinals. The square is overshadowed by the immense church of St Sulpice, built between 1646 and 1780. The classical façade was designed by a Florentine architect but the interior is more Jesuit in character. The first chapel on the south side was decorated by Delacroix.

Head north along Rue des Canettes, so named after the bas-relief of ducklings at no.18 on the left. Turn right into Rue du Four and veer left across Boulevard St-Germain to walk up the narrow Rue de l'Échaudé. Turn left and first right into Rue Cardinale that winds around into a charming square in Rue de Fürstemberg, laid out in 1699 to replace a stableyard. The Romantic artist Delacroix had his studio at no.6, now a museum.

Fontaine de Médicis

Turn left into the quiet Rue de l'Abbaye, passing the 1586 **Palais Abbatial** with its Renaissance façade. Around the corner is Place St-Germain-des-Prés, the social hub of the quartier and an old meeting place of artists and intellectuals during the 1920s. Across the square is Les Deux Magots café and just around the corner is its main rival, the Café de Flore. You may need some physical sustenance before visiting the church of

⑫ **St-Germain-des-Prés**. A monastery was built here in the open fields (*prés*) in 542 to house relics and the tombs of Merovingian kings. St Germanus, bishop of Paris, was also interred here in 576, contributing his name. It became a powerful Benedictine abbey and, following various sackings by the Normans, was rebuilt in the 11-12th centuries. Some sections from this period remain: the bell tower over the west entrance is original. Despite its 19th-century frescoes, the interior still has clean Romanesque lines.

Métro St-Germain is just nearby, but should you wish to walk north to the river, you'll find the streets pleasantly lined with boutique art galleries and antique shops and booksellers.

< Jardin du Luxembourg

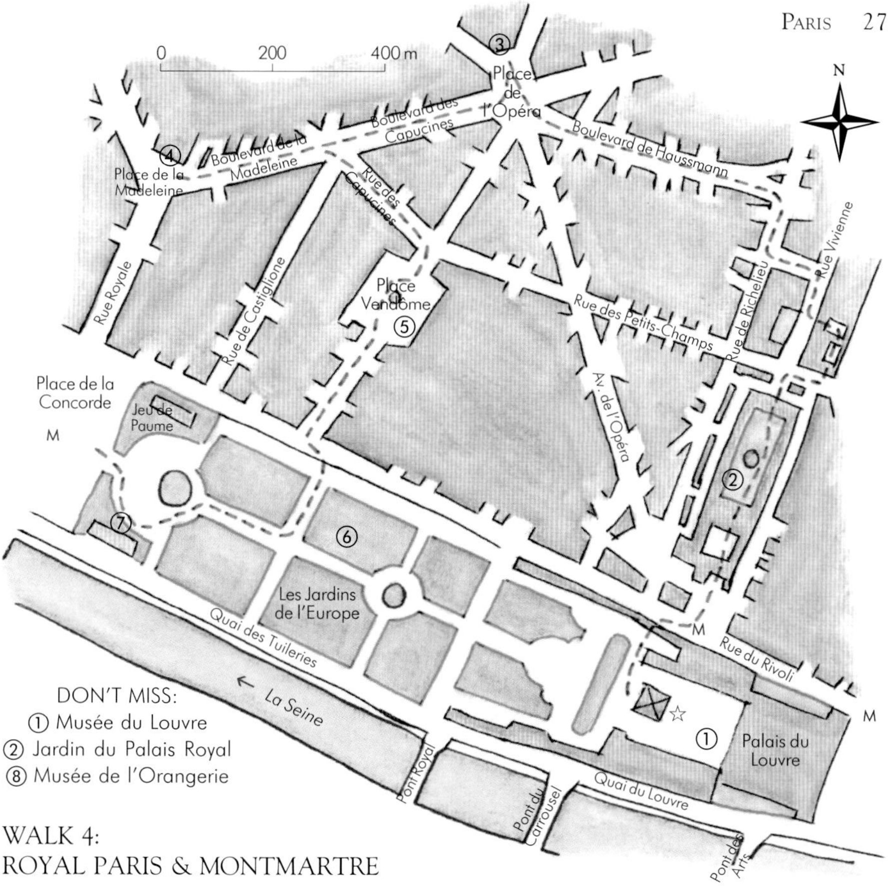

DON'T MISS:
① Musée du Louvre
② Jardin du Palais Royal
⑧ Musée de l'Orangerie

WALK 4: ROYAL PARIS & MONTMARTRE

A métro ride links these two short walks on the Right Bank to make a full day's sightseeing.

The world's largest royal palace, the
① **Palais du Louvre**, was begun in 1200 by Philippe-Auguste as a fortress rather than a residence. Royalty continued to live elsewhere until Francois I had it rebuilt in the mid-16th century. Successive monarchs modified and added to it until Louis XIV decamped to Versailles in 1682. The city enveloped it: a group of artists set themselves up in the galleries, rough dwellings were built in the courtyard. In 1793 a museum was opened for the people to see the royal collections. Since then, changes have made the building more suited to its new role, the latest being the **Pyramide** that serves as the main entrance.

It will take many visits to appreciate the collected art in this wonderful museum. It covers: antiquities from the Orient, Egypt, and the classical world; paintings, sculptures and objets d'art from the 13th to the mid-19th century; arts of Islam; and prints and drawings. There is also a section covering the history of the palace itself.

Cross the Rue de Rivoli and walk through the **Palais Royal**, built originally by Cardinal Richelieu in the early 17th century but passed to the Crown on his death. The palace is not open to the public but you can walk through the courtyard and into the
② **Jardin du Palais Royal**. During the Revolution, this was a popular meeting place and it went on to feature a circus, a cabaret and various gambling dens. Today formality has been restored, although a few frivolous sculptures lighten the tone.

Leave the garden at the north end and cross Rue des Petits-Champs to walk through **Galerie Vivienne**, one of numerous 19th-

< Along the Seine

Jardins du Palais Royal

century covered passages in this area. Turn right along Rue Vivienne and then left into Rue Colbert, skirting the massive **Bibliothèque Nationale** that is worth peering into.

Turn right into Rue de Richelieu and then left along Rue du Quatre Septembre. This brings you to **Place de l'Opéra**, planned by Baron Haussman when he made major changes to the Paris streetscapes in the mid-19th century. Its star performer is the

③ **Opéra-Garnier**, named after its architect and opened in 1875. Its lavish interior features marble quarried from all over France and a false auditorium ceiling painted by Chagall. Operas are now performed elsewhere, leaving this as the centre for ballet.

Walk around the busy square and pass the Café de la Paix to walk along Boulevard des Capucines, which was the scene of street fighting in 1848 just before Louis-Philippe abdicated and made way for the Second Republic. In 1895 the Lumière brothers staged, at no.14 on the left, the first public screening of a film. Continue ahead to Place de la Madeleine, where there is a flower market each day except Monday, and ④ **La Madeleine**, a church modelled on a Greek temple. Although begun in 1764, two attempts were razed before this design was settled upon. It was almost requisitioned as Paris' first railway terminal, but was finally consecrated in 1845. Opposite the northeast corner of the church is the city's most exclusive gourmet food shop, Fauchon.

Head back along Boulevard de la Madeleine and turn right onto Rue des Capucines, where the writer Stendhal collapsed on the footpath and died in 1842. Take the first turn right to walk through

⑤ **Place Vendôme**, lined with arcaded and colonnaded buildings built between 1687 and 1721. Napoleon married Josephine at no.3 in 1796. In 1848 the official measure for the metre was inlaid in the façade of no.13; the following year, Chopin died at no.12. The central column is a stone core wrapped in a spiral made from the bronze of 1250 cannon captured by Napoleon at the battle of Austerlitz, topped by a statue of the man himself.

Walk down Rue de Castiglione and cross Rue de Rivoli to enter the formal

⑥ **Jardin des Tuileries**, laid out in the mid-17th century by the designer of the Versailles gardens. The clay soil from here was once used to make tiles or *tuiles*. When Louis XVI fled the mob with his family in 1792, some 600 of his Swiss Guards were slaughtered here. At the western end of the gardens are the **Jeu de**

Paume – former royal-tennis courts and now a gallery for innovative art – and the
⑦ **Musée de l'Orangerie**. This houses a private art collection given to the public on condition that it stays as a whole. It includes works by Renoir, Cézanne, Modigliani, Matisse and others; most visited is the room of Monet's huge waterlily canvases.

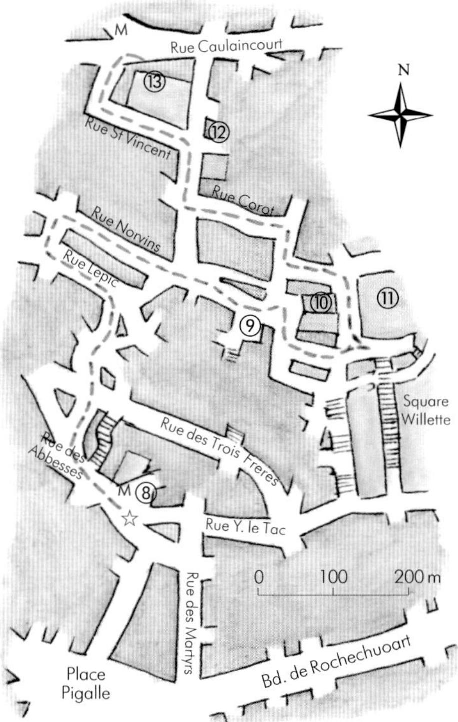

If you wish to continue the visit to Montmartre, walk to the nearby *métro Concorde* and catch the no.12 line north to *métro Abbesses*. You emerge from one of the original art nouveau métro exits at the foot of the *butte* or hill in
⑧ **Place des Abbesses**, which alludes to the mother superiors of a convent that once stood nearby. The name Montmartre possibly refers to a temple to Mercury, but it could allude to martyrs killed here around 250AD. A chapel at no.11 Rue Yvonne-le-Tac marks the likely site where St Denis was decapitated; according to legend, he then picked up his head, hiked over the Butte and walked 6 km north. Here also, Ignatius Loyola founded the Jesuit movement in 1534.

Leave the square via Rue des Abbesses and soon turn right into Rue Ravignan. A steep climb leads to Place Goudeau and the site of the **Bateau-Lavoir** where, in the years before WWI, artists and poets lived and made major leaps in art, including the birth of Cubism. The modest house was rebuilt after a fire in 1970.

Rooftops of Montmartre

Climb steps on Rue de la Mire and turn left into Rue Lepic. This leads to **Moulin de la Galette**, the last of Montmartre's many old windmills. In the 19th century this was a dance hall that inspired such artists as Renoir and Van Gogh.

Climb the street by the mill and turn right into Rue Norvins. These street scenes were painted many times by the alcoholic Utrillo, who was confined by his mother nearby. Nearby, an eye-catching bronze figure emerges from a wall, created by Jean Marais in tribute to the author Marcel Aymé. Keep straight on to walk through
⑨ **Place du Tertre**, a hive of frantic tourist activity, filled with portraitists and overpriced cafés. Artists started exhibiting here in the 19th century and in the early morning it still has a village atmosphere.

Sacré-Coeur

Just east of the square is the church of ⑩ **St-Pierre**, one of Paris' oldest, begun in 1134, although the west façade was remodelled in the 18th century. Four marble columns inside (two by the door, two in the choir) were reused from the Roman temple to Mercury.

Turn left out of the church and skirt the Montmartre reservoir to reach the terrace of ⑪ **Sacré-Coeur**, with a fine view over rooftops towards the Seine. This immense, Neo-Byzantine affair was completed in 1910. Its marble becomes whiter over time, making it an eye-catching landmark on the Paris skyline. The belfry holds the Savoyarde, cast in 1895 at Annecy and one of the world's heaviest bells.

Skirt the west side of the basilica and turn left into Rue du Chevalier de la Barre then cut right and first left into Rue Corot. No.12, once tenanted by famous artists, is now the **Musée de Montmartre**. A right turn into Rue des Saules leads you down past a tiny vineyard, the last one in Paris, to the ⑫ **Lapin Agile**, once known as the Cabaret des Assassins. It gained its present name in 1880 when André Gill painted a decidedly agile rabbit as its sign: a copy adorns the building that still operates as a cabaret with literary leanings.

Now walk down Rue St-Vincent and, at Place Pecqueur, keep right to visit the ⑬ **Cimetière St-Vincent**, a small cemetery where Utrillo and Marcel Aymé lie buried. If you find this interesting, you might want to follow Rue Caulaincourt around to the larger **Cimetière de Montmartre**, the resting place for a host of creative luminaries.

Return to the square and descend steps to find *métro Lamarck-Caulaincourt*.

FURTHER AFIELD

Bois de Boulogne

Once part of the Forêt du Rouvre, this 865-hectare park stretches along the edge of the 16e *arrondissement*. In good weather, it offers an excellent break from museums and monuments. Bikes can be hired from Jardin d'Acclimatation (south of *métro Les Sablons*). Further southwest, flowerbeds brighten Parc de Bagatelle; the far southwest corner is more wild and wood-like.

Père-Lachaise Cemetery

This city of the dead, opened in 1804, contains tombs bearing many famous names, including Oscar Wilde, Marcel Proust, Honoré de Balzac and Frédéric Chopin. A plan of the cemetery is available at the entrance on Rue des Rondeaux, just south of *métro Gambetta*.

The Lapin Agile >

Père-Lachaise

Canal walk

The Canal Saint-Martin, in the city's northeast, was opened in 1825 as a short-cut for river traffic between loops of the Seine. It flows underground from the Bastille to surface in Boulevard Jules-Ferry (near *métro République*, its cobbled *quais* lined with plane trees. Beyond Place de Stalingrad, the canal passes through locks to become the Bassin de la Villette, once the city's industrial port. Follow the Quai de la Loire on the south bank and, past a hydraulic bridge, the Quai de la Marne along the Canal de l'Ourcq. This leads through the Parc de la Villette, a vast urban park redeveloped from old abbattoirs, where there is a wonderful science and technology museum.

OPENING HOURS

Les Invalides	daily 10-5 (10-6 Apr-Sep); closed first Mon of each month
Musée Rodin	daily except Mon 9.30-4.45 (9.30-5.45 Apr-Sep)
La Tour Eiffel	daily 9.30-11pm (9-midnight Jun-Aug); stairs close 6.30
Arc de Triomphe	daily 10-10.30pm (10-11pm Apr-Sep)
Conciergerie	daily 9-5 (9.30-6 Mar-Oct)
Sainte Chapelle	daily 9-5 (9.30-6 Mar-Oct)
Cathédrale de Notre-Dame	daily 8-7; crypt daily except Mon 10-6; towers 10-5.30
Musée Carnavalet	daily except Mon 10-5.30
Musée Picasso	daily except Tue 9.30-5.30 (9.30-6 Apr-Sep)
Centre Georges Pompidou	daily except Tue 11-9
St-Eustache	daily 8.45-7, except Sun 8.15-12.30, 3-7
Musée d'Orsay	daily except Mon 10-6; open until 9.45 on Thur
Musée du Moyen-Age	daily except Tue 9.15-5.45
Panthéon	daily 10-6 (10-6.30 Apr-Sep)
Mosquée de Paris	daily except Fri and Muslim holidays 9-12, 2-6
Musée de Louvre	daily except Tue 9-6; open until 9.45 on Wed
Opéra-Garnier	daily 10-5
La Madeleine	daily 8-12, 1.30-8
Musée de l'Orangerie	check new opening times
Sacré-Coeur	daily 6-11pm
Musée de Montmartre	daily except Mon 11-6

Seine Valley

One of France's great rivers is undoubtedly the Seine, flowing from near Dijon in Burgundy, through Paris and Rouen to empty into the Channel at Le Havre. The Seine's name derives from the Celtic *squan*, meaning tortuous; beyond Paris this is a river with many tight loops or *boucles*. In its meanderings, it has cut steep-sided valleys through the chalklands on the edge of the Pays de Caux, creating white cliffs along parts of its route. For those who walk the *grande randonnée* that follows its course, this means a surprising amount of ups and downs, as the path ascends to the fertile plateau for good views and then drops to riverside villages.

Our suggested walk follows a section of the GR2 that takes in several boucles south of Rouen. We start, just off the GR2, at the medieval town of Pont-de-l'Arche, reached from Rouen by bus or by rail to Alizay and then a short road walk. From here we walk upstream along the Seine valley, through tiny villages until Les Andelys, overlooked by Richard the Lionheart's castle of Château-Gaillard.

NOTES
Type: a 4-day walk - 81 km (50 miles)
Difficulty: easy-medium
Start: Pont-de-l'Arche (bus from Rouen)
Finish: Giverny (bus to Vernon then rail)
Tourist Office: Rue Philippe Auguste, 27702 Les Andelys
☏/Fax: 0232544193
E: otsi.andely@wanadoo.fr
www.tourisme-seine-eure.com
Map: IGN 1:25000 #2012OT
Best timing: Apr-Sep

After another loop, the Seine straightens out to pass by some charming villages before passing Vernon, founded by Rollo, the first Duke of Normandy. The final destination is Giverny, a village that was home to the artist Monet and his magnificent garden.

Along the way, the route traverses rural Normandy, a tranquil, agricultural region. Up on the plateaux, the chalk is covered with a rich soil and you'll encounter old farmhouses, expanses of cereal crops and fields of bright poppies. Woods dot the hillsides and, draped over the chalk cliffs are lawns known as *pelouses calcaires*, with a botany unique to this environment. There are encroachments on this pleasant landscape – the industry of Rouen and Vernon is visible from afar – but the middle views are quite delightful.

The river, once a major thoroughfare for boats to Paris, has been controlled by locks and is now a placid waterway. Despite its proximity to the capitals of the province and the nation, this area is unexpectedly tranquil. So tranquil, in fact, that you'd be wise to book accommodation ahead, as there isn't a huge choice on offer. Good Norman hospitality includes the wonderful local cuisine; this is the province that produces France's richest dairy products and excellent *cidre* and *calvados* from its apple orchards.

< A Normandy cottage

Banks of the Seine >

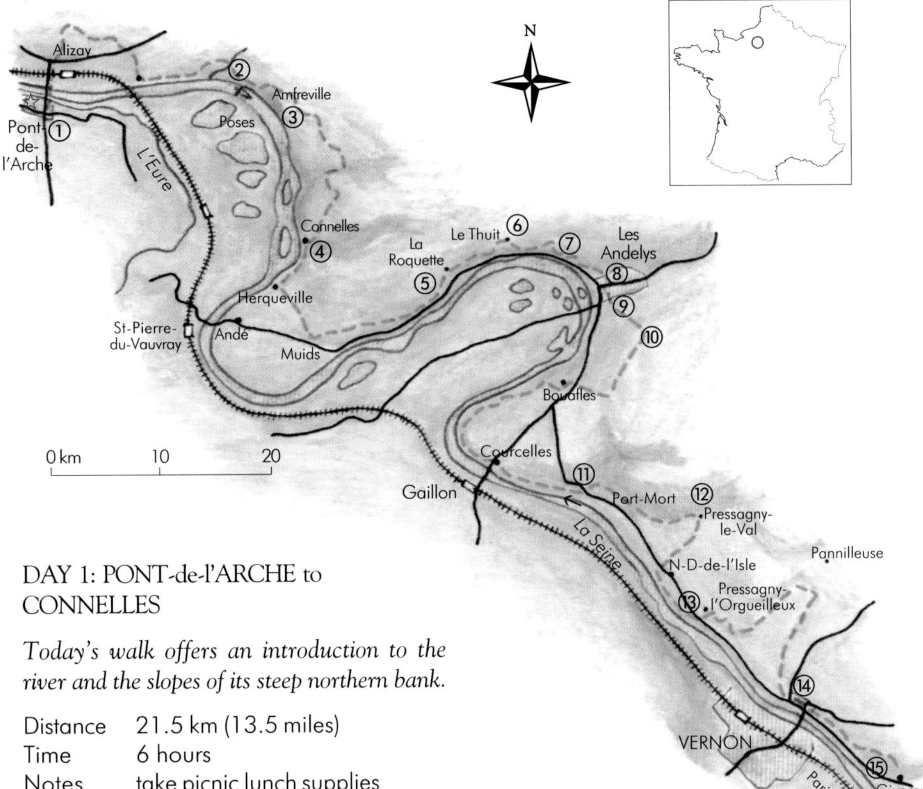

DAY 1: PONT-de-l'ARCHE to CONNELLES

Today's walk offers an introduction to the river and the slopes of its steep northern bank.

Distance	21.5 km (13.5 miles)
Time	6 hours
Notes	take picnic lunch supplies

Although off the GR route, our walk begins in the medieval town of

① **Pont-de-l'Arche**, spread along a bank of the Eure river. The quiet town features the Cistercian abbey of Bonport, founded in 1189 by Richard the Lionheart, and the 16th-century church of Notre-Dame des Arts. In the town square you'll find a *boulangerie* and other shops.

Cross the bridges over the Eure and then the Seine on the N15 and pass by a huge supermarket. At a large junction turn right into the village of **Alizay**. Follow Rue de Andelle through Alizay for 500 m and turn left into Rue de la Justice. This becomes Rue de la Garenne after veering right and, at the end of the road, becomes a footpath. Pick up the GR2 waymarks and follow them to reach a T-junction and turn left, following the road steeply uphill.

The road ends at a barrier and becomes a steeper dirt path through woodland, eventually becoming a wide and level farm track. Pass a farm building on the left and another road joining in from the right. Keep ahead for a few hundred metres and go right onto another farm road, perhaps not clearly waymarked. Turn off the road as it begins veering right, onto a dirt track by a poppy field. This becomes paved and veers right downhill towards the Seine.

Reach a T-junction with an old road, paralleling the N321. Go left and soon mount a verge to turn left onto the main road. After 100 m turn right onto a blocked farm lane, waymarked with blue footprints. This runs straight through fields, crosses the rail line and continues, now paved, through the hamlet of **Le Manoir**. There appears to be a *pension* attached to the Café de la Mairée.

Reach a T-junction: go right and immediately left on a gravel lane with a barrier. Turn left at the river onto a grassy, unwaymarked path. Follow this towpath along the Seine, staying close to the bank and avoiding the boat ramp. The route is often narrow. It widens as it diverges from the river as a farm lane.

When you reach a farm lane coming in from the left, go right on a footbridge crossing a tributary of the Seine. Continue on, soon joining another paved road. Follow the river to ② **the Seine locks** where there is a footbridge over the weir to the village of **Poses** across the Seine. A short distance on, the road turns inland. Cross the D19 road, go right and, very soon, go left uphill by a GR signboard. Climb a forest path until waymarks lead right to traverse the slope with good views down the Seine and inland. After a while you descend steeply to a road barrier where you turn left. Follow waymarks up a gully on a forest track.

Emerge on farmland and continue ahead, then veer right on a farm track. Reach a signboard at a three-way path junction. One path leads to the ruined château of **Deux-Amants**, a detour of 20 minutes return. Go right through fields and soon reach another path junction; turn right on the path signed to La Vallée. A steep descent through pretty forest leads, via a barrier and steps, to a minor road.

Turn right and then left on the D19. Very soon, leave the road up left on a grassy path that winds up past a classified church and cemetery to reach the D20 at a war memorial.

Towpath building

Leave the road up right to cut off a hairpin bend. Rejoin the D20 to climb to a hairpin bend that offers

③ **a fine panorama** and a seat. Now fork off

Mist over the Eure at Pont de l'Arche

The looping Seine

from the road down a grassy spur on a footpad, taking care as it drops steeply. The path levels, meeting a forest road at an old well. Turn left onto this road, ascending quite steeply through forest. Make a short detour to La Roche Rolline for another panoramic view. The path now levels and exits woods into farmland. Take a track to pass between farm buildings, turn right then left to leave the plateau and drop down through forest.

Reach a T-junction and turn right. The path reaches Rue des Falaises; go left. Diverge right uphill on a steep footpad to reach a path junction with great views. Continue ahead, though it may not be clearly waymarked. After a long, gentle descent on a paved lane, turn right on a dirt lane. Turn right onto Rue de l'Église to pass the church of

④ **Connelles** and reach the D19. This small hamlet boasts a four-star hotel-restaurant, Le Moulin de Connelles (☏ 0232595333). If you want more simple accommodation, you could use the public telephone to call a taxi. There are hotels in Porte-Joie and Louviers (across the Seine) and at your second day's destination, Les Andelys.

DAY 2: CONNELLES to Les ANDELYS

After crossing a finger of farmland, the route contours the dramatic chalk cliffs of the Boucle des Andelys.

Distance	16.5 km (10.3 miles)
Time	5 hours
Notes	carry lunch supplies

From Connelles, walk along D19 to **Herqueville**. At a junction of the D11, D65 and the GR2. The GR2 route goes straight on a narrow road into forest. Turn right at a crossroads and eventually reach the D65 road. Turn left, briefly following this, before going left onto another forest road. Beyond the forest, continue through open farmland for some distance. At a T-junction, turn right past La Ferme Blanche and left at the next road near the *château d'eau* or water tower.

< Château-Gaillard

Les Andelys >

Walk along this lane for 1.2 km then, at a junction, fork right to descend steeply towards the Seine. Reach the D313 by a former gatekeeper's house at a level crossing and follow the road up river for 200 m to the hamlet of

⑤ **La Roque**, named for the nearby outcrop shaped uncannily like a man's head. Fork left on a side road and then left again to climb the slope on a pretty path to the 12th-century chapel of **Notre-Dame-de-Bellegarde**, from where there is a fine view.

A short way on is the hamlet of **La Roquette**, where you keep right to pick up a track that descends to contour below the cliffs of the Côte de la Bouteillerie. Near the Roche Percée, the route turns sharply left to climb back onto the plateau. Follow a dirt track north and then pick up a paved lane for 100 m. Turn right, passing a pond to walk by the wall of the 19th-century château of

⑥ **Le Thuit**. This village, offering a fine vantage point, suffered occupation by the Romans and, later, the Merovingians.

Follow the D126 along the walls and then fork right onto a dirt track. After almost 250 m the route turns left and then rejoins the D126. Follow this for 100 m then fork left to walk through woods, cross the D126 and descend through woods again before joining the D126 into the hamlet of **Val St-Martin**.

Turn left on a paved lane, heading north up the gully. After 300 m or so, fork right on a footpath through the edge of the Hogue woods. The path climbs and then contours the slope to reach the

⑦ **Roche de l'Ermite**, a huge cave dwelling. The route weaves over the cliffs and then descends the hill, passing a reservoir. The path reaches a road near the hospital, on the edge of

⑧ **Les Andelys**, consisting of Petit Andely, once a fishing settlement by the river, and Grand Andely, a Roman town that lies up the side valley. Both villages have hotels and there is a tourist office by the river. Worth a visit are Petit Andely's 13th-century Saint-Sauveur (the interior of which leans jauntily) and the collegiate church in Grand Andely that boasts dramatic stained glass.

DAY 3: ANDELYS to PRESSAGNY-le-VAL

A stiff climb up to the castle ruins and a wonderful river view is followed by easier walking through some picturesque villages.

Distance	21.5 km (13.5 miles)
Time	6 hours
Notes	carry lunch supplies

Near the tourist office, leave the main road left on the waymarked Rue Richard Coeur de

Normandy forest

Lion. As this climbs you gain good views back over the Norman church. The route then swings right steeply uphill. Leave the path to visit the observation platform, with good information boards and views of the Seine, before visiting

⑨ **Château-Gaillard** (or the 'Saucy Castle'). This imposing château-fort was built in a single year by Richard the Lionheart to protect the extremities of his empire from the French king. It was besieged for eight months before it fell to the French in March, 1204. The castle changed hands during the Hundred Years War but remained intact until 1603 when it was partly dismantled under instruction from Henri IV. Entry to the ruins is possible between mid-March and mid-November for a small fee.

The GR path leaves from the top of the castle and becomes a dirt footpad. Go straight ahead to enter forest at a wooden barrier. There are many tracks here but keep straight to reach a forest gymnasium where you turn left, passing more equipment to reach a gate and sign 'Forest de Guillaume'. Turn right onto a paved road and, after 500 m, go right at a baseball enclosure onto a dirt farm lane. Continue straight between forest and farmland, eventually walking through the hamlet of **Cléry**. As you leave it, detour left on Chemin de Vanniers to see the overgrown

⑩ **medieval *motte***; a picnic setting also makes this a good place to rest and enjoy the ducks.

The route between Cléry and Bouafles is straightforward and well waymarked. It eventually descends through woods to pass under the D313 and enter **Bouafles** by its church. Walk through the village and, by the school, turn right towards the river. Turn left onto a lane and continue on the Chemin de l'Epingle. Fork right where the lane divides and follow around one of the Seine's many *boucles*.

At the village of **Courcelles-sur-Seine**, turn right onto the D316 and then immediately left onto a farm lane along the river. Later it becomes a muddy footpad that exits at a paved farm lane. Continue ahead to soon meet the river, and briefly follow the paved towpath road beneath La Roque. Turn left onto a paved lane and follow waymarks between the beautiful buildings of

⑪ **Château Neuf**, finally crossing the D313 onto a farm track that closely parallels the road. This broad, gravel track passes between new houses on the right and, on the left, open farmland with the wooded slope beyond. Cross a lane leading to Port-Mort and continue ahead on a gravel lane. The route goes up the Gatanay valley to reach the lovely hamlet of

⑫ **Pressagny-le-Val**. Here, just off the GR route in a back lane, is an excellent chambre-d'hote (☏0232525401) that can, given notice,

< Poppies on the plateau

A *laverie* or washhouse

supply evening meals. There is also a bar-épicerie here and a charming old *laverie*.

DAY 4: PRESSAGNY-le-VAL to GIVERNY

Pretty villages and woodland lead to a brush with civilisation and then to Monet's garden at Giverny; allow plenty of time to enjoy this popular attraction.

Distance 21 km (13 miles)
Time 6 hours

Follow waymarks out of Pressagny. Shortly, the route leaves the road right, forking onto an unpaved lane to pass between reservoirs. Cross the D313 diagonally to pick up a narrow farm track. This soon reaches a T-junction; turn left along the Seine on a paved lane through lower **Notre-Dame de l'Isle**, a village with a hotel/restaurant.

The route becomes the Chemin de Pieds-Carbons, leading along the Seine. At a T-junction, detour right a short way to a seat by the Seine, before returning to the junction and heading up through pretty

⑬ **Pressagny-l'Orgeuilleux** or 'Pressagny the Proud', where you'll find a shop and a chambre d'hôte. Leave the village by turning right on a grassy lane. Join a minor road and, just before the D313, turn left to walk up through the wooded Vallée de la Courbe for 2 km or so. After emerging from woodland, turn right by the walls of the Malira farm onto a paved lane through wheat fields.

The route touches the D117 and immediately leaves right on an unpaved farm lane, passing through the beautiful oak woods of the Vernon forest. Keep on, passing a shrine known as the *Mère de Dieu* or 'Mother of God' tree, and eventually begin to descend, gradually at first. As the path swings left, a grassy bank on the right offers an excellent view over the Seine and a splendid picnic spot.

The path now descends steeply under power lines and becomes a paved lane that meets the road. Make your way through

⑭ **Vernonnet** along well waymarked streets to the Château des Tourelles on the Seine. By the river there is a picturesque old mill on the vestiges of a bridge to the Île de Talus. Beyond the new bridge is the bustling town of Vernon, where there are several hotels and a rail station from where tourists are bussed to Giverny.

Old mill at Vernonnet >

Monet's garden at Giverny

Much as it is tempting to stay along the river in parkland, you need to cross the D5 and pick up a parallel route on a bicycle/pedestrian path named Voie Andre Touflet. At a crossing, turn up left. The route becomes a narrow footpad, climbing more and more steeply on slippery ground before emerging at a clearing with limited views up river. Continue on a level footpath that eventually swings around to meet a grassy track through farmland. This re-enters woods heading gently downhill on a broad track with filtered Seine views then climbs steeply to emerge at a house. Descend steeply to reach the outskirts of the village of ⑮ **Giverny**, made famous by the Impressionist painter Claude Monet who lived and worked here from 1883 until he died in 1926. Leave the GR2 to visit his magnificent garden and home (entry fee and many other visitors!) before catching a bus back to the rail station at Vernon. Alternatively, you can stay in Giverny itself and enjoy it without the crowds of day-trippers.

LONG DISTANCE STAGES

km	time	location	acc
		Pont de l'Arche	H
3.5	1h	Alizay	H
5	1h15	Le Manoir	H,C
3.5	0h45	(Poses)	G
10	2h45	Connelles	H
16.5	5h	Les Andelys	H,C
6.5	2h	Bouafles	C
15	4h	Pressagny-le-Val	C
3.5	1h	N-D de l'Isle	H
12.5	3h30	(Vernon)	H,C,A
5.25	1h30	Giverny	H,C

OTHER WALKS ALONG THE WAY

Across the Seine

The *passerelle* or footbridge over the Seine locks (see Day 1) offers a good opportunity to visit the charming riverside village of Poses and its floating river-transport museum. Nearby is the ornithological reserve of Grande Nöe. The *barrage* wall features a room for observing fish in the weir.

Around Les Andelys

If you have a day to spare, consider spending a second night at Les Andelys. The tourist office there has several excellent brochures outlining circuit walks nearby, including a 10-km *Circuit de Château Gaillard* that would allow a more leisurely inspection of the castle.

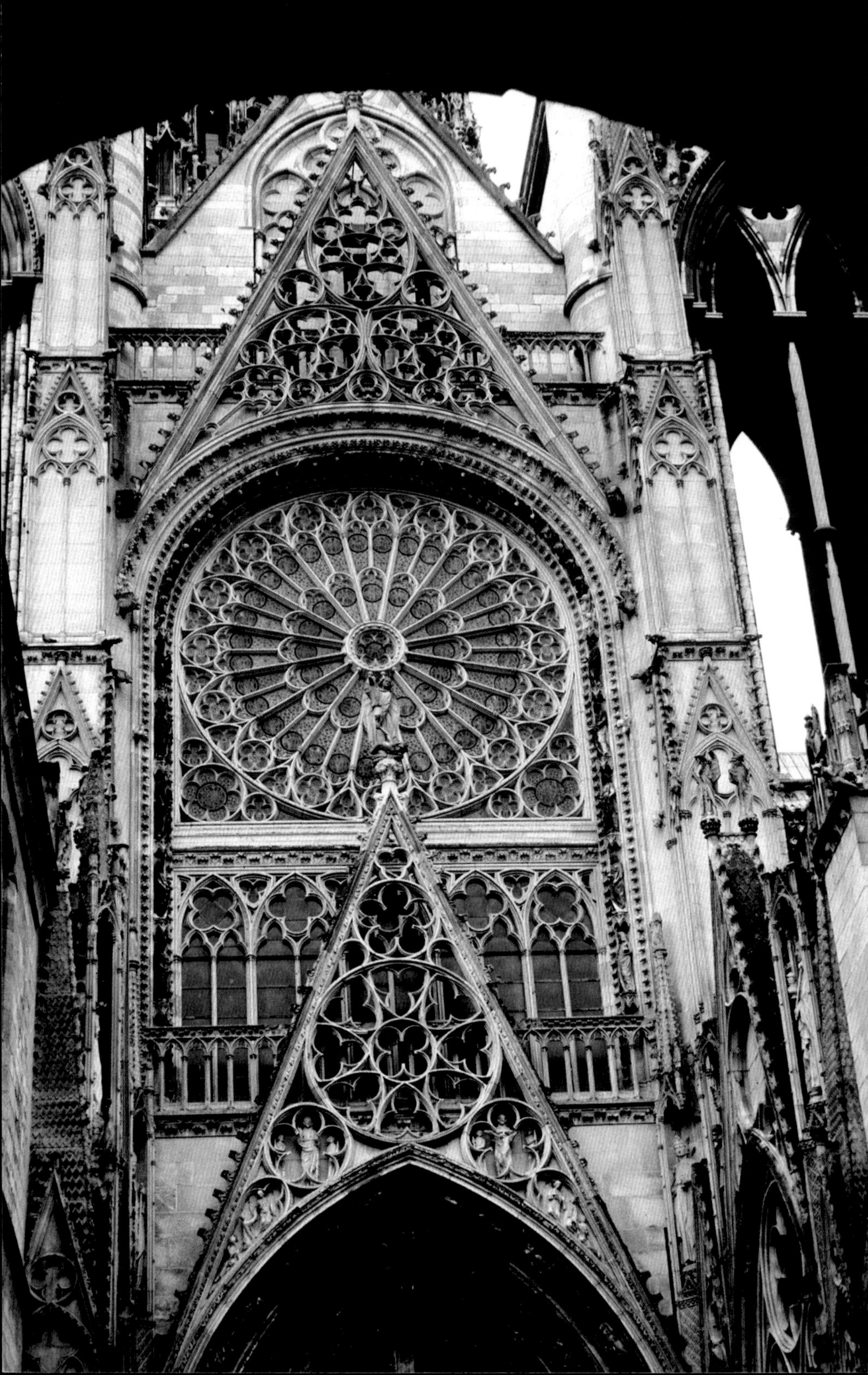

ROUEN

This northern port-city, set in a valley below wooded hills, has managed to retain a fascinating collection of treasures to tempt the traveller. It is rich in history and spends a large portion of its budget maintaining its monuments and museums. Fortunately, these are all set close to its magnificent Gothic cathedral and historic Rouen can easily be walked in a day.

Rouen's site, on a loop of the serpentine Seine, was a Celtic trading post and then a Roman garrison, established at the first place that the river could be bridged. The city was laid out by the Viking Rollo soon after a treaty made him the first Duke of Normandy in 911. His Norman dynasty went on to conquer England, Sicily and other distant parts. Duke Rollo now lies entombed in the cathedral, having died in 933, "enfeebled by toil".

Following a siege, Rouen was captured by Henry V in 1419 during the Hundred Years War and remained under English control until 1449. It was in the intervening period that the shepherdess-turned-soldier, Jeanne d'Arc, was sold to the English by their allies, the Burgundians. France's national heroine was tried for heresy in Rouen's castle and, at the tender age of nineteen, was then burned at the stake in the market place.

Rouen prospered from maritime trade and industry but immense damage was wrought by Allied bombing in WWII. Altough much of the city was meticulously rebuilt postwar, the district between cathedral and Seine remains unrestored, effectively cutting off the city centre from the river. For large container ships, this is the nearest navigable point to Paris, and Rouen's port area is understandably busy, though less so than it once was. Rouen is the only sizable town in Normandy to have preserved a medieval centre and there are many hundreds of half-timbered houses lining its streets. Rue Martainville, running alongside the church of St Maclou, is particularly picturesque.

The novelist Gustave Flaubert was born in Rouen in 1821. His father was a surgeon at the hospital and the museum that now occupies the family house – on the other side of town – displays both memorabilia of the writer and medical paraphernalia from previous centuries. Rouen also boasts suprisingly interesting museums on the history of education, ceramics, ironwork and other matters. Rouen has more than its fair share of France's wet weather, so you may find these a welcome distraction!

NOTES
Getting there: rail from Paris or Le Havre
Tourist Office: Place de la Cathédrale, 76008 Rouen
☏ 0232083240 Fax: 0232083244
E: tourisme@rouen.fr
www.rouentourisme.com
Markets: Place St-Marc: Tu, F-Sat 8-6.30
Place du Vieux-Marché: Tu-Sun 6-1.30
Note: guided walking tours available

Rue Eau de Robec

< Cathedral façade

A WALK IN ROUEN

Rouen is graced with beautiful churches and public buildings, artfully restored and set in charming streetscapes.

Start at Place de la Cathédrale, between the rail station and the Seine. Here, in the early 16th-century **Bureau des Finances**, you'll find the tourist office. Facing it is the

① **Cathédrale de Notre Dame**, built between 1201 and 1514. One of its two unequal towers is named Tour du Beurre, as it was supposedly paid for by a tax on butter consumed during Lent. The 151-m-high cast-iron spire was added in 1876; a violent storm in 1999 caused one of its supports to crash through the cathedral roof. Monet painted the west façade of this Gothic masterpiece over thirty times, studying changing light on the stonework. Inside is a semi-circular Romanesque crypt that belonged to an earlier cathedral. In the choir, along with the remains of other dukes of Normandy, is the heart of Richard the Lionheart who ordered that it be buried here.

Walk along Rue St-Romain, passing the 13th-century booksellers' courtyard at the side of the cathedral. At Place Barthélémy, you arrive at the church of

② **St-Maclou**. Erected between 1437 and 1521, this jewel of Flamboyant-Gothic style has a light and airy feel. The doors were carved during the Renaissance.

A short detour along Rue Martainville (note the half-timbered house with the drastic lean) will bring you to the curious

③ **Aître St-Maclou.** In the mid-14th century the Great Plague wiped out three-quarters of Rouen's population. This site was created as a charnel house and then an ossuary for plague victims. Carvings on the courtyard walls serve to remind visitors of their own mortality.

Retrace several steps and head along Rue Damiette, through Place du Lt. Aubert, then along the charming Rue Eau de Robec, graced by a channelled stream and lined with small galleries and antique shops. A half-timbered house on a corner boasts the **Museum of Education**; turn left here and cross Rue des Faulx to walk through pleasant gardens to the 14th-century

④ **Abbatiale St-Ouen.** This abbey-church, once part of a Benedictine monastery, is an excellent example of the High Gothic style, with a soaring interior and beautiful 14th-century stained glass. The abbey's organ, built by Cavaillé-Coll, is in great demand for recordings due to its purity of sound.

Leave the abbey via the west door and turn right to walk past the the Hôtel de Ville, occupying old abbey buildings, and continue uphill on Rue Louis Ricard. In front of a

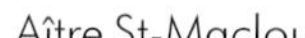

City of a hundred bell towers

Aître St-Maclou

Tour Jeanne d'Arc

grandiose fountain, turn left to walk through Square Maurois to the courtyard of
⑤ **Musée des Antiquités**, housed in a 17th-century convent. It has objects from Egypt and Greece and items dating back to the Gallo-Roman period, but its medieval art pieces are the most interesting part of the collection.

Now head back downhill and then right into Rue du Cordier bringing you to the squat landmark of the
⑥ **Tour Jeanne d'Arc**. This is the last of eight towers that ringed the castle built by the French king Philippe Auguste in 1204 and it served as a keep. After a trial conducted in the castle, the young Jeanne was threatened with torture here.

Across the road from the tower, take the lane that leads to Rue Beffroy and then take steps down past the **Museum of Ceramics**, which charts Rouen's role as a centre of *faïencerie*. Cross the shady Square Verdrel to
⑦ **Musée des Beaux-Arts**, an excellent mix of paintings, sculpture and tapestries. There are works by leading artists here, including several paintings of Rouen by Monet.

Behind the art gallery is a museum of ironwork, **Musée le Secq des Tournelles**, housed in a deconsecrated 16th-century church and more fascinating than it sounds; it contains everything from Gallo-Roman spoons to medieval tavern signs. Cross Rue Jean Lecanuet and continue south until Rue aux Juifs, where you turn right, to reach gates to the Gothic
⑧ **Palais de Justice**. Heavy bombing late in WWII left this a mere shell needing major restoration. Below the courtyard is the **Monument Juif**, a Romanesque building used as a synagogue by medieval Jews and the oldest such building in France.

Cross the busy Rue Jeanne d'Arc and keep straight on to reach
⑨ **Place du Vieux-Marché**, the old market place where the nineteen-year-old Jeanne was burnt for heresy in 1431. An unusual church in her name was built on the site in 1979 and a private museum at no.33 reviews her life. Beside the church is a covered market and there are numerous restaurants in the half-timbered houses around the square.

From here you could detour a short way west to visit the **Musée Flaubert** in Rue de Lecat, containing the novelist's famous stuffed parrot, amongst other pieces.

Gros Horloge >

Heading back towards the centre of the city, Rue du Gros Horloge leads, as you would expect, to the

⑩ **Gros Horloge**, a medieval clock mounted on an early 16th-century gatehouse. It originally adorned the nearby 14th century belfry but was moved down in 1529 so everyone could see the one-handed clock more clearly. For a fee, you can climb to see its workings and to enjoy a wonderful view over the old quarter.

As you walk under the arch, note the paschal sacrificial lamb, a feature of Rouen's coat of arms. At the street's end, return to your starting point, with a chance to view, as Monet did, the cathedral's west façade in a different light.

FURTHER AFIELD

St Catherine's hill

East of the city centre is the Côte Ste-Catherine, offering an excellent view over the Seine and Rouen. From St-Maclou, follow Rue Martainville to Place du Canada then under the rail line and a major road. Take the Chemin de la Côte and follow the GR25A up the hillside.

Route des Moulins

East of the town centre, off the Route de Darnétal are small streets – de l'Abreuvoir, du Tour and de la Petit Chartreuse – leading down to the stream of Robec, on which there are several old *moulins* or watermills. The last also contains the ruins of the Petite Chartreuse monastery. Nearby is the Pannevert mill with a restored wheel.

Jumièges & the Brotonne

A 45-minute bus trip west from Rouen takes you to the haunting ruins of Jumièges abbey, said to have been founded in 654 and destroyed during the Revolution. From here, you can follow the GR23A west to cross the Seine by ferry and climb up into the Brotonne forest, a Regional Park. There is an information centre and panorama nearby.

A farmhouse near Rouen

Long-distance paths

From Rouen's outskirts, several GR paths (including the GR2) wend their way towards a stretch of coast known as the Côte d'Albâtre. The previous chapter in this book follows the GR2 in the other direction, starting from Pont-de-l'Arche, about 35 km south of Rouen.

OPENING HOURS

Cathédrale	daily 8-6 but closed Mon am
Aître St-Maclou	daily 9-6 (until 7 mid-Mar to Oct)
Musée des Antiquités	daily except Tue 10-12.15, 1.30-5.30
Tour Jeanne d'Arc	daily except Tue 10-12.30, 2-5 (until 6 Apr-Sep), Sun 2-5.30
Musée des Beaux-Arts	daily except Tue 10-6
Musée le Secq des Tournelles	daily except Tue 10-1, 2-6
Musée Flaubert	Tue 10-6; Wed-Sat 10-12, 2-6
Gros Horloge	daily from Easter to Sept 10-1, 2-6

Brittany Coast

The coast of Brittany or Bretagne is known as Armor, or Land of the Sea; it is a rugged stretch of cliffs and coves, subject to great tidal changes that reveal rocky islands and the unearthly *bouchons* or poles of shellfish beds. This land of seafarers is proudly different from the rest of France; Celts settled here before and after the Roman occupation. It is a land rich in myths, one of which features a giant, aptly named Gargantua, who is held responsible for many of the landmarks.

Our walk traverses most of the Côte d'Émeraude, the name given to the stretch between Pointe du Grouin and Le Val-André. It is well named: the water here is a sparkling emerald when the sun shines. We follow the GR34 red-and-white waymarks on customs paths, across beaches, and along *polders* or sea walls as the route weaves into deep bays and out to scenic promontories.

Along the way, the GR passes through villages and small towns – some old and venerable, some claimed by holidaymakers – and makes use of these for overnight stops. Gîtes d'étape are rare here, but there are chambres d'hôtes and small hotels.

NOTES

Type: a 6-day walk - 128 km (79.5 miles)
Difficulty: easy-medium with long stages
Start: Cancale (bus from St Malo)
Finish: Erquy (bus to St-Brieuc)
Tourist Office: Esp. St-Vincent, 35400 St-Malo, ☏ 0825135200 (timed fee)
Fax: 0299566700
E: info@saint-malo-tourisme.com
www.annuaire-emeraude.com
Maps: IGN 1:25000 #1116ET, #1016ET & #0916ET
Best timing: Apr to Jun; Sep to Nov

In plentiful supply are restaurants offering fresh, inexpensive seafood. The movement of the tides along this coast is phenomenal: the difference in height of sea level can be over 11.5 metres. These tidal waters are rich in nutrients for oysters, mussels and other shellfish. Harvesting the seabeds is a serious small industry here but lone locals are often to be seen wading in the estuary with a net in hand. When the tide is low, vast bays are emptied and boats lie stranded like toys. Walkers are also affected: high tides may mean an estuary must be circled rather than crossed.

Inland, quiet hamlets boast tidy stone cottages, their gardens brimming with brightly-coloured flowers. Vegetation along the coast changes constantly. Exposed tracts of land are covered with gorse and heather and even the dunes and mudflats have been colonised by plants. The natural highlights, however, are the jagged headlands, blasted by strong winds but bedecked with myriad hardy flowers. Birds also find sanctuary on these cliffs and, in spring and summer, kittiwakes, fulmars, cormorants, razorbills, guillemots and various types of gull compete for nesting space on rock shelves and stacks.

Low tide in the bay of Arguenon

Brilliant colours near Cap d'Erquy >

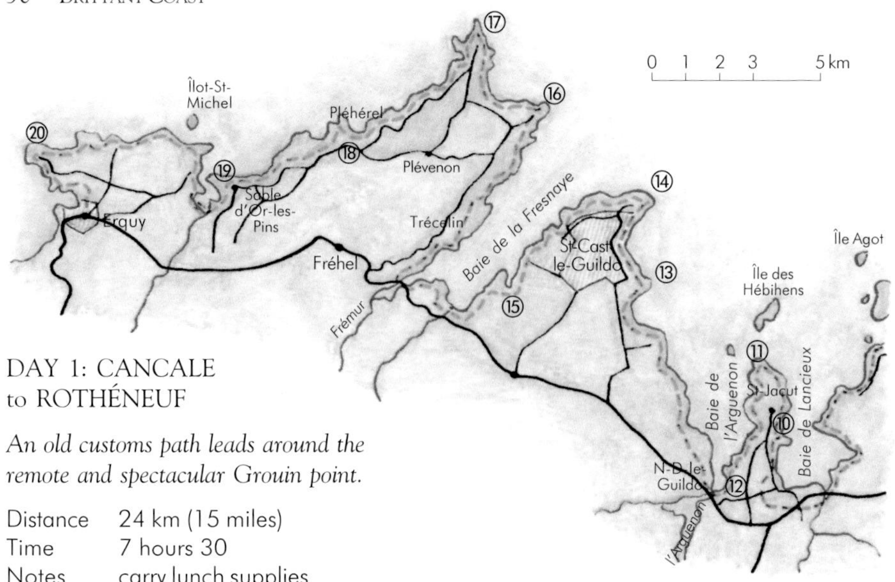

DAY 1: CANCALE to ROTHÉNEUF

An old customs path leads around the remote and spectacular Grouin point.

Distance	24 km (15 miles)
Time	7 hours 30
Notes	carry lunch supplies

Pick up the GR34 at **Pointe du Hock**, a short walk from the church of St-Méen at Cancale. The point offers a view of the bay and the oyster beds that stretch south from here. Cancale's oysters have been highly prized since the time of Julius Caesar.

The path passes beneath a high stone wall, before undulating (at times steeply) to reach **Pointe de la Chaîne**. Offshore you can see the Rocher de Cancale, rising from one of two islands. The coastal path continues undulating above the sea to reach Port Briac, a popular beach for gathering winkles. Some 500 m further on is Port Pican, a small sandy beach where there is a youth hostel.

Chapelle du Verger

This strategic stretch of coast features several *blockhausen* or gun emplacements, built by the Germans during WWII; some now shelter the endangered greater horseshoe bat. Past Pointe de Barbe Brûlée, the path nears the tip of

① **Pointe du Grouin**, covered with coastal heath and grasses. A narrow channel separates it from the Île des Landes, a bird sanctuary that is home to the largest colony of cormorants in Brittany. Views from the point take in the Baie du Mont-St-Michel and west to Cap Fréhel.

The GR path leaves from the edge of a car park, heading right over the exposed cliff tops on a level, sandy track. Pass more *blockhausen* and continue level to pass above a beautiful sandy beach that can be accessed. Past the Pointe de la Moulière (or 'mussel collector') you reach the Plage du Verger. The route passes between beach and a lagoon and gives you a view of the nearby

② **Chapelle du Verger**, rebuilt in 1867 and an ancient place of pilgrimage for local sailors. The GR path continues and passes Les Daules, an 18th-century customs house that is open to the public. Nearby is a pleasant spot for lunch: a grassy clearing among rock formations with

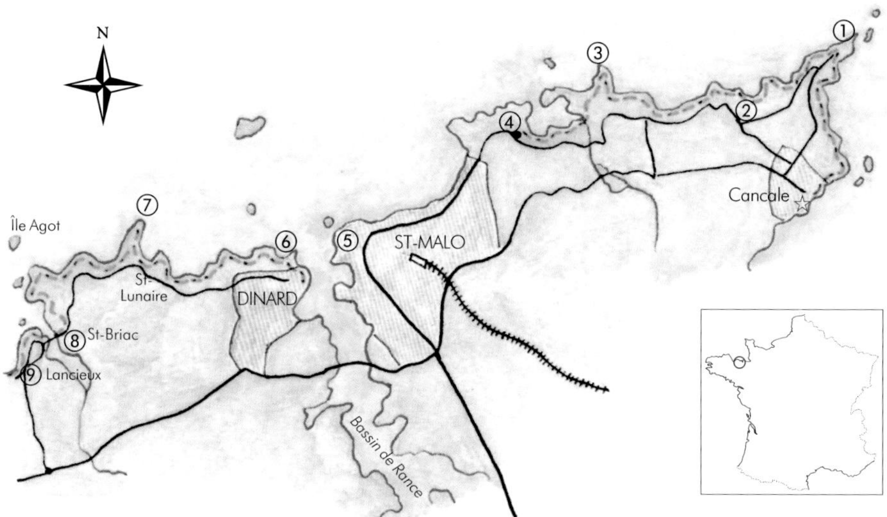

views out to sea and inland.

Round the points of Daules and Nid and pass left of the Fort du Guesclin, accessible only at low tide. Continue along the beach, the Anse du Guesclin. Pass a junction with the GR34A and, after a short road walk, turn right uphill to an old, partly ruined building. A level footpad leads to the Pointe des Grandes Nez (or Big Noses). Beyond this is Roz Ven, where the writer Colette lived. Descend to the Anse de la Touesse, negotiable at low tide; at high tide you must detour behind the rock outcrop on the beach.Towards the end of the beach, veer up left on steps and follow the fence line.

Traverse the slope to round the ③ **Pointe du Meinga**, gaining fantastic views of islands and islets, particularly at low tide. Proceed inland to reach, and go straight ahead, on an unsealed lane. Follow waymarks through the pretty hamlet of **La Guimorais**. Head down to water level; at low tide you can wend around the rocks to a concrete causeway, allowing a crossing of the inlet of Havre du Lupin. The large cove, hemmed in by Presqu'Île Benard, is a saltwater lake at high tide.

Continue along an eroded bank where storm damage has caused trees to fall. Scramble down onto rocks and then beach level at low tide and keep along Rothéneuf beach. Leave it by Chemin du Havre to soon reach the village of ④ **Rothéneuf**. Here you can catch the #5 bus to St-Malo, saving an 8.5-km walk. The bus stops just outside the citadelle of ⑤ **St-Malo**. Originally an island, this strategic site was fortified early. Its inhabitants were a fierce breed and during the Middle Ages, it flourished as an independent port. By the 15th century, it was notorious for harbouring *corsaires* or pirates who plundered ships in the Channel. Trade with the New World brought immense wealth to shipowners, who built fine mansions or *malouinières* here. Towards the end of WWII, the port was all but destroyed by Allied bombing, but it was rebuilt post-war with historical accuracy.

Its walled citadelle is a maze of lanes and granite buildings. The ramparts offer wonderful views all around. At low tide you can walk to the island of Grand-Bé, where the 19th-century writer-politician Chateaubriand is buried

St-Malo >

The view back to Dinard

Ferries leave from the quay just outside the Porte de Dinan and take you across the Rance estuary to **Dinard** in 10 minutes.

DAY 2: DINARD to LANCIEUX

A day of genteel towns and villages, including a walk along the sea wall below mansions.

Distance 19.5 km (12 miles)
Time 6 hours 30

Dinard was a sleepy fishing village until the English and Americans made it their resort of choice in the 1850s. The GR34 hugs the coast around the Pointe du Moulinet. If you wish to see Dinard's centre, you could instead pick the path up from the pretty beach of
⑥ **L'Ecluse**. Follow the *Promenade Picasso* (Picasso painted here during the 1920s) behind the beach, then continue on a concrete walkway between high walls and low rocks.

Walk along the beach of St-Enogat. At low tide, you can take a causeway at the far end of the beach and then steps onto the headland. At high tide, take the public steps off the beach about two-thirds along, and follow lanes to the headland. Take a rest on seats here and enjoy the fine views out to nearby islands and back over the clifftop mansions of Dinard.

The path meanders above beaches, affording magnificent views, then descends steps to Port Blanc. A detour inland avoids private land; the route then returns to the coast near a ruined semaphore. By rocks at the end of the beach, ascend left on steep steps and contour above rocks and sand. After rounding the headland, you can take a footpad (not the very steep one!) down to cross the inlet at low tide; the high tide alternative crosses the inlet some 500 m further inland.

Pick up the GR by a yacht club on the edge of **St-Lunaire**, named for a 6th-century monk who settled here. He is entombed in the 11th-century church, one of Brittany's oldest. The GR route doesn't go to the town centre but follows coast roads out to
⑦ **Pointe du Décollé**. This narrow headland features an orientation table and viewfinders. Detour right, down to the Rocher Napoleon for another excellent viewpoint. Backtrack, descend steps and walk around rocks to pick up a promenade along **Longchamp** beach. At the end, climb steps to a path that passes through bracken to **Pointe de la Garde Guérin**, a pleasantly remote headland.

You then skirt a golf course (take care) and descend steps to rejoin a coastal path. Cross a beach and continue along a path around the headland, gaining views of rocky islands in both directions. Eventually, with the golf course on

Low tide at St-Lunaire

A Breton garden

your left, walk through a high hedgerow and follow lanes inland, regaining water views near a mansion on a small promontory.

The GR route follows the busy D786, but you should detour briefly inland to visit
⑧ **St-Briac-sur-Mer**, an old fishing village once frequented by artists, where you can find shops, refreshments and accommodation.

Return to the GR to cross the inlet of the Frémur river. Continue ahead on a minor road uphill and into the old section of
⑨ **Lancieux** with its square bell tower, topped with a dome and lantern turret. A restaurant and boulangerie are nearby. Detour south onto the D786 to reach Lancieux's two hotels.

DAY 3: LANCIEUX to St-CAST-le-GUILDO

A long day with possible shortcuts, around the bays of Lancieux and the Arguenon.

Distance 31 km (19.25 miles)
Time 8 hours 30
Notes a 5-km shortcut is marked with *

Walk down to Lancieux's beach of St-Sieuc and pick up the GR between houses and beach. Leave the beach on Boulevard de la Mer. Turn right on a path above the coast, divert back onto the road briefly, then follow an open and level coast path, providing beautiful views south to **Tertre Corieu** and west to Presqu'île St-Jacut. This protected site has seats and tables.

The route becomes muddy, passing between *polders* (manmade dykes) and the shallows of the Baie de Lancieux. A footbridge leads over an estuary and, about 1 km further south, a path (negotiable at low tide) follows another estuary inland. Turn right onto the D768 to cross the bridge over the inlet. Immediately leave the road left through wheat fields and farmland. Arrive at a lane by a château, at la Ville Guerif, and then cross the D26 by a gravestone. Continue on to a grassy path ahead. A brief forest walk leads onto the D786, which you leave at a shrine right onto a lane.

Pass through the outskirts of **Trégon** hamlet leaving it on a well-churned bridle path. Turn right when you reach the paved road. Pass by a chambre d'hôte and go straight at crossroads (*to shorten the day, turn left here and follow the road for 2 km to le Guildo, detouring briefly to visit ruins at ⑫). Further on, join the D26 road for 150 m and turn off right on a footpad near a sign for St-Jacut. The path reaches wetlands and leads above a polder by a caravan park. It then swings left across the point of la Justice and joins a road, soon swinging off right onto Chemin de la Pissotte, to the
⑩ **Plage de la Pissotte**, offering a pleasant spot for a rest.

The GR keeps along Presqu'île St-Jacut (an 'almost-island' or peninsula) to the panoramic
⑪ **Pointe du Chevet** on the tip and then turns south. However, walking this section would add a further 4.5 km to this day's total. To avoid this, take the road inland through St-Jacut-de-la-Mer, cross the D26 and continue west to the other side of the spit, where you

can pick up the GR34 on top of a sea wall.

The path reaches the D62 road and follows it for 500 m. Branch off right after you pass an old shrine in the shape of a well. The GR nears the coast again and follows it, then takes steps before turning inland. Follow waymarks around minor points to the evocative ruins of the

⑫ **château** of le Guildo, set among shady woods by an old theatre cut in stone. In the 15th century, the château was the seat of poet Gilles de Bretagne who was murdered by his brother, the reigning duke.

Reach the road at the château car park and take it briefly downhill before going up right on a narrow path. Reach the shoreline and scramble back up to the D786 at the bridge. Cross the inlet of the Arguenon and turn right on a lane to the strange **Pierres Sonnantes** or 'singing rocks': their density produces a metallic sound when struck by another such rock. The road swings left to rejoin the busy D786; follow it for 300 m then turn right onto a quiet lane.

The pleasant road passes by a small château and several well-kept gardens filled with flowers. After nearly 2 km, descend steeply to the **Plage de Quatre Vaux**, popular with bathers. Cross a footbridge at the end of the beach and take a path through woods across a steep slope. Continue through lush woodland to gain views out to the oyster beds and islands beyond. After several ascents, reach a high point with a sign 'St-Cast 1hr30'. Soon after, at a junction with a GR de Pays, continue on the GR34 to the Pointe du Bay. Descend steeply, sharp right, to the long beach of Pen-Guen.

Walk the beach to meet the D19. At a roundabout, turn right on a minor road in the direction of la Garde. Back lanes lead to the

⑬ **Pointe de la Garde** where there is a statue of the Virgin and an orientation table. Continue to the tip for excellent views in all directions, including out to the **Ebihens archipelago**. Heading back, take a narrow footpath down right from the orientation table. Wend down to the long beach, Grande Plage, and reach the centre of **St-Cast-le-Guildo**.

Now a popular holiday destination, this was the scene of a failed British attack in 1758 that marked the end of British designs on France. A column, back from the beach, commemmorates the event. The town has a plenty of good restaurants: the local fishing fleet specialises in scallops and clams.

< Stacks off Cap Fréhel

Bouchons near St-Cast

DAY 4: St-CAST to FORT de la LATTE

From one picturesque headland to the next, via the deep bay of Fresnaye.

Distance	23 km (14.25 miles)
Time	7 hours
Notes	carry lunch supplies

From the end of the Grande Plage, follow a road winding uphill. At a Y-junction take a minor road signed 'port'. Reach the port, walk through a car park and up steps to

⑭ **Pointe de St-Cast**, marked by a memorial to escaped prisoners of WWII, a cannon used in 1758 and panoramic views.

Pick up the coastal path at the cannon. About 750 m along the cliffline, you pass a memorial to the crew of a frigate mined in 1950. Descend to beach level and fork right, avoiding the road, to pick up a paved lane. At a T-junction, turn right onto Rue de la Corbière, signed to Plage de la Pissotte. This passes left of a chapel before narrowing into an overgrown footpath. At one point, steps lead down to a lookout over an

Near Pointe de St-Cast

isolated beach. Later, the path broadens and winds down to a small car park where there are toilets and a water tap. The GR climbs, hugging the coast, and emerges from thick vegetation for great views at le **Grouin de la Fosse**.

Soon descend to a boat ramp; at low tide you could cross rocks here to reach the remote and tempting beach of **la Fosse**. From the boat ramp, climb high above the beach and continue through dense vegetation before descending to another boat ramp at **Port St-Jean**, where the water is muddied by the oyster-harvesting boats that launch here.

Wend through woodland, then follow the right bank of a stream for almost 500 m to the ⑮ **Moulin de la Mer**, the ruins of an old mill near a small waterfall. A picnic table and bench stand nearby in a picturesque setting.

The path soon trisects; take the middle path uphill. It broadens and meets a paved lane; continue ahead, slightly left. Waymarked lanes lead through the hamlet of **St-Germain**. Take a farm road for over 1 km and turn right on the D786. Cross a polder wall and follow waymarks (the GR may not be as per your map) to le Fournel. From here, take lanes to eventually reach the shallows of the Baie de Fresnaye.

At **Port à la Duc**, cross the Frémur inlet on the D786 and turn right in front of a hotel-restaurant to follow the water's edge. A lane forms the top of a polder; follow it for 1 km to Port Nieux. Turn uphill on a minor road and follow waymarks through the hamlet of **Grand Trécelin**. (There is a hotel in nearby Petit Trécelin.) The way descends through woods towards Pointe de Château Serein. Here the route was officially closed in 2004, possibly due to tree-fall. It is quite negotiable, however, and passes through beautiful woodland.

At **Port St-Gerin**, you should detour if you plan to stay at the nearby *auberge de jeunesse* (youth hostel; open May to mid-September ☏ 0296414898). To get there, take minor roads inland, crossing the D16A and heading northwest through Quérivet hamlet. About 350 m further on, turn right to reach the quiet hostel (bring all food supplies).

Otherwise, continue on the path signed to **Fort de la Latte**. This hugs the coastline, staying high, with excellent views, including those ahead to the fort. Turn inland just before the fort and walk past a tall menhir known as the Doigt de Gargantua, or 'giant's finger'. Beyond this is the D16A and a two-star hotel, the Ushuaia (☏ 0296414161).

DAY 5: FORT de la LATTE to PLÉHÉREL

An easy day's walk allowing a leisurely visit to a coastal fort and time to view the bird sanctuary off the stunning Cap Fréhel.

Distance	12 km (7.5 miles)
Time	5 hours
Notes	carry lunch supplies

Return past the menhir to the impressive ⑯ **Fort de la Latte**. Built in the 13th century by the Goyon-Matignon family, it fell into the hands of the French, English and the Holy League at various times. It was restored in the 17th century under orders of Vauban and more recently by private owners. It's well worth the entry fee to cross its two drawbridges, walk the parapets and see the foundry for cannon balls.

From the fort, the GR34 hugs the coast staying high above the water passing sections of forest and patches of bracken, brambles and gorse. Contour above the **Anse de Sevigne**, walking through coastal heathland of gorse and heather; the cliff edge is dotted with a variery of rare Mediterranean flowers in season.

Eventually you reach a spot near huge sea stacks of pink sandstone where seabirds nest in their thousands; this designated ornithological reserve shelters gulls, cormorants, kittiwakes, fulmars and oystercatchers. With binoculars, you can view nestlings in season: March to June is best. Nearby, a footpath winds precariously half-way down the 70-m cliffs to excellent observation spots and around the tip of ⑰ **Cap Fréhel**. If you don't have a head for heights, stick to the path on the cliff top. The view stretches in clear conditions as far as Pointe du Grouin to the east, Île de Bréhat to the west and sometimes out to the Channel Islands.

Head to the newer lighthouse (which can be climbed for more views) and find the GR path near toilets. Go right and stay as far right as possible: some paths have been blocked off to allow vegetation to regenerate. It is worthwhile detouring out to **Pointe du Jas**, some 15 minutes' walk from the lighthouse.

There are myriad track variants on the next stretch; paths rejoin and sometimes touch the road. The GR34 is only sporadically waymarked but you can't get lost. Pass high above Port au Sud-Est with views of cliff formations. Pass several tempting beaches and descend to the D34A at a junction. Here you could detour left to the village of **Plévenon**, an alternative overnight stop. Otherwise keep along the coast; at low tide walk the beach; at high tide you must walk behind it, through a caravan park.

Forte de la Latte

View from the fort

Exit the beach of **Anse du Croc** at the boat ramp at the far end and follow the road uphill to a signpost. For the centre of ⑱ **Pléhérel** turn left onto the D34, passing a chapel on the right. Pléhérel is a popular holiday location and has hotels and chambres d'hôtes.

DAY 5: PLÉHÉREL to ERQUY

The final day takes in both tidal inlet and beautiful headland as you approach Erquy.

Distance 18.5 km (11.5 miles)
Time 6 hours

Retrace your steps to pick up the GR34 and round the **Pointe aux Chèvres**, then rejoin the D34A road to avoid a limestone quarry. Go uphill a short distance before branching off up right on a narrow, well-waymarked path through bracken and woods. The path traverses heathland before crossing the D34A again and continuing between houses and road. It joins an unpaved lane veering right and reaches a

Îlot St-Michel

vacation village. Leave the lane and proceed ahead on a grassy track between woodland and the rear of houses. Rejoin the D34A briefly, then branch off right at another signpost.

The path cuts back sharply and makes a steep descent to beach level. It meets the gravel quarry road at a locked gate; proceed along this, behind the long beach of

⑲ **Sables-d'Or-les-Pins**, a bland resort town established in the early 1920s as a rival to Deauville. You might enjoy an ice-cream or drink from one of the bars.

At low tide you can cross the nearby tidal inlet from the tip of the sandy spit of Sables-d'Or heading SSE to the other side without getting your feet too wet. You should regain the track at a three-way junction at the locality of Vallée Denis. (At high tide you must follow the GR34 around the inlet, over a disused railway bridge and right to reach Vallée Denis.) The GR follows the road NW, then takes a paved lane above the bay before descending to the sea near **Pointe du Champ du Port**.

Go left, walking between the beach and a camp ground and then continue on a path ahead, below the hills. There is a beautiful view of cliffs ahead and a vista out ot sea of the chapel on Îlot St-Michel. Walk around the foreshore on a narrow path and then join a road, Rue de la Fosse Eyrond, to walk below imposing granite rocks. A concrete path leads onto the beach of Guen. Climb steps and walk through bracken high above the shore and through a well-kept community. Leave via a barrier and cross a wooden bridge.

The GR continues along the coast, perhaps not as per your map, to the isolated, sandy beach of **Portuais**. Some way on it reaches a protected area on the beautiful headland of

⑳ **Cap d'Erquy**, carpeted with flower-studded heath. Various paths criss-cross the headland, some closed for regeneration. One path detours to an *oppidum* known as **Camp de César**, actually a Gaulish earthworks. Round the tip of the point for spectacular views west across the Baie de St-Brieuc.

Beyond the point, the GR reaches a car park and follows the road. Turn right to descend steeply to an old kiln for cannon balls and then traverse between ochre-tinged cliffs and the harbour of Erquy. Pass right of quarry lakes, known as Lacs Bleus for their hue, before rejoining the road. After 500 m or so, take steps down right and follow roads down to the Plage du Bourg and the centre of Erquy.

This port hosts a fleet of deep-sea trawlers and is renowned for its scallops and clams. There are hotels, a gîte d'étape and, in season, boat trips on offer. Near the post office, you can catch a bus to the rail station at St-Brieuc.

The harbour at Erquy

Mont-St-Michel

LONG DISTANCE STAGES

km	time	location	acc
		Cancale	H,A
24	7h30	Rothéneuf	H
8.5	2h30	St Malo	H,A
-	-	Dinard	H
9	2h45	St-Lunaire	
8.5	2h45	St-Briac-sur-Mer	C
2	1h	Lancieux	H,C
13	3h30	St-Jacut-de-la-Mer	H
7.5	2h	le Guildo	H,C
10.5	3h	St-Cast-le-Guildo	H,C
17	5h	Trécelin	H
6	2h	on Cap Fréhel	H,A,C
12	5h	Pléhérel via cape	H,C
4.5	1h30	Sables-d'Or	H
14	4h30	Erquy	H,G

OTHER WALKS NEARBY

Mont-St-Michel

East of Cancale, at the mouth of the river Cousenon in a large tide-affected bay, is the remarkable Mont-St-Michel. From the 8th to the 16th centuries, in an amazing feat of engineering, a fortified abbey was built on this 80-metre-high granite island. Reached by a dyke that connects it to the mainland, the island can only be explored on foot. When the tide is low, the island sits surrounded by sand banks and it is possible to walk out to the small island of Tombelaine. But beware: the shifting sands can develop soft patches and the tides can reach speeds of 30 km/hr in spring.

Between Rothéneuf and St-Malo

The stretch of the GR34 between Rothéneuf and St-Malo is mostly along straight beaches; a walk you may prefer to do without a heavy pack. The point north of Rothéneuf, facing the Presqu'île Benard, has more interest.

Follow the GR34 waymarks north from Rothéneuf to Notre-Dame des Flots, an oratory in a converted coastguard's house on the edge of the cliffs. The path now heads west on the *Chemin des Rochers-Sculptés* to the garden for which it is named. Abbé Fourré was a partly paralysed priest who carved some 300 naive figures – human, animal and monster – out of the granite rockface.

Continue on to the Plage du Val, from where you can keep on the GR to Pointe de la Varde or take a road south, back into Rothéneuf.

NANTES

NOTES
Getting there: rail from Paris
Tourist Office: Place du Commerce, 44041 ☏ 0240206000
Fax: 0240891199
E: office@nantes-tourisme.com
www.nantes-tourisme.com
Markets: Tue-Sun am, Marché de Talensac
Note: Nantes City Card available

Nantes is a difficult city to pigeon-hole. It is a port, but the city centre has almost lost touch with its waterways. It has a number of modern developments and yet its green spaces are charming. Even the bureaucrats have found it awkward: despite being the historic capital of Brittany it was transferred to the Pays de la Loire in 1962.

Its position on the lower reaches of the Loire – where ships could enter from the Atlantic – and on the confluence with the Erdre made Nantes a promising site for settlement. First Gallic and then Roman, the town was caught up in the struggle between Frankish kings and Breton nobles before an 843 attack by Viking raiders. In 939, Alain Barbe-Torte established the duchy of Brittany and made Nantes his capital. Later rulers, Francois II and daughter Anne, built the stout ducal palace before Brittany lost its independence.

Throughout the 18th century, merchants of Nantes profited from the slave trade although human cargo didn't pass through the port. In a 'triangular trade', ships sailed from Nantes to West Africa carrying cheap goods that were exchanged for slaves. These were then shipped, often with great loss of life, to the Antilles, where they were bartered for commodities such as coffee, tobacco and unrefined sugar. Back in Nantes, these goods made the shipowners huge profits, some of which funded the lavish building projects on the Île Feydeau.

A mansion on Île Feydeau

The Revolution brought another dark period for the city. Carrier, the man sent to represent the Convention, found a solution to the problem of jails crowded with Royalists. He designed boats with a hull that could be opened mid-Loire, drowning a hundred people at a time. His barbarity was punished with the guillotine but thousands perished under his regime.

When ships increased in dimension, a new port was built downstream at St-Nazaire and Nantes turned to other industries. In 1885, a couple who had owned a pâtisserie opened the LU biscuit factory, quite near the château. A decade ago the factory was saved from demolition and turned into a cultural centre, now known as the Lieu Unique.

Nantes' most famous son is the writer Jules Verne, born in 1828, who grew up in Nantes when it was a hive of industrial activity. His birthplace is now a museum dedicated to his futuristic world.

Between the two world wars, various sections of the Loire and the Erdre were filled in, but visitors to the city can still enjoy walks or boat cruises along its various rivers: the Loire, the Erdre and the Sèvre. These, together with Nantes historic quarters and parks, offer the walker plenty to enjoy.

Île de Versailles >

DON'T MISS:
① Château des Ducs
⑥ Place Royale
⑦ Cathédrale
⑧ Île de Versailles

A WALK IN NANTES

Despite its modern developments, Nantes retains pockets of historic charm and some surprising green spaces.

As a reminder of Nantes' history as the capital of independent Brittany, we begin at the ① **Château des Ducs**. The fortification was begun in 1466 by François II and continued by his daughter Anne, who became queen of France. It held captive various individuals, including Bluebeard and John Knox, and played host to many of France's kings at some point, including Henri IV who signed the Edict of Nantes here in 1598.

Originally the castle was surrounded by the Loire but, as various waterways were filled, it became landlocked. The centuries have seen much damage to its various buildings and a major restoration program has recently fitted it out as a museum complex.

Turn left out of Rue du Château into the busy Rue du Strasbourg and then first right into Rue de la Juiverie, admiring the half-timbered house at no.7. Now turn left to reach ② **Place du Bouffay**, site of first settlement, near the confluence of the Loire and the Erdre. During the Middle Ages, this was the location of public executions. The car-free alleys behind the square are well worth a wander and include plenty of cafés and restaurants.

Leave on Cours Franklin-Roosevelt and turn left along Cours de Clisson to gain the ③ **Île Feydeau**, which was a true islet before the branches of the Loire were filled in during the 1930s and 1940s. Its streets, including Rue Kervégan, are lined with the 18th-century mansions of ship-owners and many of the carvings make reference to the sea and new trading lands. At the end is a square, once a covered market, now a sunken garden.

Turn right and leave Île Feydeau to arrive at Place du Commerce, where a tourist office is to be found. From the western corner you can walk up through

④ **Passage Pommeraye**, an elaborate three-floor arcade, built in 1843. The sumptuous decoration highlights just how much money flowed through the city at its zenith.

Turn left into narrow and busy Rue Crébillon to soon reach the neoclassical

⑤ **Place Graslin**, on the corner of which you'll find Nantes' most famous *brasserie*, **La Cigale**, crammed with colourful mosiacs and stucco work. The square is dominated by the **Grand Théâtre**, built in 1783 in Corinthian style, which you should keep on your right.

Now turn right to follow Rue Scribe, then Rue Rubens and then zigzag to enter

⑥ **Place Royale** which, though bombed heavily in 1943, was rebuilt in replica. The 1865 granite fountain symbolises the city as a female figure, overlooking the Loire and its tributaries, the Erdre, Loiret, Cher and Sèvre.

The château moat

La Cathédrale

Leave at the southwest corner and take Rue d'Orléans to cross the Cours des 50 Otages, named in honour of the fifty resistance hostages killed by the occupying Germans in 1941. Continue straight on, through Place du Pilori where stocks once stood, then fork left up Rue de Verdun to gain the

⑦ **Cathédrale St-Pierre-et-St-Paul**. This edifice, begun in 1434 and not completed until 1893, has a surprising Gothic integrity. Its white stone has been recently cleaned, increasing the airy feeling of its soaring nave. The elaborate tomb of François II and his wife Marguerite was carved in 1507 by Michel Colombe.

As you leave the cathedral, detour left along the Impasse St-Laurent to La Psalette, a charming 15th-century Gothic house that once contained the chapterhouse. Nearby, at no.3 Rue Mathelin-Rodier, the Duchess of Berry (who had tried to stir rebellion against Louis-Philippe) hid for 16 hours in a chimney cavity to avoid capture by troops. She was forced to give herself up when soldiers unwittingly lit a

< Detail, tomb of François II

fire to keep themselves warm.

Return to the cathedral and skirt its northern edge to pass through the **Porte Saint-Pierre**, a 15th-century gateway to control the road to and from Paris. You can still see the brick remains of the original Roman wall on which it was built. The Gothic building on top served as an Episcopal palace.

Beyond this is the large **Place Maréchal-Foch**, decorated with a statue of Louis XVI and flanked by two 18th-century mansions. From here, a detour along the Cours St-André and then along the bank of the Erdre river brings you to

⑧ **Île de Versailles**. This island was once an industrial district, packed with odiferous tanneries and laundry boats. Today it is a delightful garden laid out in Japanese style.

Retrace your steps to Place Maréchal-Foch and then continue along Cours St-Pierre, a popular spot for a game of *boules* under the shady chestnuts and oaks. There is a good view over the castle from the end of the avenue. Now follow Rue Clemenceau, passing on your left the Chapelle de l'Oratoire and then the

⑨ **Musée des Beaux Arts**, housed in a building constructed for the purpose in the late 19th-century. It has a good collection of European paintings, displayed well in galleries around a central courtyard.

At the end of the street, a gate leads into the ⑩ **Jardin des Plantes**, created in 1805. This is one of the best botanical gardens in France, partly due to the numerous exotic specimens that reached Nantes' port from the New World during the great days of 19th-century plant collecting. There are over 500 varieties of camellia, and a magnolia tree planted in 1807.

If you leave the park by the southern gate, you are very close to Nantes' rail station.

< La Cigale

The Erdre river

OPENING HOURS

Château des Ducs	reopening in 2006; daily 10-6
Passage Pommeraye	daily 8-8
Musée des Beaux-Arts	daily except Tue 10-6; Fri 10-8

FURTHER AFIELD

Along the Sèvre Nantaise

This pretty river flows into the Loire south of the Île de Nantes. Catch a tram south to Place Pirmil and walk down to the Sèvre Nantaise river to pick up a path on its right bank.

About 7 km upstream you reach the ancient weir of Chaussée des Moines, where you can cross the river and return on a path along the left bank. Alternatively, you can continue along the right bank for a further 4 km through countryside and make a crossing there for a long walk of 22 km. *Allow 4 hours return to the weir; allow 6 hours for longer walk.*

Along the Erdre

The Erdre river, its banks dotted with manor houses, joins the Loire from the north. From the Île de Versailles, a path follows the left bank of the Erdre river upstream, crossing it on the Pont de la Tortière and continuing north along the right bank to pass the Tertre château and, later, the Château de la Desnerie. Some 9 km from the start, near the 16th-century Château de la Gascherie, you can take a road west to the rail station at La Chapelle-sur-Erdre and catch a train back to Nantes. Alternatively, you could retrace your steps to cross the river on the A11 and then return along the left bank, passing the Parc Floral de la Beaujoire and the Château de l'Eraudière. *Allow 2.5 hours one-way; 5 hours return.*

The GR3

The first part of the route along the Erdre coincides with that of the GR3 which runs through the very heart of Nantes. North of the city it veers west, away from the Loire, towards the town of Orvault. Leaving Nantes in the opposite direction, the GR3 route leads along the eastern bank of the Canal St-Félix and then follows the Loire east along its right bank towards Ancenis.

Loire Valley

France's longest river, the Loire, runs through the heart of the country, from its southeast to its western coast. It is also the least tamed: though it may look broad and languid, it is a river of whirlpools and strong currents, with a tendency to flood. On its course to the Atlantic, the Loire runs through the regions of Touraine and Anjou and it is this stretch, now a regional nature park, that we traverse on the GR3.

The Val de Loire is an unusual landscape. Deposits from a time when the land was covered by sea have formed a bed of tufaceous limestone or *tufa* that has a fine grains and is easily carved. The Loire has carved a valley through it and, along the cliffs that rise from the river bank, humans have quarried the rock for building material and hewn out caves in the process. These caves were then used as shelters by the poorest workers; by the 17th century, a large portion of the population inhabited these troglodyte dwellings. Today, locals mostly use them for storage, as garages, or to raise mushrooms, for which the region is famous. A few caves are open to the public as museums, restaurants or wine cellars.

Boats on the Loire

NOTES
Type: A 6-day walk - 108 km (67 miles)
Difficulty: easy
Start: Erigné (bus from Angers)
Finish: Chinon (train to Tours)
Tourist Office: Pl. de la Bilange,
49418 Saumur
☎ 0241402060 Fax: 0241402069
E: info@ot-saumur.fr
www.saumur-tourisme.com
Map: IGN 1:100000 #25 *Angers Chinon*
Best timing: Apr-Jun; Sep-Oct

Wine is a major industry here and much of your walk will be through vineyards up on the fertile plateau above the tufa cliffs. Saumur produces an excellent *méthode champenoise* sparkling wine and Chinon a ruby red that tastes of raspberries. The food is equally good here, with plenty of fish from the river on offer. Not on the plate, but enjoyable to watch, is the rich birdlife that inhabits the many islands and embankments of the Loire.

This countryside is also rich in history, with visible remains of prehistoric and Gallo-Roman settlement. More obvious are the signs of medieval settlement: the great châteaux of the royal court that took such pleasure in the Val de Loire. Some royal personages reside here still, entombed in the great abbey of Fontevraud.

Our walk begins just south of the town of Angers, the capital of ancient Anjou, and heads upstream, via Saumur and a host of smaller villages, to the confluence of the Loire and its tributary, the Vienne. Here we leave the Loire to visit Fontevraud and finally Chinon, a well-preserved town on the Vienne. The walk is spread over six days, allowing time to visit the many historic sites along the way. To shorten the route, we suggest you catch a train from Angers to Les Rosiers-sur-Loire and begin the walk at Gennes.

Château de Poce >

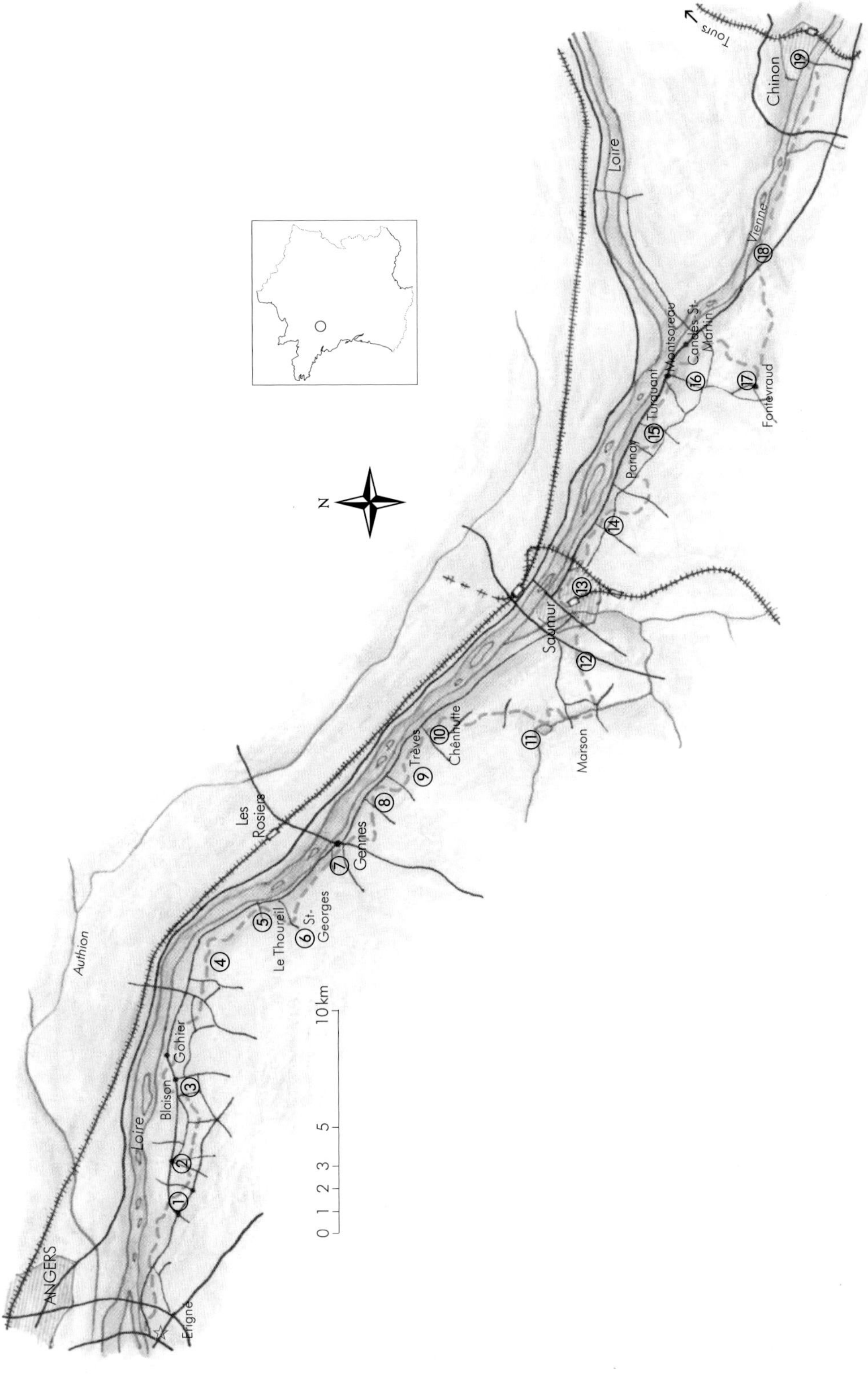

ANGERS
Érigné
Loire
Authion
1
2
3
Blaison
Gohier
4
5
Le Thoureil
6 St-Georges
7 Gennes
Les Rosiers
8
9 Trèves
10 Chênehutte
11
Marson
12
Saumur
13
14
Parnay
15 Turquant
Montsoreau
16 Candes-St-Martin
17 Fontevraud
18
Vienne
Loire
19 Chinon
Tours
N
0 1 2 3 5 10 km

DAY 1: ERIGNÉ to BLAISON

An easy day's walk starts along the Louet, a tributary of the Loire, and leads via farmland to the quiet village of Blaison.

Distance	16.5 km (10 miles)
Time	4 hours 30
Notes	carry lunch supplies

In Angers, catch a #8 bus from Boulevard Foch (or Place Marengo by the rail station) towards Murs Erigné. This heads south and crosses over the Loire, and soon after, over the Louet. Alight here, cross the road and descend on steps to pick up the GR3 route (waymarked with red-and-white stripes) heading east on a path following the Louet through woods. The path becomes a forest track. At a T-junction, turn right onto a farm lane, then left onto the D132 and follow it for a few hundred metres.

Turn right onto a dirt forest track. Eventually this passes under a motorway, loops and then swings right through cornfields. Reach the D132 again at **Juigné-sur-Loire** and take a minor road forking left down to the languid river Louet. Follow GR waymarks through back lanes alongside a lake, passing

① a **junction of walking routes**. The GR follows sealed lanes lined with poplars, some pollarded, then between high schist walls along the back lanes of **St-Jean-des-Mauvrets**. Some 1.25 km further on, the route enters

A moulin a vent

② **St-Saturnin** at a church and near the village's only shop, a boulangerie-pâtisserie.

The GR is waymarked poorly out of the village. Follow yellow duck symbols (truly!) and leave the newly developed outskirts to pass by a tiny vineyard and turn right at a sign 'La Guessière'. Pass left of the pretty farmhouse of La Fosse and immediately left onto an unpaved farm lane. Reach a T-junction with another lane. There are no waymarks, but turn left and then soon right on a grassy track between vineyards. This eventually becomes a paved farm lane veering left; follow this for some time. The GR passes right of an old windmill, one of the 640 that stood in 19th-century Anjou.

Turn right at the farm of Jourallan with its picturesque chapel. Turn left, signed to Château de Bois Brinçon. Reach a paved road and turn left at a T-junction. There is a good view across the valley to the château ahead. Soon turn off the road right at the farm of La Refiviére. The route arrives at

③ **Blaison**, a quiet village that has a Gallo-Roman history as Blasius. Here you'll find a gîte d'étape, a chambre d'hôte, a small supermarket and a bus stop.

< Ducks on a still lake

A troglodyte dwelling

DAY 2: BLAISON to GENNES

Pleasant lanes lead cross country to rejoin the Loire at Le Thoureil before an ascent of the valley side and a descent to Gennes.

Distance 22 km (14 miles)
Time 6 hours 15

Follow waymarks on a road north out of Blaison and cross the Petit Louet stream. Turn sharp right at a sports field and follow a track all the way to the hamlet of **Gohier**. Walk through Gohier and skirt north of woodland. Turn right onto a road and then left to the hamlet of **Chauvigné**, sharing the route with a yellow PR.

After Chauvigné, turn left at a T-junction onto a paved road, then turn right onto a grassy track. The route skirts south of the village of **St-Rémy-la-Varenne** and passes by an excellent drinking fountain from the St-Maur spring. Reach a T-junction where the route goes right, but you can detour left downhill to the former Benedictine monastery of

④ **St-Maur** (now a religious centre) and its small church-cemetery.

From the point of detour, walk up the road and then turn left, signed 'la Bois Chattonier'. Eventually, join the D132 on the Loire at

⑤ **Le Thoureil** where you will find a welcome café/bar. Stroll for a few minutes up river to view houseboats that may be moored here, or to enjoy the charming riverside houses of this former Loire port.

From Le Thoureil, the GR heads away from the river and follows lanes then climbs over a wooded hill. It skirts the wall of an estate and passes by the hamlet of **Cumeray**. The route swings west to cross the D156 road and turns left onto a lane to reach a T-junction with the D751. Cross this and follow a path through woods to then turn right onto the D156 and follow it into the hamlet of

⑥ **St-Georges-des-Sept-Voies** where there is a Romanesque church.

Follow GR waymarks on a path west through woods to a crossroads. (There is a gîte d'étape at St-Pierre-en-Vaux, a detour of 20 minutes if you were to turn right here.) Turn left onto a minor road. Leave this left to cut across more land to pass near a ruined mill. A broad path takes you past a dolmen and through woods to then enter the town of

⑦ **Gennes**, by the banks of the Loire. Turn left on the Trois Lapins or 'three rabbits' road. Keep straight on at crossroads to reach the 12th-century belfry of St-Eusèbe. There is a memorial here to the cavalry cadets of Saumur who died

St-Eusèbe at Gennes

Notre-Dame de Cunault

defending the hilltop against the Germans in WWII. The GR now turns away from the river up through the village where there are hotels, chambres d'hôte and various shops.

DAY 3: GENNES to CHÊNHUTTE

A short day's walk with time to enjoy a parade of ancient buildings, including a magnificent Romanesque church at Cunault.

Distance 10.5 km (6.5 miles)
Time 3 hours

Past the *mairie* of Gennes is the 10th to15th-century church of St-Vétérin. Detour here to visit the ruins of the nearby Gallo-Roman amphitheatre and an archaeological museum.

The GR leaves Gennes, passing a gigantic supermarket to walk through Joreau forest along car-free tracks. Pass left of the Etang du Cunault, a popular spot for fishing, and continue through forest to emerge at a barrier. Turn right onto a paved lane. The GR passes by a ruined Romanesque church and walled cemetery, worth exploring. It then wends downhill on a paved lane into **Cunault**, where there are several chambres d'hôtes. Allow plenty of time to enjoy the magnificent Romanesque church of

⑧ **Notre-Dame de Cunault**, built by the Benedictines from the 11th to 15th centuries. Its vast interior has clean lines and plenty of light by which to examine the 223 carved capitals (bring binoculars) and frescoes. There are also some fascinating treasures including a 13th-century wooden reliquary, carved and painted, holding the bones of Maxenceul, who founded a church here in the 4th century.

Leave Cunault on the D751, following the Loire and turn right on a wide, grassy path uphill to enter forest. Turn left off the forest lane onto a paved road and presently reach the junction with the GR3D variant. We continue ahead, passing fields on the right. Watch for a waymarked left turn that descends to

⑨ **Trèves**. This village is dominated by a tower built of tufa, once the *donjon* of an important 15th-century chateau. Beside it is the 12th-century church of St-Aubin, in Angevin style, featuring a lovely baptistry built of porphyry. By the river, you'll find a picnic table. There is a restaurant deep in the hillside in the nearby **Cave aux Moines**, worth peeking into just

The *donjon* at Trèves

Le dolmen de Bagneaux

for a cave experience. You can even take a tour to see a troglodyte dwelling and cave cultivation of champignions and snails.

The GR follows the D751, then turns right into a working forest. The rutted forest path ascends steadily before swinging left to pass between forest and cornfields. It emerges onto a paved lane, passing right of a former priory-château, now a four-star restaurant-hotel.

Saumur's château, above the Loire

After passing a field of sunflowers, turn right on a dirt lane to pass right of an old **Roman encampment** where there are remains of ramparts. A dirt footpath descends very steeply left off a Roman road built on a *levée* embankment. The path emerges at a field, where you turn left onto a farm track. This enters and leaves the D214 and passes behind a large house with a formal rose garden. Wend down to the D751 and cross a bridge over the tributary stream of Fontaine de l'Enfer to enter

⑩ **Chênhutte-les-Tuffeaux**, so named for its many tufa caves. Here you can visit the church of Notre-Dame des Tuffeaux, dating back to the 11th century but later enlarged. There are also the Gallo-Roman ruins of the Temple du Villiers, discovered in 1981. Chênehutte has a chambre d'hôte and a shop serving as boulangerie, pâtisserie and épicerie.

DAY 4: CHÊNHUTTE to SAUMUR

The GR3 leads inland through forest to a village of troglodyte dwellings and then via an ancient monolith to fascinating Saumur.

Distance	18 km (11.5 miles)
Time	4 hours 30
Notes	carry lunch supplies

Leave Chênhutte on the Route de Petit Puits to climb to the plateau, then follow farm lanes to cross a D road at a four-way junction, taking an unpaved road signed to Puits. The route swings left through forest on a level track and emerges onto a wide, grassy path. It passes through the hamlet of Villemolle, crosses a road, and continues straight on as an unpaved track through wheat fields. It then swings left then right and enters the forest of Saumur, where you may see deer, and skirts the
⑪ **Étang de Marson**.

Follow waymarks through the village of **Marson** where there are troglodyte cave dwellings, through the hamlet of **Riou**, and then cross country on tracks, passing the privately-owned Château de Poce, to the village of Bagneaux. Stop at the restaurant-bar for refreshments and to visit its garden (entry fee) containing the largest dolmen in Europe,
⑫ **le Dolmen de Bagneaux**. This massive gallery grave comprises numerous 3-m-high stone uprights supporting four gigantic slabs of stone. Its builders were probably people who migrated to the region from the Near East from about 3000 BC. Its present owner, who is an enthusiast, sometimes serves meals inside it.

Cross the road and wend down to cross the pretty Thouet river on a footbridge. The GR follows the river through beautiful parkland to a road junction. Rue du Maréchal Leclerc leads to the banks of the Loire and the centre of
⑬ **Saumur**, the 'pearl of Anjou'. By the river you'll find a large tourist office with lots of shops, restaurants and hotels nearby; there is a hostel on the southeast tip of Île d'Offard.

The lovely old quarter of cobbled lanes and medieval houses lies at the foot of the white, turreted château-fort that looks magical in misty mornings or illuminated at night. In the late 14th century, Louis I of Anjou transformed his ancestors' fortress into a residence. It was made more palatial by his grandson, King René, before passing into the hands of the king of France. An entry fee gives access to dungeons, the watchtower, a decorative arts collection and a fascinating equestrian museum.

DAY 5: SAUMUR to FONTEVRAUD

This is a long but interesting day through vineyards between tufa villages along the Loire and then diverting to the royal abbey of Fontevraud. You might want to break it up with an overnight visit to Candes-St-Martin.

Church amid vines on the plateau

Distance 24 km (15 miles)
Time 7 hours

Follow signs through the lanes of old Saumur to climb to the château. Leave its walls, crossing a footbridge and walking through a parking area. Turn left onto the Rue des Moulins and swing right past steps to an excellent panorama over the Loire and the Île d'Offard.

Follow waymarks along back lanes high above the river. Cross the D145 below a water tower and continue on a narrow footpath that skirts the edge of vines before turning left and descending steeply. The path turns right, levelling, before going up right quite steeply. The path eventually joins a narrow lane downhill and passes a parish church at
⑭ **Dampierre-sur-Loire**.

The church lane climbs right and forks left; you ascend moderately steeply on a beautiful walled and wooded lane. It finally emerges onto the plateau between vines on a level vineyard

track. The GR path coincides now with a mountain bike route. We pass by the 11th-century church of **Parnay**, with its Romanesque nave and Renaissance portal.

The route is now through vineyards before descending steeply to the hamlet of **Parnay**. Pass right of a well-restored *lavoire* or wash-house and soon take a steep path right up to reach more vines on the plateau. The GR then descends to the river at

⑮ **Turquant** and passes close to Troglo des Pommes Tapées, the last producers of once-common Saumurois preserved apples, dried in ovens and flattened slightly by tapping before bottling (tours available in season). It then passes right of the tufa church of St-Aubin, which had its floors raised in the 17th century after repeated flooding. The path then wends up steeply to the right of a hotel that has some troglodyte rooms carved into the cliff. Here the route wends steeply uphill through a break in the cliff line and then passes through vineyards. Head towards a water tower and turn left just before it. Take the path down to the lively riverside village of

⑯ **Montsoreau** where there are hotels, chambres d'hôtes, a bus stop and shops. Its 15th-century fortified château (entry fee) overlooks the wide confluence of the Loire and the Vienne. A very short way down the D751 is **Candes-St-Martin**, classified as one of France's beautiful villages and a possible overnight stop.

The path leaves the road uphill to gain river and château views before climbing to parkland where there are remnants of a ruined windmill. From here the panorama includes the nuclear power plant upstream on the Loire, from which we now diverge. Walk inland on a farm lane crossing the D751. The GR route follows three sides of a square, taking you through farmland before entering the forest of Fontevraud. Follow woodland tracks for 2 km before descending to a paved lane on the edge of the village of

⑰ **Fontevraud-l'Abbaye**. Its centrepiece, the abbey of Fontevraud, is one of the most remarkable sites in France. Founded in about 1101 in the middle of a large forest, this was a double community with both a monastery and

< Montsoreau château

Fontevraud cloister

a convent, the whole of which was run by an abbess, usually a woman from a noble family. Eleanor of Aquitaine died in the abbey and is buried here, alongside her husband, Henry II of England and their son Richard the Lionheart (*sans* the heart that lies in Rouen), along with other royal figures.

The complex includes a Romanesque church (1119) with an immense nave and beautiful cloisters, along with other monastery buildings that survived the Revolution. The most fascinating of these is an octagonal building, now recognised as the kitchen. Fontevraud served as a state prison from 1804 until 1963; today it is a cultural centre.

The village offers two hotels, a chambre d'hôte and various shops. Be sure to visit St Catherine's chapel, dating back to 1245.

DAY 6: FONTEVRAUD to CHINON

A relatively short walk through farmland to the banks of the Vienne and then along its course to the historic town of Chinon.

Distance	17 km (10.5 miles)
Time	4 hours 45
Notes	carry lunch supplies

< The kitchen at Fontevraud

The GR route passes right of the Chapel Royale. Leave the village up left on the Rue de l'Hermitage. You reach, on the right, the small chapel of

⑱ **Notre-Dame de Pitie**, dating from 1579. From here, there are good views back across fields to Fontevraud.

The way leaves farmland to enter forest on a broad path and eventually crosses a paved road and continues straight on, signed Chemin St-Vienne, on a paved lane. Soon, turn off right, initially through forest on a gently rising track. Skirt between fields and defence-owned land. The lane becomes paved on reaching a small hamlet. Go ahead to crossroads, where you turn right, signed Vallée des Vaux.

Pass by a walled château. The lane reaches a T-junction with good views back over the château. Turn left and, after 150 m or so, turn right onto a farm track. After a few hundred metres, turn right at another T-junction, picking up the GR waymarks and heading towards Thizay. The path soon doubles back and descends to the hamlet of

⑲ **La Chaussée**. Turn right to walk briefly along the main road. At the bar, cross the road and cross a small stream. The lane swerves right to follow the course of the Vienne river. It becomes an unsealed lane out of sight of the river. Soon, you can follow a parallel, grassy track close to the river bank with good river views. Eventually, you must return to the lane but you soon get river glimpses from here.

The farm lane becomes paved and continues by the river and passes under the D751 road. The route continues ahead, before turning off right and then left. Presently, good views open up of Chinon's château across river. Turn left at a T-junction onto a paved road. Soon, turn right at another T-junction and then left to cross the Vienne on a 12th-century bridge into ⑳ **Chinon**. There has been a fortress of various kinds here since prehistoric times. Henry Plantagenet (and II of England) rebuilt the castle and later died here. It was here that, in 1492, Jeanne d'Arc picked the disguised Charles VII from a crowd of courtiers and asked to lead his army against the English. The castle was later neglected and is today a ruin, though one with an entry fee.

Chinon was also home to François Rabelais, the scholar and writer of ribald satires, who

Fields above the Vienne >

Chinon

was born here in 1494. The old quarter is filled with well-preserved medieval houses, one of which is said to have received the dying or dead Richard the Lionheart from the battlefield. There are also several troglodyte dwellings and wine caves in and around the town. The rail station lies at the western extreme of Chinon; you can walk along the river to it.

LONG DISTANCE STAGES

km	time	location	acc
		Erigné	
16.5	4h30	Blaison-Gohier	G, C
12	3h	Le Thoureil	C
4.5	1h30	St-Georges	G, C
5.5	1h45	Gennes	H, C
4.75	1h15	Cunault	C
2.75	0h45	Trèves	G
3	1h	Chênhutte	H, C
18.2	4h30	Saumur	H, C, A
10.2	3h	Parnay	H
3	1h	Turquant	H, C
3.3	1h	Montsoreau	H, C
1	0h 15	(Candes-St-Martin)	H, C
7.5	2h	Fontevraud	H, C
17	4h45	Chinon	H, C

OTHER WALKS ALONG THE WAY

Chinon

The tourist office at Chinon has a *sentier pedestre* brochure for an 8.5-km circuit northwest of the town. This *petit randonnée* or PR, waymarked in yellow, departs from the car park for Chinon's château and visits the priory of Saint-Louans further down the Vienne river. It then turns north through vineyards to a viewpoint over protected land known as Le Pérou, rich in wildflowers. The PR then heads east, skirts a château and turns south to return to Chinon via two *loges des vignes*, old shelters for vine workers. *Allow 2-3 hours.*

Azay-le-Rideau

Beyond Chinon, the GR3 continues northeast through the forest of Chinon to the village of Azay-le-Rideau, reached after 26 km. Here you'll find what is perhaps the most perfect Renaissance château, floating serenely in the Indre river. If your time is limited, catch the train from Chinon to the station near Azay-le-Rideau and visit the château before continuing on to Tours.

Tours

Tours, which has given its name to the surrounding region of Touraine, is the principal town of the Loire valley. It has a reputation as a conservative city; its inhabitants claim to speak the purest form of French. However, its pleasant setting between two rivers, its historic riches and its dedication to fine living, including good wine and cuisine, makes this a palatable place for the traveller to pause.

Tours was founded under the Romans as Caesarodunum, later changed to Turones. Fragments of the Gallo-Roman walls can be found near the cathedral. In the 4th century, Tours became an important centre of Christianity under its bishop, St Martin, renowned for having given a beggar half of his cloak. After his death in 397, his relics became a pilgrimage drawcard and, in the Middle Ages, a huge basilica was built to receive his shrine and a large congregation.

Louis XI made Tours the capital of France in 1461 and the city flourished on the silk trade: two great fairs were held each year to sell the fabric. Unfortunately for Tours, Henri IV took a dislike to the city and returned the court to Paris.

Half-timbered houses

NOTES

Getting there: rail from Paris; there is an airport 6 km northeast

Tourist Office: 78-82 Rue Bernard-Palissy, 37042 Tours
☏ 0247703737 Fax: 0247611422
E: info@ligeris.com www.ligeris.com
www.tourism-touraine.com

Markets: M-Sat, Sun am, Place des Halles

Note: museum pass available

A section of the medieval town was cut away in the 18th century to accommodate the Rue Nationale, linking Paris to Spain. Redevelopment continued with an array of public buildings, designed by Victor Laloux, a native of Tours. During the Franco-Prussian war, the provisional government fled Paris and established itself at Tours until the city fell following Prussian bombardment in 1870. History repeated itself in 1940 when the French government removed to Tours in the face of German invasion. Again, the city suffered heavy bombing, this time combined with a firestorm.

After WWII the damaged buildings were carefully restored, but by 1960 the medieval quarter had virtually become a slum. It narrowly avoided being demolished and after much work visitors can now enjoy this maze of alleys with names such as Rue des Balais, du Serpent Volant and des Cerisiers, respectively 'brooms', 'flying serpent' and 'cherry trees'. Here, half-timbered houses lean and bulge alongside more sturdy Renaissance buildings.

Fairs are still a major part of life here. Each Wednesday and Saturday, the Marché aux Fleurs, one of France's oldest flower markets, is held in Boulevard Beranger. On the first Friday of each month, Tours hosts a Marché Gourmand for the finest local produce; the city even boasts an Institut Français du Gout or 'school of taste'.

Cathédrale façade >

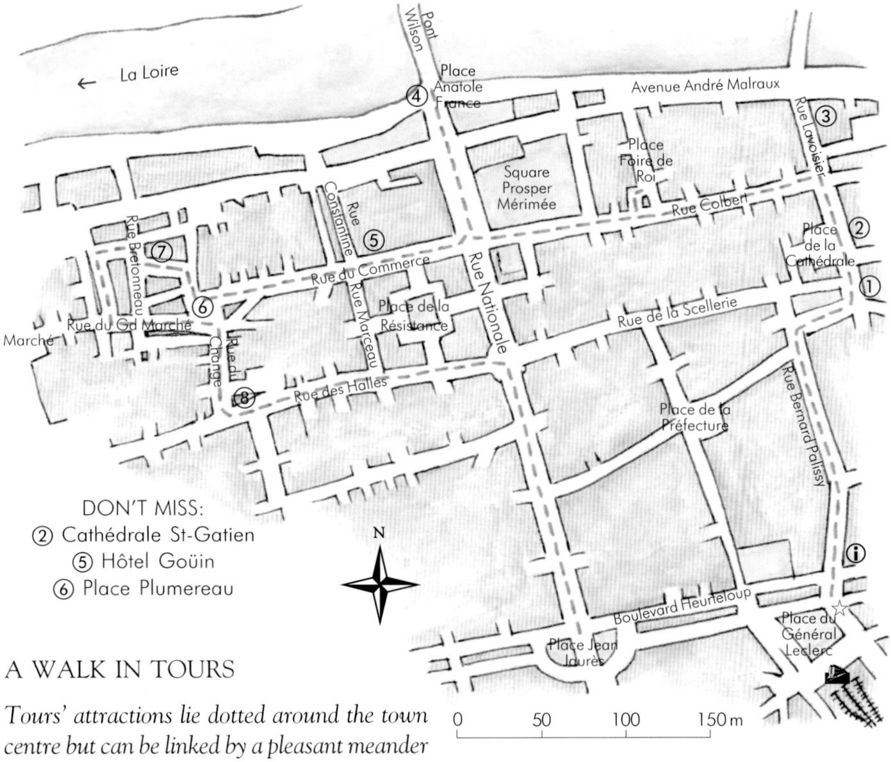

La Loire
Pont Wilson
Place Anatole France
Avenue André Malraux
Rue Lavoisier
Place Foire de Roi
Square Prosper Mérimée
Rue Colbert
Place de la Cathédrale
Rue Constantine
Rue Bretonneau
Rue du Commerce
Rue Nationale
Rue de la Scellerie
Place de la Résistance
Rue Marceau
Rue du Gd Marché
Marché
Rue du Change
Rue des Halles
Place de la Préfecture
Rue Bernard Palissy
Boulevard Heurteloup
Place Jean Jaurès
Place du Général Leclerc
N
0 50 100 150 m

DON'T MISS:
② Cathédrale St-Gatien
⑤ Hôtel Goüin
⑥ Place Plumereau

A WALK IN TOURS

Tours' attractions lie dotted around the town centre but can be linked by a pleasant meander along broad boulevardes and the winding alleys of the old quarter.

We start at Place du Général Leclerc, by the rail station. The station's façade was designed by a local, Victor Laloux, who also created the old Orsay station in Paris. Cross Boulevard Heurteloup and pass the **tourist office** to walk north up the quiet Rue Bernard Palissy. Cross Place François Sicard to the

① **Musée des Beaux-Arts**, housed in the former palace of the archbishop, built in the 17th and 18th centuries. This art museum (free entry) contains a good collection of Loire landscapes, plus some fine 15th-century paintings by Mantegna taken from Italy by Napoleon. The courtyard is filled by an enormous cedar of Lebanon, planted in 1804, and behind this is a pretty flower garden.

Next door is the impressive

② **Cathédrale St-Gatien**; you will need to stand well back to take in its Flamboyant Gothic façade. It was begun in the early 13th century and not completed until the 16th, and various parts of the church reflect the changes of

Cathédrale St-Gatien

Château Royal

architectural taste over that period. Much of the wonderful stained glass dates from the 13th to 15th centuries. You can visit the Renaissance cloisters with a guide for a small fee and see the unusual spiral staircase there.

Turn right out of the cathedral and follow Rue Lavoisier to view the ancient

③ **Château Royal**, now reduced to two medieval towers. One of these holds the **Historial de Touraine**, portraying fifteen centuries of local historical events with 165 wax figures.

Retrace your steps a short way and turn right along Rue Colbert. This was the main road through the medieval city and is lined with houses from the 15th and 16th centuries. No.39 is reputedly where Jeanne d'Arc's armour was fashioned. The passageway of Coeur Navré (or *distressed heart*), off to the left, was the path taken by condemned prisoners about to be executed or pilloried in nearby Place Foire le Roi. This square was also the site of the great silk fairs in the 15th and 16th centuries.

Further along, on the left, you can enter the garden of **Beaune-Semblançay**, where a 16th-century fountain stands beside the sheer façade of an old mansion. A passage leads through to Rue Nationale where, just past **St-Julien**, are two museums in monastic buildings. The 12th-century abbey cellars are dedicated, fittingly, to a museum of regional winemaking, **Musée des Vins de Touraine**. Dormitories contain the **Compagnonnage** museum, a celebration of ancient guilds and their crafts.

Continue up Rue Nationale to reach

④ **Place Anatole France**, where statues of Rabelais and Descartes ponder the view over the Loire. The 18th-century Pont Wilson had to be rebuilt after it collapsed in 1978. Retrace your steps and turn right into Rue du Commerce. The amazing Renaissance façade of no.25 belongs to the

⑤ **Hôtel Goüin**, built around 1510 for a merchant. The rest of the building, which now houses an archaeological collection, was destroyed in 1940.

Beyond Rue Constantine, you enter the traffic-free old quarter, crowded with half-timbered and oddly-shaped buildings. At the centre of this is the picturesque

⑥ **Place Plumereau**, an ancient market place that is still the hub of the town, but is now crammed with cafés and restaurants. A gateway at the northern edge leads through to Place St-

Carved detail

Hôtel de Ville

Pierre-le-Puellier, a small square with sunken Roman ruins.

Leave the place on Rue Briçonnet and have a look at the delightful sculpted detail on the **Ecoles des Langues Vivantes**. Turn left into the narrow Rue du Mûrier, where you'll find, at no.7, the

⑦ **Musée du Gemmail.** *Gemmail* is a 19th-century art form in which pieces of coloured glass are embedded and then lit from behind; there are examples in the collection by Picasso and Jean Cocteau.

Cross Rue Bretonneau and turn left into Rue des Cerisiers, entering the quarter now inhabited by artisans. Turn left down Rue Etienne Marcel then left into Rue du Grande Marché, lined with stalls on market days. Back at Place Plumereau, head south down Rue du Change and see if you can walk straight past the *pâtisserie*, La Marotte. Turn left at Rue des Halles to view the Romanesque

⑧ **Tour Charlemagne,** once the north tower of a massive 12th-century church dedicated to St Martin, the 4th-century bishop of Tours. The tower is said to have been built over the tomb of Charlemagne's wife Luitgarde, who died in 800. The new basilica stands just nearby, a neo-Byzantine affair designed by Laloux and built from 1886 to 1924.

From here, a stroll along the shop-lined Rue des Halles and then south along Rue Nationale will bring you to Place Jean Jaurès, dominated by the law courts and the **Hôtel de Ville**, another work of Laloux. You are not far now from your starting point.

Basilica St-Martin >

FURTHER AFIELD

Parks and Gardens

Tours is well-supplied with public parks and gardens. Its botanic gardens, dating back to 1843, lie 750 m east of Place Jean-Jaurès. North of old Tours, across the Loire on the Pont Mirabeau is the vast Parc de Sainte Radegonde. Another large green space is found 800 m south of the rail station on Île Honoré de Balzac, an island in the Cher river.

Villandry

Some 17 km southwest of Tours is the Château de Villandry, set in five hectares of the most elaborate formal gardens in France. The gardens (entry fee) are most colourful in spring and autumn but are open daily throughout the year. Public transport from Tours is limited: a train runs occasionally to Savonnières, 4 km east of Villandry. A better alternative is to hire a bicycle in Tours (Amstercycles, 5 Rue du Rempart, near the rail station, ☏ 0247612223) and cycle along the D88 along the Loire, south on the D288 across the Cher and into Savonnières, then east on the D7 to the village of Villandry and its château. *Allow a full day.*

Long-distance paths

Several GR paths pass through or near Tours. The GR3 closely follows the left bank of the Loire; a section downstream is described in the previous chapter.

A possible circuit to the east of Tours follows. From old Tours, cross to the right bank of the Loire on the footbridge Saint Symphorien and follow the GR3, heading east. The first destination is **Vouvray**, famous for its white wines; the village boasts 40 or so *caves* or cellars. Soon after, the GR heads south, crossing to the

The Loire at twilight

Loire's left bank to pass through Montlouis-sur-Loire before reaching **Amboise**. The château here is of great historical importance as the home of several French kings and the site of a Huguenot conspiracy. Leonardo da Vinci spent his last years here and his home, Clos-Lucé, is a museum.

Continue on the GR3 to **Chaumont-sur-Loire** and its fortified château. From here, pick up a GRP that diverges from the Loire and heads south to the Cher river, where you turn west onto the GR41. This soon leads to **Chenonceau**, renowned for its magnificent Renaissance château that spans the Cher. From here the GR41 crosses to the south bank of the Cher and heads west to **Bléré**, then joins the the GR46 to enter Tours. *Allow 4-5 days.*

OPENING HOURS

Musée des Beaux-Arts	daily except Tue 9-12.45, 2-6
Cathédrale St-Gatien	daily, closed 12-2; cloisters closed Sun morning
Historial de Touraine	daily 9-12, 2-6 (Jul-Aug 9-6.30; Nov-Mar 2-5.30)
Musée des Vins de Touraine	daily except Tue 9-12, 2-5
Musée de Compagnonnage	daily except Tue 9-12, 2-5 (daily 9-6.30 summer)
Hôtel Goüin	daily 10-7 (shorter hours and closed Fri in winter)
Musée du Gemmail	Tue-Sun 10-12, 2-6.30 (closed mid-Oct to mid-Mar)

THE DORDOGNE

NOTES
Type: a 5-day walk - 123 km (76 miles)
Difficulty: easy-medium with long days
Start: Martel (rail from Toulouse or Brive)
Finish: Rocamadour (same rail line)
Tourist Offices:
www: tourisme-lot.com
www: tourismelimousin.com
Map: IGN 1:100000 #48 *Perigeux Tulle* or 1:25000 #2136ET, 2135E & 22360
Best timing: April-October

The Dordogne is one of France's longest rivers and is said by many to be its most beautiful. This walk is centred on the upper Dordogne river valley and surrounding plateaux formerly known as Haut-Quercy. Unmarred by large industrial cities and away from teaming tourist haunts, the area provides a wealth of opportunity for the walker and is crisscrossed by long distance footpaths, several of which form the basis of this near-circular walk. Here are uncluttered landscapes of wooded hills and lush farmland, open limestone plateaux or *causses* carved through by pretty river valleys and deeper gorges, and unspoilt medieval villages linked by twisting lanes. The valleys of the Dordogne, the Cère, the Bave, the Autoire and the Alzou all make for superb walking. The Martel and Gramat Causses, though more remote and arid, are equally interesting; the Gouffre de Padirac, a dramatic chasm on the Gramat Causse, is one of France's natural wonders.

The region's tranquillity is largely the result of depopulation. The rural exodus continued throughout the 20th century, stemmed only partly by the advent of tourism. The quietude is in stark contrast to the region's tumultuous past, evidence of which can be seen in the fortifications surrounding its châteaux, churches and indeed its towns and villages. This was long disputed territory between the English Plantagenets and French Capetians, the river Dordogne acting as a natural dividing line. Quercy was ceded to the English by the 1259 Treaty of Paris but fighting during the Hundred Years War restored it to French ownership in 1369. Later, the area was racked by the Wars of Religion between Huguenot Protestants and Catholics.

This route encompasses many sites attesting to these bloody struggles: old, walled towns such as Martel, Turenne and Rocamadour; the *bastide* (planned) town of Bretenoux; Castelnau-Bretenoux château and the ruins of other fortifications. You'll also see exquisite artifacts that once drew fervent pilgrims through these parts on their way both to Santiago de Compostela and to the shrine of St Amadour at Rocamadour where this walk concludes. The Quercy Romanesque style of architecture was rich in sculptural decoration, creating carved doorways known as *tympana*; excellent examples are to be seen along the way.

Much of the time you will be walking through pasture, farmland and orchards. Walnuts, tobacco, strawberries, ducks and geese (for *foie gras*) and maize (to fatten the ducks and geese) are all plentiful and a hardy breed of sheep is grazed on the causse pasture. Dining certainly is no hardship in the Dordogne, famed for one of France's greatest regional cuisines.

Evening sky over Rocamadour

Farmland below Castelnau >

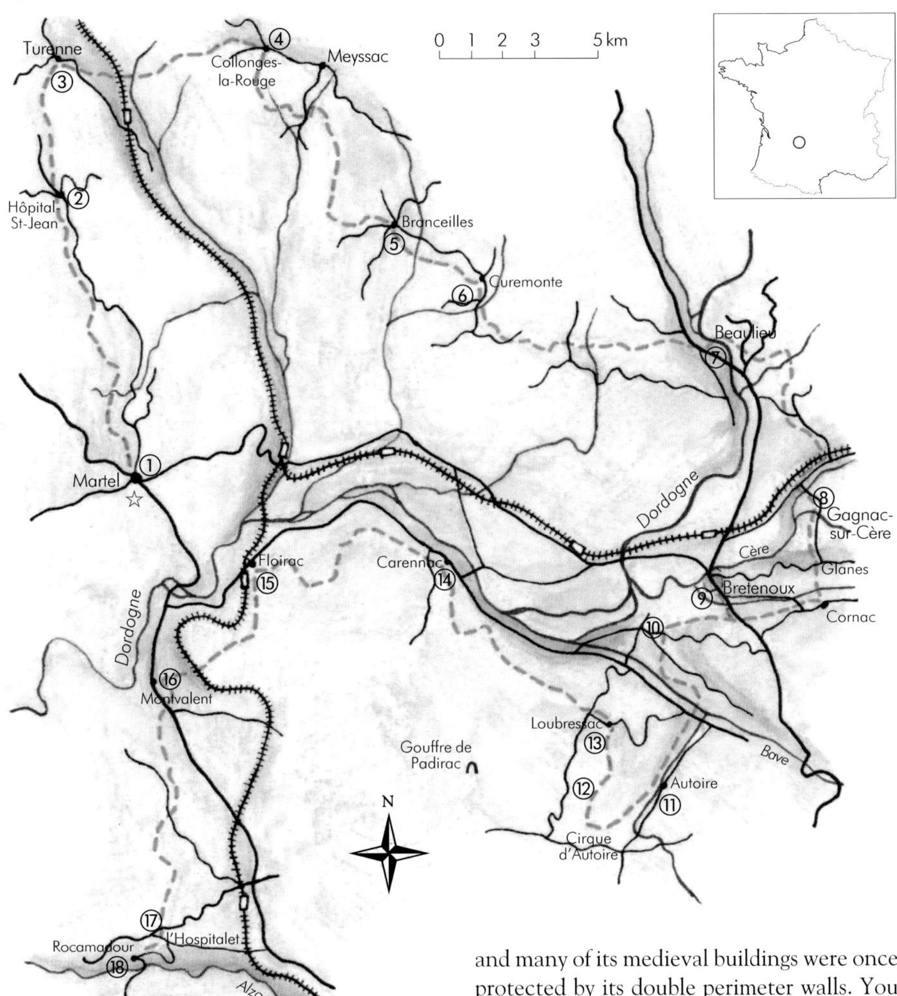

DAY 1: MARTEL to COLLONGES

The first day's journey follows the GR 446-480 over the Martel Causse, through farmland and woodland to the ancient hilltown of Turenne and then east to Collonges-la-Rouge with its unique red sandstone architecture.

Distance	22.7 km (14 miles)
Time	6 hours
Notes	take lunch provisions

Our route begins in

① **Martel**, a picturesque market town 7 km by road from St Denis-pres-Martel rail station. Martel is known as the 'town of seven towers' and many of its medieval buildings were once protected by its double perimeter walls. You should take time to inspect the Gothic St-Maur church with its Romanesque tympanum depicting the Last Judgement, its buttressed bell-tower and other towers with battlements. There is an 18th-century covered market or *halle* in the Place des Consuls and the nearby town hall, the Hôtel de la Raymondie, is an elegant mansion originally built as a fortress in the 13th and 14th centuries.

Leave Martel on the GR 446-480 which heads off north and can be joined from the north side of the N140 road to the right of its intersection with the D23. The path soon crosses but stays close to the D23 for 1 km; there are views back to Martel's distinctive skyline. The path then veers off to the left (NW) and heads into woodland and after another

1 km it swings right (NE) and later joins a minor road. Turn left at a T-junction, crossing the stream, and follow the D23. After 500 m you turn left on a forest path which joins a minor road at **Maslafon** hamlet. From here it is under 5 km to

② **Hôpital-St-Jean**, the site of a medieval leper hospice, first on woodland paths and then following the D23 once more.

About 2 km north of Hôpital-St-Jean, you leave the region of Midi-Pyrénées and enter Limousin. At the hamlet of **La Gironie**, the path forks left following the D150 before crossing the D8 to climb the narrow cobbled streets of medieval

③ **Turenne**. Overlooking a delightful landscape of wood and meadow, the hilltop town of Turenne nestles sleepily around the ruins of its fortified castle. Its size belies its former importance as the capital of the viscounty of Turenne that held power over more than 1200 villages and abbeys in the 15th century. Under the Tour d'Auvergne dynasty, Turenne remained the last independent feudal fiefdom in France until the ninth viscount sold the viscounty to Louis XV in 1738. All that remains of the fortress are the 11th-century Tour de Cesar (with panoramic views east to the Monts du Cantal) and the 13th-century Tour de l'Horloge. The 15th- and 16th-century town houses around the Place de la Halle attest to Turenne's former wealth.

A Martel doorway

Our route leaves the town eastwards downhill along a minor road passing under a railway line after about 1 km. Soon after turn right onto a minor road and in 500 m turn right again onto a path through a strip of woodland and orchards to rejoin a road and pass through the small hamlet of **Ligneyrac**. Continue past the church and, as the road bends sharply, the path continues off to the left. About 1 km further on, the path veers left and skirts a hill, above a road, to reach orchards. From here the route follows minor roads into

④ **Collonges-la-Rouge**. The distant prospect of Collonges in the late afternoon light is quite beautiful, its deep red sandstone buildings set amidst verdant countryside. The village dates back to the 8th century but it later became a halt for pilgrims en route to Santiago de Compostela in Spain. Collonges is graced by châteaux and manor houses with pepper-pot turrets and towers dating from the 16th century when it became the holiday retreat for Turenne's nobility. The whole village repays thorough

< An alley in Turenne

Collonges-la-Rouge

exploration but particularly the covered market with its communal oven and the 13th-century penitents' chapel. The church dates from the 11th century but was fortified during the Wars of Religion. The beautiful 12th-century tympanum is carved from white Turenne limestone, contrasting with the building's red sandstone. Nearby **Meyssac**, another picturesque market town of red sandstone, is an alternative overnight stop, with shops (there are none in Collonges).

DAY 2: COLLONGES to BEAULIEU

Still following the GR 446-480, we journey southeast through undulating country and the isolated villages of Branceilles and Curemonte before descending east to Beaulieu on the banks of the Dordogne.

Distance 27 km (16.8 miles)
Time 7 hours
Notes buy a packed lunch in Collonges

Leave Collonges on the road to Saillac. In 500 m the path forks left from the road and heads SSE. For the next 10 km the route heads generally S to SE, following paths and short stretches of road through orchards, farms and woodland. The tiny settlements of Pevridieu, Cruze and Coquart are passed and then

⑤ **Branceilles** can be visited by making a short detour on the D10. Otherwise the path skirts north of the village, heading SW from the junction through orchards, crossing the Ruisseau le Maumont and veering left to follow a lane. A minor road is reached and followed right into the village of

⑥ **Curemonte**, one of France's classified villages and set on an escarpment overlooking the valley of the Soudoire. The village was named after a knight of the First Crusade in 1096, Raymond de Curemonte, and has seen little change in recent centuries. Full of turreted and towered old houses, Curemonte also boasts three churches and three châteaux plus a gîte d'étape 1.5 km north.

The GR 446-480 wends through the village and leaves on the D15. Soon you follow a minor road left to a T-junction. Here the path leaves the road and contours around a small hill. On reaching a crossroads, the route heads S then, 100 m on, turns left onto a footpath to the settlement of **Sennac**. From here, follow the road east for 1 km then turn right onto the D153 and left at the next T-junction. The route zigzags down through woods and then on the winding D153E to pass a communications pylon. Turn left onto a minor road for a short distance then right onto an ancient cobbled mule track that descends the river valley steeply. Soon the Dordogne is glimpsed through the trees and the path descends to cross the main road (D940) and enter the charming

⑦ **Beaulieu-sur-Dordogne**, an attractive old riverside village which lines a gentle curve in the upper Dordogne. Beaulieu centres around its famous church, the majestic 12th-century Romanesque abbey church of Sainte-Pierre, once a pilgrim halt en route to Santiago de Compostela. The south portal features a tympanum, carved from limestone around 1140, depicting Christ's second coming. Christ is represented as a triumphant Roman emperor while the double lintel below depicts the seven-headed monster from the book of Revelations. Nearby, on the riverbank is the restored 12th-century Chapelle des Penitents, now a religious art and history museum. Beaulieu has a tourist office.

DAY 3: BEAULIEU to BRETENOUX

A climb out of the Dordogne valley takes you through farmland and forest on backroads. In the valley of the Cère you join a new GR and reach the former bastide town of Bretenoux.

Distance 22 km (13.7 miles)
Time 5 hours 30

Following the GR 446-480, cross the Dordogne on a footbridge near the Chapelle des Penitents. The path crosses parkland to reach a riverside road which is followed right with beautiful views left through a vineyard to a château. After 700 m the path veers away from the river and crosses first the D116 and soon after the D41, zigzagging uphill to a communications pylon. Less than 1 km on, the route heads E along a minor road through the settlement of **La Borderie**. After 1 km, leave the waymarked GR route and turn right (S) at a crossroads onto a minor road. Continue on this road through two sets of crossroads to reach the bucolic hamlet of **Fontmerle** after about 4 km. Now descend the winding D116E, turning left (SE) at an intersection and descending more gradually towards the river Cère. Near the river, turn right onto the busier D14 and follow this through Port de Gagnac then turn left over the river and into

⑧ **Gagnac-sur-Cère**. There are pleasant picnic spots by the river if you arrive here at lunch time. Leave Gagnac, keeping the church on your right, and soon turn left onto the D134 and left again at a small cemetery to go through **Glanes**, the centre of a small wine-making area. Keeping the church on your right, soon cross the D3 and continue south on a minor road to reach picturesque **Cornac**. Pick up the GR 480-652, leaving Cornac westwards on the D134. Where the road forks, the path bisects the two roads and leads beside orchards for 2 km to reach the major D940 road. Here you detour right on the D940 for 1.3 km to the overnight stop of

Beaulieu-sur-Dordogne

⑨ **Bretenoux**. Sitting astride the river Cère, Bretenoux is a *bastide* town with a well-preserved medieval centre. Bastides were the 'new towns' of the 13th century, built hurriedly in France's southwest by both the French and English in the lead up to the Hundred Years War. Some were built on near-impregnable clifftops while others like Bretenoux depended on perimeter walls punctuated with gates and towers for protection. All bastides were built to a grid plan around a central square containing a wooden

< A cave or cellar door

Autoire

covered market (*halle*) surrounded with covered arcades (*couverts*). Old Bretenoux retains its grid plan, halle, couverts and sections of ramparts. It has since acquired hotels, restaurants, shops and a tourist office.

DAY 4: BRETENOUX to CARENNAC

A long but spectacular walk takes in the awesome Château de Castelnau, the charming villages of Autoire, Loubressac and Carennac and the scenery of the Bave valley, Autoire gorge and the Gramat Causse high above.

Distance 26 km (16 miles)
Time 7 hours
Notes take lunch provisions

Leave Bretenoux and return to where you left the waymarked path the previous day. Turn right onto the footpath, ascending gently through wood and farmland to reach the

⑩ **Château de Castelnau-Bretenoux** with the hamlet of Prudhommat lying at its foot. Visible from afar, the massive red bulk of Castelnau is truly imposing at close quarters. It was built in the 11th century on a spur of rock by the powerful barons of Castelnau and the huge outer fortifications (more than 5 km around the perimeter) were added during the Hundred Years War. Its sheer scale – its garrison comprised 1500 men and 100 horses – makes it one of the finest examples of medieval military architecture. Tours are in French; the castle closes on Tuesdays. At its foot stands the beautiful St Louis Collegiate Church and canons' residences.

The path now descends through fertile farmland to the Bave valley, crossing the pretty river Bave after a few kilometres. You soon enter the narrow valley of the Autoire near its confluence with the Bave. Cross the river Autoire and then follow it upstream. Here, set exquisitely at the mouth of the gorge, is the delightful Quercynois village of

⑪ **Autoire**. This is a miniature showcase of Quercy architecture, replete with turreted and towered châteaux and mansions, quaint houses, and farm buildings with elegant dovecotes (built to keep the prized pigeon droppings rather than the pigeons). The steep roofed, half-timbered buildings are made of Gramat limestone and have small balconies reached by stone steps. The route leaves Autoire on a footpath behind the 10th-century

Ruins of the Château des Anglais >

church of St Pierre. Soon there is a short diversion to a superb 30 m waterfall, one of several over which the Autoire plunges from the Gramat Causse. Returning from the waterfall, you now climb steeply out of the gorge. At a path junction, a short diversion right takes you to the dramatic ruins of the
⑫ **Château des Anglais**, built out of the sheer cliff face by the English during the Hundred Years War to keep watch over the gorge. The views down to Autoire are indeed spectacular. Back at the junction, continue the ascent to the limestone plateau with wonderful views back to the natural amphitheatre of the Cirque d'Autoire. Out of the gorge, the path loops around north through the dry pastureland, eventually picking up a minor road NW towards Loubressac.

The path skirts just to the right of
⑬ **Loubressac** but a brief detour is warranted. Built on a spur of rock occupied since ancient times, Loubressac commands splendid views eastward to the Bave valley and north to the Château de Castelnau. It has a hotel and restaurants and would make a suitable overnight stop if you plan to visit the **Gouffre de Padirac** (see the end of this chapter).

From Loubressac, rejoin the GR 480-652 heading west through the hamlet of La Poujade. It continues along a minor road for about 3 km when the path branches off right along a track and then left along a path, passing some ruins to the right. From here the path descends steeply towards the Dordogne, crossing the Gintrac road at the tiny settlement of **Taillefer**. The route descends left, overlooking the Dordogne, before looping back uphill to reach the hamlet of **Magnagues**.

The path descends again, crosses the D3 and reaches the riverside village of
⑭ **Carennac**. Here is a beautiful Quercy village showcasing 16th-century golden stone houses and turreted manor-houses clustered around the priory and church of St Pierre. The priory, which was damaged in the Revolution, still retains its fortified gateway and a hexagonal priory tower. The Romanesque church, next to the castle, is noted for its superb 12th-century carved tympanum and its restored two-storey cloisters. The religious writer Fénelon is supposed to have written his masterpiece, *Télémaque*, at Carennac where he spent 15 years as senior prior.

DAY 5: CARENNAC to ROCAMADOUR

The final day's walk wends high above the Dordogne to the grand Cirque de Montvalent before heading inland over the Gramat Causse towards the amazing site of Rocamadour on the cliff face of the Alzou gorge.

Distance	25 km (15.5 miles)
Time	6 hours 30
Notes	start early

The GR 480-652 path climbs out of Carennac NW, high above the course of the

Tympanum, Carennac >

Rocamadour rooftops

Dordogne for several kilometres, providing filtered views of the river. It contours around a gentle bend in the river and then climbs up to a farm where you turn left onto a lane, following it south through woodland. The route leaves the lane right (W) and soon joins another to cross a minor road. The path enters more woods, descends a gully, skirts left around the village of

⑮ **Floirac** and crosses the Floirac road. A detour into Floirac for lunch provisions is easily made. The walk can be substantially shortened to allow an afternoon exploration of Rocamadour by catching a train from the Floirac train halt to the Rocamadour-Padirac station. Soon the path turns sharply S and climbs up to the causse cliffs of the **Cirque de Montvalent**, affording picturesque views of the valley and a *cingle*, a meandering loop in the Dordogne below. The path soon joins a farm track and you head SW through **Veyssou**. In a further 2.5 km, mainly on farm tracks, you reach the village of

⑯ **Montvalent** where the GR 46 is joined and followed to Rocamadour. Head S on the east side of the busy N140 for almost 1 km. Cross the road and continue S, passing to the right of a château at La Sarladie and dropping through woodland. The D15 is crossed and the path climbs again, joining a minor road SW for 1 km when you turn right to follow a farm track to the buildings of Les Alis. Turn left onto a minor road leading, after a kilometre, into the hamlet of

⑰ **L'Hospitalet** where there are excellent views of the Alzou gorge and Rocamadour, less than 2 km away. The route takes the pilgrims' 'holy road', passing near l'Hospitalet's 13th-century chapel and the ruins of the pilgrim hospital, then under the Porte de l'Hôpital before joining the D32 road. At the Porte du Figuier or 'fig tree gate' you enter

⑱ **Rocamadour**, one of the most famous pilgrimage sites of the 12th to 14th centuries. Rocamadour is still a shrine and a well-touristed village best seen out of season or late in the day when the coaches have left. Inside its gates, houses and souvenir shops line its single pedestrian street, above which rise the buildings of the ecclesiastical city, accessed by climbing the 223 steps of the Grand Escalier. The whole site is crowned by a château and ramparts from where there are panoramic views over the roofs of the churches and houses below. From the Grand Escalier you enter the churches' parvis, the Place St-Amadour, around which are grouped seven churches. Of these, the most hallowed shrine is the Chapelle Notre-Dame containing the venerated 12th-century Black Madonna, a wooden reliquary. Rocamadour, with its rich history and spectacular setting, is a fitting end to our walk.

LONG DISTANCE STAGES

km	time	location	acc
		Martel	H,C
15.5	4h	Turenne	H,C
7.2	2h	Collonges-la-Rouge	H,C
14	3h30	Curemonte	G
13	3h30	Beaulieu	H,G,A
14	3h30	Gagnac-sur-Cère	H
8	2h	Bretenoux	H,G
10	2h45	Autoire	H,C
5.5	1h45	Loubressac	H
10.5	2h30	Carennac	H
25	6h30	Rocamadour	H,C

OTHER WALKS IN THE REGION

Gouffre de Padirac

If you can add a day to your itinerary, make a side trip to this extraordinary site from Loubressac (see Day 4). This collapsed cave provides access to a subterranean river 100 m below ground and to a series of astonishing galleries it has hollowed out of the Gramat limestone. Explored by Edouard Martel from 1889 and opened to the public in 1898, Padirac is a deservedly popular attraction (open April to early October; guided tours).

From Loubressac, rejoin the GR 480-652 heading west through La Poujade hamlet. The Gouffre de Padirac can be reached by leaving the GR, taking the D14 SW at a crossroads and then forking left and left again on paths. *12 km (7.5 miles); allow 6 hours.*

Sarlat circuit

Further west along the Dordogne is a cluster of fascinating villages and châteaux. This loop starts at charming Sarlat and leads south over the river to visit Domme and Castelnaud then returns via La Roque-Gageac.

From the roundabout by Sarlat's *gare SNCF*, walk under the rail viaduct on the D704 and take Av. Rostand south. Fork left into Av. du

A château south of Sarlat

The view from Domme

Dr.Boissel and contine south through the hamlet of La Canéda to Montfort village on the Dordogne, overlooked by a medieval castle. Here you pick up the GR64a, following it west through woods to Vitrac. At Vitrac Port, cross the river and fork right onto a riverbank track, passing La Perpetuum camping ground. A steep climb leads via the Porte des Tours into the 1281 *bastide* town of **Domme**. It has stunning views, underground caves and is an excellent overnight stop (hotels and chambres d'hotes).

Leave via the Porte del Bos, now following the GR64 downhill to cross the D46 and then pick up a track along the Dordogne heading west. Turn right onto a road to St-Julien, where the GR64 takes forest paths to Camping Maisonneuve then the D57 to **Castelnaud-la-Chapelle** (gîte d'étape). Its 12th-century fortress has a museum of medieval warfare.

Cross the river on the D57 and then turn right to **La Roque-Gageac** (hotels and gîte d'étape). Take the minor road at the east of the village that climbs a narrow valley north and then east. Turn right at a T-junction and follow this road for 2.7 km, then fork right onto the D57 and follow this all the way back to Sarlat. *34 km (21 miles); allow 2-3 days.*

l'espri
de
famille
MARY
CÉPIÈ
l'esprit
de
famille
CADEAUX
DECORATIO

Toulouse

Toulouse has always been the hub of the southwest. Once it was the capital for all the regions united by the Occitan dialect or *langue d'Oc*. Now it is a thriving centre for the aerospace industry, but arts and culture still flourish here and it makes an excellent stopping place before you go walking in the nearby mountains of the Pyrénées or visit the historic towns of Albi, Carcassonne or Moissac.

The settlement that became Toulouse originally grew up by shallows where the river Garonne could be easily forded. It was known as Tolosa by the Romans and became a centre of new ideas, converting to Christianity in the 3rd century. The Visigoths made it their capital in the 5th century before it fell into Merovingian hands in 508. After Charlemagne, the region was ruled by the counts of Toulouse, a great feudal dynasty that kept one of the most magnificent courts in Europe.

When the Cathar heresy spread though the south in the 12th century, it was more than tolerated here. As a result, the city suffered besiegment twice during the crusade led by Simon de Montfort. Toulouse soon regained its position as a centre of culture, partly as a result of the religious turmoil. In 1229, Raymond VII was required by the Treaty of Paris to support various academics, thus founding the university that still flourishes here today. In 1324, seven leading citizens created a society to preserve the *langue d'Oc*, creating France's oldest literary academy.

From the 9th century, the city was administered by a council (or *capitol* in Occitan) comprising a number of *capitouls* who wielded significant power and enjoyed great prestige. This system allowed merchants to enter the ranks of the aristocracy: to mark their rise, new noblemen would adorn their mansion with a turret. As in the town of Albi, *pastel* or dyer's woad was a source of great prosperity here. The 16th-century merchants who grew rich on the trade built mansions known as *hôtels particuliers* and many are still found in the old quarter.

NOTES

Getting there: Toulouse-Blagnac airport is 8 km N-W; rail from Paris

Tourist Office: Donjon du Capitole, 31080, ☏ 0561110222
Fax: 0561220363
E: infos@ot-toulouse.fr
www.ot-toulouse.fr

Markets: Place Victor Hugo, Tue-Sun

As there were no stone quarries on the alluvial plain of the Garonne, the most commonly used building material was red brick, leading to the city's nickname of 'laVille Rose'. The colours shift from a hot red to a soft pink, depending on the light, of which there's plenty in this southern city.

The warm climate helps to make this a lively city, abuzz with university students and a multicultural mix of people. Many refugees from the Spanish Civil War settled here and there is a large North African population that has arrived more recently.

The Capitole

< An alley in la Ville Rose

A WALK IN TOULOUSE

A stroll between the major buildings of the old centre and across the Garonne.

We start this itinerary at Place Wilson, a kilometre southwest of the rail and bus stations. This pleasant green space is popular for an evening aperitif. The fountain portrays Godolin (1579-1648), famed as the first poet in the Occitan language. Leave Place Wilson due west along Rue Lafayette to soon reach the Charles de Gaulle square, dominated by the

① **Donjon**, or keep of the 16th-century Capitole. It was restored, a little inaccurately, by Viollet-le-Duc and now houses the tourist office. Just behind the Donjon is the back entrance to the

② **Capitole**, built in 1760. This brick-and-marble building is Toulouse's city hall and also houses a prestigious opera venue. Inside is the Salle des Illustres, decorated in the 19th century. Walk through to **Place du Capitole**, the city's main plaza, inlaid with a bronze cross of Languedoc and lined with cafés. Take a look at the ceilings of the arcade gallery facing the Capitole to see striking artworks by Moretti.

Walk north up Rue du Taur, soon passing,

on the left, the 14th-century church of **Notre-Dame-du-Taur** in Southern Gothic style. Inside you'll find a 16th-century wooden statue of the Virgin Mary, now black with age. At the end of the street is the beautiful

③ **Basilique Saint-Sernin**. St Sernin or Saturnin was a Languedoc apostle martyred in 250 by being bound and dragged down steps by a bull that he had refused to sacrifice. The basilica was built on his burial site and it received many relics from Charlemagne, becoming a focal point for pilgrims. Built, in the late 11th century, to hold huge congregations during the era of great pilgrimages, it has a 115-m-long chancel and is France's largest Romanesque building. It is very similar in style to the cathedral at Santiago de Compostela. The octagonal tower was added in the 13th century and the spire in the 15th.

Across Place St-Sernin, you'll find the

④ **Musée Saint-Raymond**, Toulouse's museum of archaeology, housed in a collegiate building. It maintains a well-displayed collection of antique sculptures, Roman portraits and sarcophagi. From its gardens, there is a good view of the basilica.

Now pick up the lane behind the museum, Rue Cartailhac, and continue along Rue

Saint-Sernin

Lautmann. Turn left and walk through Place Anatole France and down Rue Déville. Turn sharp right and then left into Rue Lakanal, passing an English-language bookshop, then right into the lane leading to the entrance of

⑤ **Les Jacobins**. Alarmed by the success of the Albigensian heresy, St Dominic founded the Jacobin or Dominican order in Toulouse in 1216. Its mother church and monastery were begun in 1230 and completed, in Gothic style, in 1385. Inside the nave is a row of 22-m-high columns with unusual fan vaulting so they resemble palm trees. The remains of St Thomas Aquinas are interred below the modern altar.

Continue south, past the Lycée Fermat, housed in the 16th-century Hôtel de Bernuy, and turn right into Rue Gambetta (note the 1504 façade of the *hôtel*), which becomes Rue Suau and then reaches Place de la Daurade, a public space that slopes down to the Garonne. From road level, you have a good view of the city's two hospitals: directly across river is the **Hôtel-Dieu St-Jacques**; just downstream is the massive dome of **Hospice de la Grave**.

Nearby, on Quai de la Daurade, is the 18th-

< Les Jacobins

Statuary in Musée des Augustins

century **N-D-de-la-Daurade**, built on the site of a pagan temple. The **Beaux Arts** school next door is often open for exhibitions.

Cross the Garonne on the 16-17th-century ⑥ **Pont Neuf**, Toulouse's oldest bridge.

On the other side is a red-brick tower, once a water tower and now a photographic gallery, **Galerie du Château d'Eau**. From this point, you could detour 750 m (straight down Rue de la République, left into Rue Reclusane and left into Allee Charles de Fitte) to visit the modern art gallery, housed in the recently restored buildings of **Les Abattoirs**. Alternatively, you could relax on the bank, known as the **Praire des Filtres** and enjoy the view across the river.

Return over the Pont Neuf and walk up Rue de Metz then turn left into the courtyard of the ⑦ **Hôtel d'Assezat**, the house of a pastel merchant who became a *capitoul*. Begun in 1555, its design comprises three classical styles with Greek columns. Upstairs is the Bemberg Foundation, a private collection of paintings, *objets d'art* and rare books.

Turn into the Rue de la Bourse; no.20 features a turret built by a would-be *capitoul*. Take Rue Malcousinat, which brings you to the pedestrian zone along the *cardo maximus*, the Roman road through the town. Turn left, passing through the junction known as Quatre Coins des Changes, and enjoy the façades and turrets of the many well-preserved buildings.

Detour briefly up car-restricted Rue des Changes to enjoy lovely façades housing boutique shops. Retrace your steps and turn left at Place Esquirol to regain Rue de Metz where you'll find the solid bulk of the ⑧ **Musée des Augustins**. This former Augustinian monastery is a perfect example of Languedoc Gothic architecture. although the building facing on to Rue d'Alsace was constructed by Viollet-le-Duc in the 19th century. The great and small cloisters shelter lovely gardens. Contained within the monastery is an excellent collection of stone carvings, including capitals and gargoyles.

Return towards Place Esquirol and turn left down Rue du Languedoc, then left into Rue Croix Baragnon, skirting the **Hôtel de Fumel** which houses the Chambre de Commerce. This is a charming street, with red-brick alley-vistas and old houses: No.15 dates back to the 13th century. in Place St-Etienne, you'll find a 16th-century fountain known as Le Griffoul, and behind it, the ⑨ **Cathédrale St-Etienne**. Begun in the 11th century, this unusual church took five centuries to complete and suffered funding

Canal du Midi >

Sunset on the Garonne

problems along the way. As a result it has a variety of styles and architectural peculiarities.

From here, you could wander north to return to Place Wilson, south to the various gardens or east to pick up the Canal du Midi.

OTHER EXCURSIONS

Canal du Midi

This canal meanders over 240 km to link the Mediterranean with the Atlantic. Completed in 1681, it is now a UNESCO World Heritage Site. It loops around the town, passing by the rail station, and is lined with beautiful plane trees. Shaded footpaths along the banks provide easy walking beyond Toulouse.

Gardens of Toulouse

Just 400 m south of St-Etienne is a green space of public gardens, including the Jardin Royal, Grand Rond and the Jardin des Plantes. The last contains a memorial to the Resistance in which a set of lenses allows sunlight into the crypt only on August 19, the anniversary of the liberation of Toulouse during WWII.

Cité de l'Espace

For the astronomically inclined, this museum features lots of interactive exhibits relating to space exploration. Arranged around its 3.5-hectare park are large objects such as the Mir station. Catch a #15 bus from Allées Jean Jaures to the end of the line, then walk for some 600 m to the park on Ave Jean Gonord.

OPENING HOURS

Capitole Galleries	Mon-Fri 8.30-5
Musée Saint-Raymond	daily 10-6(Sept to May); 10-7 (June-Aug)
Couvent des Jacobins	daily 10-6
Château d'Eau Gallery	Mon, Wed-Sun 1pm-7; closed Tuesdays
Les Abattoirs	daily except Mon 11-7 (Nov-Mar); 12-8 (Apr-Oct)
Hôtel d'Assezat	Tue-Wed, Fri-Sun 10-6; Thur 10-9; closed Mondays
Musée des Augustins	Mon, Thur-Sun 10-6; Wed 10-9; closed Tuesdays

THE PYRÉNÉES

While the Alps may be France's best known mountain range, the Pyrénées offer walkers a quite different mountain experience. They form a natural frontier between France and Spain, spanning almost from the Atlantic to the Mediterranean in two ranges which overlap midway at the Val d'Aron. Despite this, the Pyrénées tend to be divided into three sections: the lush, Basque country of the Pyrénées Atlantiques, the drier Pyrénées Orientales, and the central section known as the high or Hautes Pyrénées. The latter contains the best walking and is the focus of this chapter.

On the French side, the Hautes Pyrénées rise surprisingly steeply, in deep, green valleys and huge *cirques* or corries, in contrast to the arid *sierras* across the Spanish border. Though its peaks aren't as high as those of the Alps, several rise above 3000 m: Vignemale, on the border reaches 3298 m. Indeed, it's best not to underestimate these mountains, as the walking can be as challenging as you like.

While the climate here is more settled than that in the Alps, hot summer days can bring late thunderstorms. September is an ideal month for walking. Whatever the season, carry clothing to protect you from rain and cold.

NOTES
Type: day walks and a 2-day trek
Suggested base: Cauterets
Getting there: rail from Toulouse then bus from Lourdes
Tourist Office: Place M.Foch, 65116
☏ 0562925050 Fax: 0562921170
E: accueil@cauterets.com
www.cauterets.com
Map: IGN *Vignemale* 1647OT 1:25000
Best timing: late May to mid-Oct

Our base is Cauterets, a pleasant town on the edge of the *Parc National des Pyrénées* that began its life as a spa town as far back as the 10th century. It has shops dedicated to selling *berlingots*, boiled sweets that were originally curatives made from the mineral-rich water. As well as a tourist office, Cauterets also has a National Park office and a mountain guides' bureau that organises walks.

Several walks begin further up the Val de Jéret at the Pont d'Espagne, where there is a hotel. In season, a shuttle runs there regularly from Cauterets; out of season a taxi service is available. We recommend that you undertake the lovely return walk downhill from Pont d'Espagne to Cauterets on the *Sentier des Cascades*; it's described at the end of the chapter.

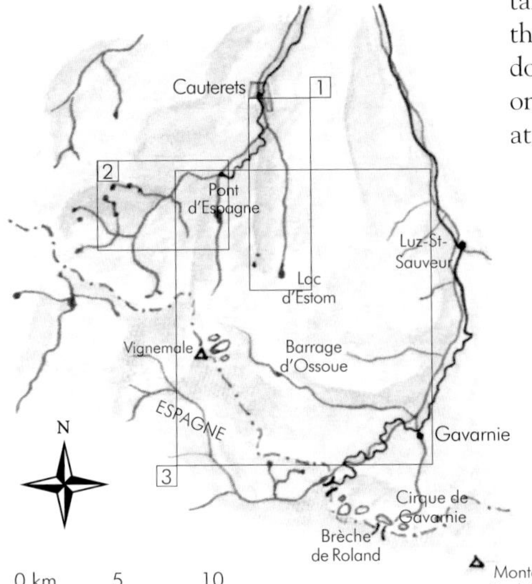

Barrage d'Ossoue >

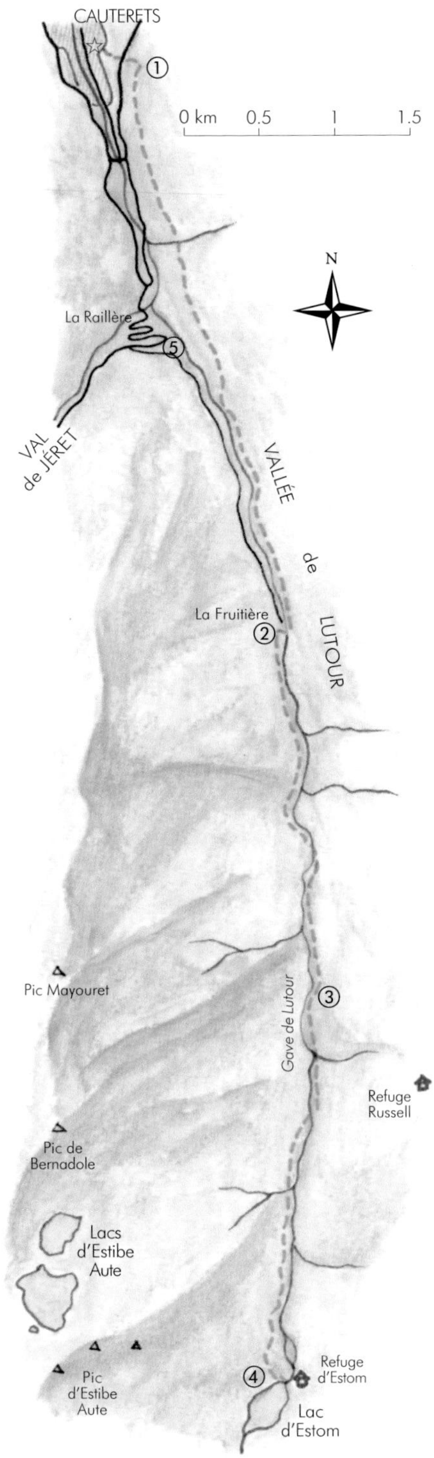

WALK 1: VALLÉE DE LUTOUR

This return walk involves a gradual ascent up a beautiful valley to the serene Lac d'Estom. Transport, parked at either La Raillère or La Fruitière, would shorten the route.

Distance	20.5 km (13 miles)
Time	6 to 7 hours
Difficulty	medium
Start/Finish	Cauterets

From Cauterets' Place Foch, walk up the Allée du Parc and up steps to the left of the yellow Maison du Curistes. A signpost leads you left, up past the church steeple to zigzag up through woodland. Cross the D12 road at ① **Pauze Vieux**, ancient site of thermal waters, and join the GR10 path which climbs further before it levels as *Chemin des Pères* and heads up valley.

Cross a stream, the Coume de Prébendé, and reach a path junction above the old thermal spa of La Raillère (which means *scree* in local dialect), where you fork left uphill. The path continues through beech woods and then passes through a gate into a pastoral zone at **Le Pradet**. From there the path follows close by the pretty Gave de Lutour to reach the small hotel at

② **La Fruitière**, which serves local cuisine. From here, the path continues, unmarked but clear, on the east bank of the river, through pasture and past alpenrose. It ascends more steeply by some lovely cascades and passes the

Crocus flowers by the path

Horses graze in the Lutour valley

③ **Cabane de Pouey-Caut**, a small hut.

About an hour from La Fruitière, the path crosses the river and continues up along the other bank, along the border of the National Park: you will see stencils indicating this. The climb becomes steeper as the valley narrows and rises through conifers and past another cascade to finally reach the northern end of ④ **Lac d'Estom**. At the lake edge, the Refuge d'Estom offers refreshments. Beyond the lake tower the Pic de la Sède (2976 m) and Pic de Labas (2946 m).

If you have time and are sure-footed, you might follow a faint path clockwise around the lake. The steam on the far side can be crossed a short way above the lake.

Leave the lake and return by the same route past La Fruitière to the junction above La Raillère. Here, turn left onto the footpath that zigzags down to the ⑤ **Cascade de Lutour**, crossing below the falls on a bridge. Descend from here to La Raillère, pass the string of shops selling whistling marmots, and continue along the road until a large disused building. A yellow signpost directs you down the driveway and onto a broad path, Avenue Demontzey, that drops gently through woods and then zigzags steeply down to enter Cauterets near the casino.

Lac d'Estom and its refuge

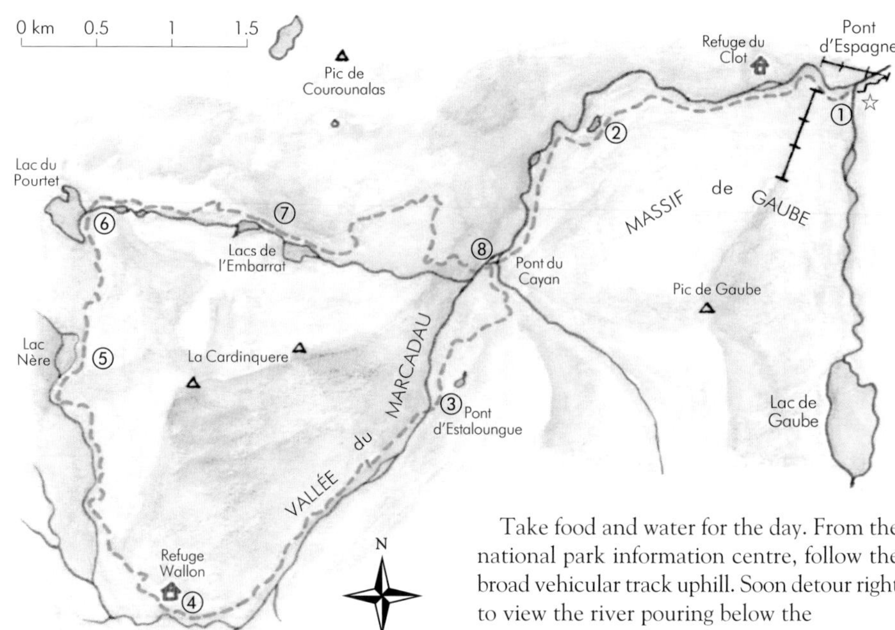

WALK 2: CIRCUIT des LACS

This day-walk of wild beauty ascends the magical Marcadau valley and then follows a string of perfect tarns. You might prefer to take two days, overnighting at Refuge Wallon.

Distance	19 km (12 miles)
Time	7 to 8 hours
Difficulty	strenuous
Start/Finish	Pont d'Espagne

Take food and water for the day. From the national park information centre, follow the broad vehicular track uphill. Soon detour right to view the river pouring below the

① **Pont d'Espagne**, an elegant arc. Return and cross over the bridge to the hotel, from where you can view another set of cascades, the confluence of the Marcadau and the Gaube. Turn left at the hotel and soon recross the Gave du Marcadau on a footbridge to the right bank. Pass by the *télésiège* (chairlift) and continue on the stony path uphill, signed to Vallée du Marcadau.

The now-bitumen road rises gently through the forest and passes above the tiny

② **Lac du Paradis**, somewhat overrated by name. The valley now opens out to pasture with mountain views. Almost 1.5 km from the lake, you reach a signed junction just before the **Pont du Cayan**. Turn left uphill, away from the river, towards Refuge Wallon.

From here you climb into forest, then drop a short way to cross to the left bank on the

③ **Pont d'Estaloungue**, in a bucolic valley setting. Climb once more on a rocky path above the stream and, after a further 1.5 km through forest, the path veers west to an area where grazing rights are shared by French and Spanish herders. This has long been a place of meeting and trading; the name Marcadau derives from the Spanish *mercado* for market. Here, above the Gave des Batans, stands the

< The autumn transhumance

A tarn below Lac du Pourtet

④ **Refuge Wallon** at 1865 m. Opened in 1911, this large refuge is named after Paul Edouard Wallon, a pioneer of the Pyrénées and co-founder of the Club Alpin Français (CAF) in 1874. From the terrace, you have a wonderful view into the Arratille valley, dominated by the massif of **Pouey Laou**.

From the refuge, take the path heading northwest, signed to Lac Nère. This climbs, steeply in parts, with spectacular mountain scenery in most directions. At a junction, bear right and continue climbing to the hidden

⑤ **Lac Nère**, set in a rocky basin at 2309 m. After a rest to enjoy lunch or the sweeping views, skirt above the eastern shore of the lake and climb steeply once more. After half an hour, you reach the largest of the lakes,

⑥ **Lac du Pourtet** (2420 m), overlooked by the sharp **Aiguilles du Pic Arrouy**.

Midway along the lake, the path turns sharply and climbs a short way to a gain a magnificent new view eastwards and descends steeply to two tiny linked tarns, unnamed on the map, but charming nonetheless. The stony path continues down, passing a path turn-off, to reach the two

⑦ **Lacs de l'Embarrat**, below the **Aiguilles de Castet Abarca**. These final lakes perch on a balcony, more like widenings of the stream than the higher, enclosed tarns. At the lower lake, watch for isards on the spur across valley. The path winds steeply down, past another turn-off and drops to the valley floor at the

⑧ **Pont du Cayan**. Don't cross the bridge, but return along the left bank through the lovely meadowland of the **Cayan** and **Clot** plateaux. Watch for marmots in the late afternoon. After passing the Chalet-refuge du Clot, follow a track back to Pont d'Espagne.

< Gave du Marcadau

WALK 3: BELOW VIGNEMALE

A two-day walk takes you from Pont d'Espagne to the village of Gavarnie via the base of spectacular Vignemale. You can overnight at the refuge of Oulettes or Baysselance; the latter would break the journey more evenly.

Distance	30 km (18.5 miles)
Time	6 h Pont d'Espagne to Baysselance 7 h Baysselance to Gavarnie
Difficulty	medium-strenuous
Start	Pont d'Espagne
Finish	Gavarnie

Past the park information centre, leave the main road almost immediately, taking the paved path left uphill, signed to Lac de Gaube. You are now following the high-level variant of the GR10 footpath, which will continue all the way to Gavarnie. After 20 minutes of climbing through conifer woods, you reach a very pretty glade of moss-covered rocks. The valley opens up and you can see the *télésiège* or chairlift across valley. Pass over flat rocks with strange seams, and over clusters of exposed tree roots.

Before the path dips, you gain your first glimpse of Vignemale with its somewhat grubby glacier. The path rises and you see cascades on the Gave de Gaube. Keep a lookout for isards that sometimes graze high up on the slopes opposite. In a few minutes you reach the foot of the turquoise

① **Lac de Gaube**. Refreshments are served at the *hotellerie* on its northeastern shore. The GR10 footpath continues along the western shore and then along the steam. Ten minutes on, cross to the left bank on a footbridge that offers a fine view back over the lake.

The stony path rises, passing the unmanned Cabane du Pinet. Pass an unnamed cascade and, after a rise, you see Cascade Esplumouse, About 500 m after the cascade, cross the Gave des Oulettes de Gaube on

② **a footbridge**. Soon, you pass the dramatic cascade of **Darrê Splumouse**. The valley now broadens and the path can be boggy in parts.

Les Grottes Bellevue >

Near a smaller cascade, the path veers right up a rocky rise to reach the ③ **Refuge des Oulettes de Gaube**. This small CAF refuge (☏ 0562926297) is basic but comfortable. It sits by the meltwaters running off Vignemale's retreating glaciers and, when the clouds lift, its view of the mountain is incomparable.

From the refuge, the GR10 heads southeast (ignore the turn-off to Refuge Wallon), climbing steeply uphill. Keep right at a path junction, to climb to the right of some tiny tarns. As you climb, several spurs offer a view back down valley to the distant Lac de Gaube. The spectacle of Vignemale and its neighbouring peaks becomes increasingly dramatic. Ascend over scree to gain the pass of ④ **Hourquettes d'Ossoue**, at 2734 m, the high point of the walk. (Although, from here, an optional side path allows an easy ascent of the peak of Petit Vignemale.) After pausing to enjoy the new views, veer left to follow the footpath downhill to the nearby ⑤ **Refuge de Baysselance**, another CAF refuge (☏ 0562924025), recently renovated and the ideal place to break your journey. Perched high on a ridge, its copper roof may be seen right down the Ossoue Valley.

Lac de Gaube

From the refuge, the path descends southeast, with good views of the extensive Glacier d'Ossoue and down over the fingers of the Ossoue gorge. After rounding a spur, you pass the entrance to the three caves of ⑥ **Grottes Bellevue**, hewn into the rock by the 19th-century mountaineer Count Henry Russell, who lived here for many summers.

The path continues down, veering away from a hanging valley and passing above the converging cascades of two streams. Soon you cross the Pont de Neige below the small Montferrat glacier and then the path rises to traverse the gorge on a rocky ledge some way above the main stream. Soon, pass above a ribbon of falling water, unnamed on the map.

Watch for marmots as you continue down the flower-decked valley, then cross the stream by a large erratic at the Oulettes d'Ossoue where the valley opens. Ahead is the man-made, but attractive, ⑦ **Barrage d'Ossoue**. The path skirts the northern shore to reach the dam wall and the head of the D128 road. The GR10 continues by crossing below the spillway on a metal footbridge. A signpost directs you to Gavarnie,

< Vignemale and the Oulettes de Gaube

but it will take longer than the stated 2 hr 45.

The footpath climbs a hillside, with the road across valley in sight. As you round a spur, look back to see Baysselance in the distance. The footpath runs roughly parallel to the road, but with two deviations into side valleys. The first enters the mouth of the Vallée de la Canau to an unmanned shelter, Cabane de Lourdes; the second brings you to the

⑧ **Cabane de Sausse-dessus**, which stands at the head of the valley of the same name, below a rocky spur. Cross boggy pasture and a stile, then descend gently on a rocky path through shrubbery that includes alpenrose.

As views of mountains beyond Gavarnie open up, you reach a grassy saddle where a mark on a large boulder instructs you to veer left to a red-and-white waymark. Descend towards a large boulder then veer right to a small cairn and veer left onto a stony track. This becomes a dirt footpath and descends through pasture to cross a stream and reach the D923 road.

Turn left for a 3-km road walk down to Gavarnie, watching out for footpaths that cut out road switchbacks. Les Granges de Holle, the CAF refuge, stands along the road some way above the village of

⑨ **Gavarnie**, which also offers several hotels and two gîtes d'étape. This was once a stop for pilgrims on their way to Santiago de Compostella, as noted outside the 12th-century church. It is now a magnet for tourists visiting the nearby Cirque de Gavarnie.

A cold snap

LONG DISTANCE STAGES

km	time	location	acc
		Pont d'Espagne	H
7.5	3h30	des Oulettes	R
3	2h30	Baysellance	R
19.5	7h	Gavarnie	H,G,R

Vallée de la Canau>

Cascade du Ceriset

OTHER WALKS IN THE REGION

Pont d'Espagne to Cauterets

This route may prove useful if you need to return from a walk above Pont d'Espagne, but it is well worth doing in any case, particularly the first half: the **Sentier des Cascades**.

From in front of Hotel Pont d'Espagne, pick up the GR10 footpath, descending the left bank of the Gave du Marcadau to a viewpoint below the bridge itself. From here, the path drops through beautiful mossy woodland alongside the river as it descends the Val de Jéret. Beyond the pretty Cascade de Boussès, you soon pass the Île Sarah Bernhardt and then the cascade and bridge of Pas de l'Ours. Just beyond this is the cascade of Pouey Bacou.

A footpath for climbing Pic de Péguère diverts off to the left and you reach the spectacular **Cascade du Ceriset**. A kilometre further on, the sulphurous smell of thermal springs announces La Raillère.

Cross the road and continue on the GR10 to the Cascade de Lutour. Cross the footbridge and zigzag up the hillside to a path junction, where you turn left and follow the Chemin de Pere to Pauze Vieux and then down into Cauterets. *Allow 2 to 3 hours one-way.*

Lac de Gaube

This enchanting lake, which is passed en route in Walk 3, can be the destination point on a short walk for less ambitious walkers.

From Pont d'Espagne, follow the direction in Walk 3 to reach the lake. For the return journey, pick up the broad gravel track that leaves from the foot of the lake and traverses the slope of the Massif de Gaube. This soon brings you to a *belvédère*, just beyond the télésiège station. Here you'll find a wonderful view across to Pic de Péguère plus information boards on such topics as glaciation. Just south of the station, a gravel track or ski *piste* descends rapidly to the base station of the chairlift, from where a track leads off right, back to Pont d'Espagne. *Allow 2 hours.*

Gavarnie Cirque and Brèche de Roland

Close to Gavarnie are two wonders of the Pyrénées that shouldn't be missed. The Cirque de Gavarnie is a tight amphitheatre of towering limestone walls, adorned with one of Europe's longest falls, the Grande Cascade. Well above it lies the Brèche de Roland, a huge square cleft in the mountain wall. There are various ways of seeing these.

Both marvels can be reached in a very long day-walk with a challenging rock clamber. From the centre of Gavarnie, follow the mule track south, over the Brioule bridge to the Hôtellerie du Cirque. Soon, cross a footbridge and head for the western base of the cirque, following vague red spots and cairns. These guide you up the Echelle des Sarradets, an exposed climb which should not be attempted in bad weather or if you suffer vertigo. At a grassy slope you can rest and then head up a steep Vallon des Sarradets to gain a dramatic view across the cirque to the Pic du Marboré.

The path now rises up the Sarradets valley to the refuge of the same name (sometimes called the **Refuge de la Brèche**). From here, a scree slope and a small glacier must be crossed to reach the stunning Brèche, which stands on the very border of France and Spain. In legend, it was created by the hero Roland, nephew of Charlemagne, who tried to break his sword rather than submit it to the Saracens; instead the magical sword created

Above the Cirque de Gavarnie

an escape route. On the other side, Spain stretches away like an arid moonscape.

Return to the refuge and take the track behind it, following red spots. Soon gain a view across the valley of Pouey Aspé. Drop to cross a cascading stream, assisted by a chain. Soon after, fork right on the path to Gavarnie that zigzags down, following cairns. Recross the stream and turn sharply right. The route curves left (up valley) before weaving down to the valley floor.

Brèche de Roland

Cross the Gave des Tourettes and go uphill a short way, then turn right onto a footpad. Gently descend the valley to reach a signpost on the Plateau de Bellevue; turn left and soon gain a wonderful view back into the cirque. Zigzag steeply downhill and then make a gentle descent into Gavarnie by its 12th-century church. *Allow 9 hours.*

Alternatively, make the Cirque de Gavarnie your destination and, from the Hôtellerie du Cirque, return on the path via the Refuge des Espuguettes. This path climbs through pine forest to meadows on the eastern side of the Gavarnie valley, with fine views of the cirque and the Brèche. From the refuge, descend back to a fork and turn right for a winding descent to the main valley path, just south of the Brioule bridge. *Allow 3 to 4 hours.*

The easiest route to the Brèche requires transport to Port de Boucharo, at the end of the D923. From here a footpath heads east to climb below the north face of Le Taillon. It joins the trail from Vallée de Pouey Aspe and climbs steadily to the Refuge de la Brèche, and thence to the Brèche itself (see above). Return by the same route. *Allow 4 hours 30.*

Strasbourg

This 'City of Roads' (as it translates from the German) is aptly named. Strasbourg has long been a crossroads where ideas and culture have been exchanged and today it is the cosmopolitan Alsatian capital and one of the capitals of the European Union. It also happens to be one of France's prettiest cities, centred on the Grand Île afloat in the river Ill, with many of its charming alleys closed to cars.

In 12 BC the Roman camp Argentoratum stood here, with the present Rue du Dome and Rue des Juifs as its main thoroughfares. Located only a few kilometres from the Rhine, a major transport artery linking central Europe with the Mediterranean, the settlement prospered from trade. It was part of the Germanic Holy Roman Empire but during the Middle Ages developed a surprisingly democratic constitution. Guilds of craftsmen played an important role in the city's life and fortifications were built to protect its status as a free city.

A university was founded in 1566 and Strasbourg became a centre of reform, home to several Protestant leaders. The ideas developed here were disseminated quickly by the invention of Johannes Gutenberg who perfected his printing press with moveable type. Religious factions created turmoil in the city and, in 1681, Louis XIV took the opportunity to acquire Strasbourg for France. The city gained a dynasty of prince-bishops who governed from the Rohan Palace until the Revolution; under their rule, the upper classes adopted French over the Alsatian language. It was in Strasbourg in 1792 that the *Marseillaise*, despite its title, was composed as a battle song for the army of the Rhine, preparing to fight Austria.

After France lost the Franco-Prussian war in 1871, Strasbourg – along with the rest of Alsace – was annexed by Germany until the end of WWI, and again from 1940 to 1944. The large buildings around Place de la République, north of the branch of the Ill known as Fossé du Faux Rempart, date from the period of Prussian occupation. A memorial here depicts a mother bearing the bodies of two sons, one French and the other German, a testimony of the trauma suffered by this frontier city during the world wars.

Despite the cultural restrictions imposed by both the French and the Germans, the local Alsatian culture survived, affecting the language spoken here and the cuisine favoured. Like many of the villages of Alsace, its half-timbered houses – especially in the quarter known as 'Petite France' where tanners and dyers once used the canals – are beautifully maintained and bedecked with flowers.

NOTES
Getting there: rail from Paris;
airport 12 km south with shuttle to city
Tourist Office: Place de la Cathédrale,
67082 Strasbourg
☎ 0388522828 Fax: 0388522829
E: info@ot-strasbourg.fr
www.ot-strasbourg.fr
Markets: Sat 7-1, Place du Marché Neuf
& Place du Vieux-Marché-aux-Poissons
Note: a tourism pass is available

< La Petite France

Half-timbered houses >

Lohkäs
Maison

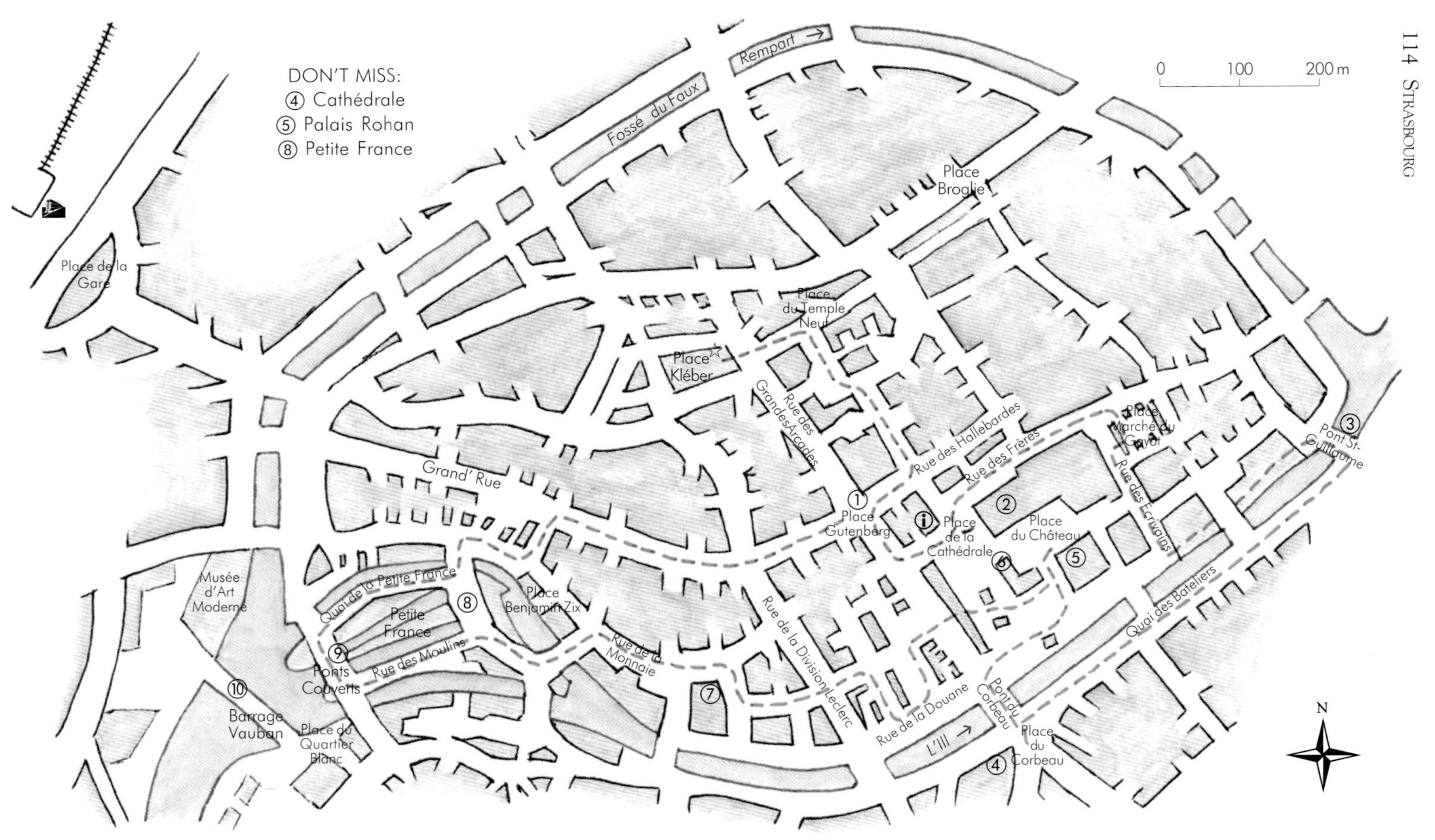
DON'T MISS:
④ Cathédrale
⑤ Palais Rohan
⑧ Petite France
0
100
200 m
N
Rempart
Fossé du Faux
Place Broglie
Place du Temple Neuf
Place Kléber
Rue des Grandes Arcades
Rue des Hallebardes
Rue des Frères
Place Marché du Gayot
Rue des Ecrivains
Pont St-Guillaume
Place Gutenberg
Place de la Cathédrale
Place du Château
Quai des Bateliers
Pont du Corbeau
Place du Corbeau
Rue de la Douane
L'Ill
Rue de la Division Leclerc
Rue de la Monnaie
Place Benjamin Zix
Grand' Rue
Quai de la Petite France
Petite France
Rue des Moulins
Ponts Couverts
Place du Quartier Blanc
Barrage Vauban
Musée d'Art Moderne
Place de la Gare

A WALK IN STRASBOURG

Picturesque waterways and winding alleys make it difficult to keep a straight path in Strasbourg's old centre.

Perhaps it's best to start at **Place Kléber**, the vast, open square in the centre of Strasbourg's island, some 800 m west of the train station. From here, take the narrow Rue de l'Outre that leads to Place du Temple Neuf, and then the narrow Rue des Orfevres. Turn left at Rue des Hallebardes to reach

① **Place Gutenberg**, named for the innovative printer who worked in the city for a decade in the mid-15th century; a statue of Johannes Gutenberg graces the square.

Follow Rue Mercière towards the beautifully carved rose sandstone of the

② **Cathédrale de Notre-Dame**. The Gothic façade was begun in 1277 but the delicate 142-metre spire was not completed until 1439; the missing southern spire was never built, giving the edifice a slightly lopsided effect. The building has had a rocky history, enduring Protestant control following the Reformation, suffering vandalism during the Revolution, being mortared in the Prussian attack of 1870 and bombed by the Allies in 1944.

The cathedral clock

Cathédrale de Notre-Dame

Inside, the 13th to 14th-century stained glass windows glow like jewels and an elaborate astronomical clock has the apostles parading for Christ's blessing at 12.30 pm. Nearby, look for the Pilier des Anges, carved around 1230. It's possible to climb to a viewing platform in the spire, for wonderful views over the old town and beyond to the Vosges and the Black Forest.

Also to be found in this square are **Maison Kammerzell** – a 16th-century mansion with elaborate wooden carvings and bottle glass – and the **tourist office**.

Walk alongside the cathedral and along Rue des Frères, then turn left to visit **Place Marché du Gayot**, an attractive square lined with cafés. Now walk down Rue des Ecrivains to reach the banks of the Ill river. A footpath leads downstream to

③ **Pont St-Guillaume** which gives you a view of Église St-Paul. Cross the bridge and wander back upstream along the Quai des Bateliers to arrive at the medieval Cour du Corbeau. Just beyond it is the

④ **Musée Alsacien**, a display of local traditions housed in a series of interconnecting

Église St-Paul on the river Ill

Renaissance buildings.

Cross the Pont du Corbeau and turn first right to weave through several places named for the markets once held there (*cochon de lait* means a suckling pig) and along Rue de Rohan to gain the Place du Château. Here you can enter the grand

⑤ **Palais Rohan**, built in the 1730s for the powerful Rohan family who kept the office of cardinal for a number of succeeding generations. It houses three museums, displaying fine arts, archaeological items and decorative arts, in a series of lavish state apartments.

Next door, in a charming medieval building that was once the seat of the stonemasons' guild, is the more interesting

⑥ **Musée de l'Oeuvre Notre-Dame**, a collection of artefacts related to the cathedral, including its original sculptures and some ancient stained glass.

Return along Rue Rohan but then turn right to weave through medieval alleys named for trades – cordmakers and stone-cutters – and cross the streets of the old hospice and fish market to reach Place des Tripiers. Turn left into Rue des Tonneliers (where barrels were made), right along Rue de la Douane (alongside the old customs house) and right up Rue de l'Ecurie (where stables once stood). Turn left along Rue de l'Ail to reach

⑦ **Église St-Thomas**, with its Romanesque façade and Gothic towers. Strasbourg was a bastion of Reformist zeal and since 1549 this has been a Protestant church. Behind the altar stands an amazing piece of sculpture, the tomb of the Marshal of Saxony, created in 1777 by Jean-Baptiste Pigalle.

Now take Rue de la Monnaie and cross Pont Saint-Martin to enter the district known as

⑧ **Petite France**. This quarter of canals and half-timbered houses was home to the city's tanners and dyers. It would have been less picturesque in the 16th century and certainly more pungent.

Walk up Rue des Moulins, passing a *lavoire* on your right and then turn left along Quai du Woerthel. This brings you to the fortified

⑨ **Ponts Couverts**, once roofed with tiles. Today they are uncovered but the watchtowers still stand. Beyond the bridges are yet another defence against waterborne assault,

⑩ **Barrage Vauban**, built by the military engineer whose name it bears. If you make the detour, via Place du Quartier Blanc, there is a good view to be had from the dam's grassy panoramic terrace.

Now stroll along the green Quai de la Petite France and cross back to the main island on a

Canals once used by tanneries

A quiet waterway

bridge that swivels open for boat traffic. Just around the old tannery is Place Benjamin Zix, bedecked with flowers and offering a lovely view over the waterway.

To head back to the town centre, take the Petite Rue des Dentelles and then follow the flag-lined Grand' Rue back to Place Gutenberg.

FURTHER AFIELD

The Orangerie & European Quarter

Just 1.7 km northeast of the island is Strasbourg's oldest and largest park, the Orangerie. To reach it, follow the river Ill upstream on its quays, then turn right. A pavilion in the park was a favourite haunt of Empress Josephine. There are also a lake, a waterfall and a breeding area for storks or *cigognes*.

Immediately northwest, standing on the junction of the river and a canal are the buildings of various European institutions. The Palais de l'Europe, built in 1975, is home to the Council of Europe and may be visited by reservation (☏ 0388412029). Across the river is the 1999 structure housing the European Parliament. Diagonally across from this is the European Court of Human Rights, inaugurated in 1995.

Contemporary Art

Set on the river bank just beyond the Barrage Vauban is Strasbourg's museum of modern and contemporary art. The glass-fronted gallery, opened in 1998, follows developments from Impressionism to video art.

OPENING HOURS

Cathédrale de Notre-Dame	daily 7-11.40, 12.40-7; spire 10-5.30 (4.30 Nov-Mar)
Musée Alsacien	Mon, Wed-Sat 12-6; Sun 10-6; closed Tue
Palais Rohan	daily except Tue 10-6
Musée Oeuvre Notre-Dame	daily except Mon 10-6
Église St-Thomas	daily except Sun am 10-12, 2-5 (until 6 May to Oct)
Barrage Vauban	daily 9-7.30
Musée d'Art Moderne	Tue, W, F & Sat 11-7; Th 12-10; Sun 10-6; closed Mon

Alsace & the Vosges

The province of Alsace has been disputed territory for much of history. Torn, in recent centuries, between Germany and France, it has developed a character and dialect of its own. The mountains of the Vosges that line its western edge were once part of the same massif as those of Germany's Black Forest. The shifting of the earth's crust that created the Alps also formed the wide valley of the Rhine river.

Strewn around the valley floor on the French side are impossibly picturesque villages, their narrow alleys lined with brightly-painted medieval houses and shops. These, in turn, are decorated with geraniums or charming hanging shop signs. To top it off, some roofs and towers feature huge storks' nests, a remarkable sight to those unfamiliar with these gangly birds.

Our walk begins in the village of St-Hippolyte, one of the gems along the Route du Vins. Wine-making is a serious Alsatian preoccupation – the district is renowned for such whites as Gewürtztraminer, Tokay and Riesling – and much of the walking at low altitude is alongside tidy vineyards. The route takes in several well-touristed villages as well as a few quieter ones, and also visits castles, both restored and ruined, up on the wooded hills above them.

NOTES
Type: A 6-day walk - 96 km (60 miles)
Difficulty: medium with some long days
Start: St-Hippolyte (rail to Sélestat, then taxi; or bus from Colmar)
Finish: St-Amarin (rail to Mulhouse)
Tourist Office: BP28, 68340 Riquewihr
☏ 0389490840 Fax: 0389490849
E: info@ribeauville-riquewihr.com
www.parc-ballons-vosges.fr
Maps: IGN 1:25000 #3718OT, 3618OT and 3619OT
Best timing: May-Oct

Those who want an easy few days' walk might choose to end the itinerary in Orbey, from where you can catch a bus to Colmar. Hardier souls will want to push on up into the Vosges, to reach and roughly follow the *Route des Crêtes*, a road built for defensive purposes during WWI and which marked much of the Franco-Prussian frontier from 1871 to 1918. Boundary stones marked D for Deutschland on one side and F for France on the other still lie along the way, as do the ruins of gun emplacements and trenches. These hills were fiercely fought over in the First World War.

The route wends its way along the high ground of the Vosges, through woods and over exposed slopes where cows graze in summer months, to gain its highest point on Grand Ballon. Along the way are *fermes-auberges* – farmhouses that offer simple accommodation – and chalet-refuges that are either privately run or operated by the Club Vosgien. This august walking club, founded in 1872, was the first to plan and mark out a long-distance path, long before the concept of the grande randonnée arose elsewhere in France. For this reason, you'll find that the GR5 is uniquely waymarked as it traverses the Vosges.

Storks nesting in Hunawihr

A village of Alsace >

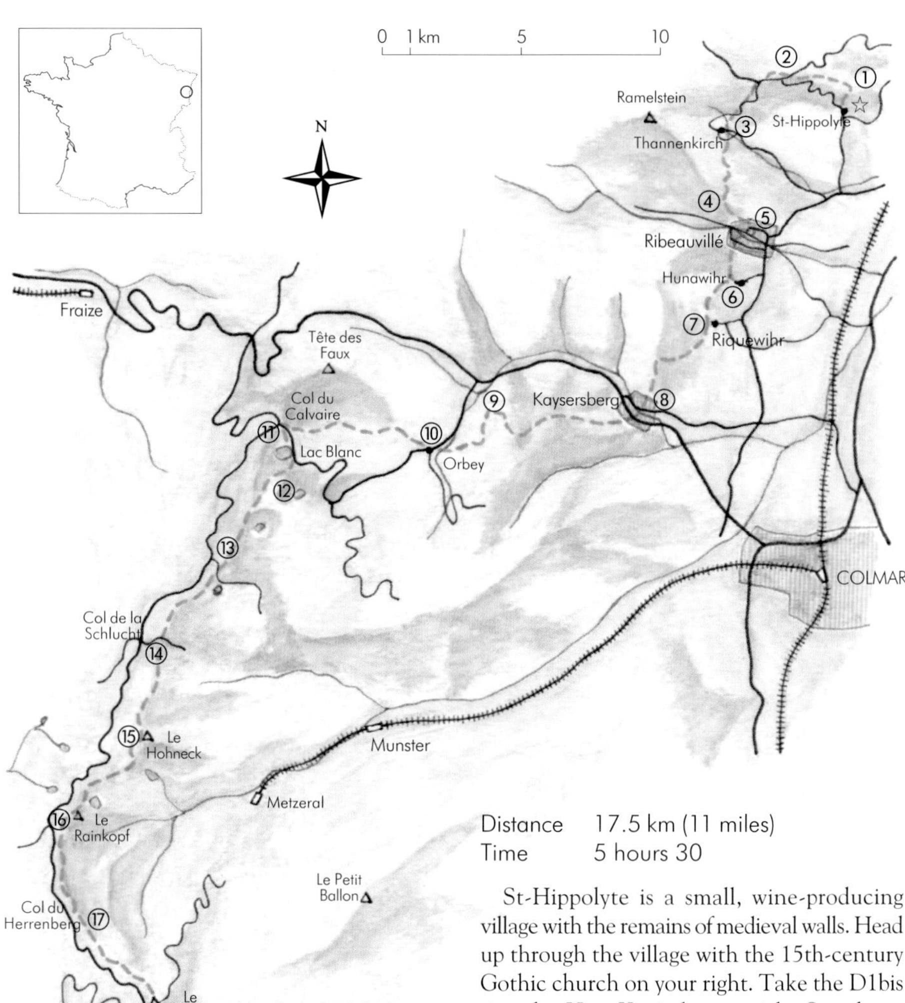

Distance 17.5 km (11 miles)
Time 5 hours 30

DAY 1: St-HIPPOLYTE to RIBEAUVILLÉ

After a quick climb up to a restored fortress, a meander through woods leads to a string of ruins above the lively town of Ribeauvillé.

St-Hippolyte is a small, wine-producing village with the remains of medieval walls. Head up through the village with the 15th-century Gothic church on your right. Take the D1bis signed to Haut Konigsberg up right. Soon leave this up right at a large sign, following waymarking with red-white-red vertical stripes (RWR). Leave the RWR path for a higher way to reach ① **a table of orientation**, from which, on a very clear day, you can see Feldberg in the Black Forest and the Swiss Alps beyond. To the SSW, you might pick out Grand Ballon.

The path continues gently uphill, providing great views of the castle ahead, before merging with a wider, unpaved forest road from the right to rejoin the RWR path. Join a paved road at Schaflager; the path traverses just above the road to reach a fountain from a spring. Later, cross another forestry track. Continue uphill, following the yellow-diamond and the RWR path. Follow a path up from the paved road to

Alsace's most visited château-fort of ② **Haut Konigsberg**. First mentioned in the 12th century, the castle stood at the crossroads of important trade routes. Owned for a while by the Hapsburgs, it was abandoned for over two centuries before becoming the property of the German Kaiser. It was extensively restored in the early 1900s. For an entry fee you can wander through its rooms, courtyards and ramparts; allow an hour for the visit.

From the castle, turn right on the level footpath. Soon, detour right to climb to the ruins of Oudenbourg (or 'abandoned castle') to see the remains of 13th-century outer walls. Back at the path junction, take the higher of two descending paths to reach and cross a road, then descend to cross it again. Continue down on the GR5 (red-rectangle) through forest to reach the road at a car park with picnic tables.

Cross the D42, follow the other joining road for less than 50 m before going up right on a narrow forest footpad, parallel above the road. The path descends once more to the D42 at a parking area on the outskirts of ③ **Thannenkirch**. Shortly after, you could detour right to the centre of this mountain village for food supplies or to visit a restaurant. Otherwise, continue to the church of St-Annekeirch (1682) and its little cemetery, from where there are views back to the castle.

Haut Konigsberg

Ribeauvillé

Continue on road to reach a large rock, hollowed to trap water from a spring. Reach a three-way junction at a sharp hairpin bend; you take the right road uphill on a broad, gravel forest track. Soon, reach a T-junction where you turn right and, a few metres later, left uphill on a gravel path.

At a four-way junction, you have a choice of GR routes to St-Ulrich ruins, right is the easier and more direct of the two. If you go straight ahead uphill, however, you can also visit the **Haut Ribeaupierre** ruins on the hill top by detouring briefly uphill off the path. The route then becomes a steep and uneven switchback descent on a footpad, passing beneath some impressive rocks, before levelling at a clearing just below the ruins of ④ **St-Ulrich fortress**. Take time to explore these, as you gain views over the Rhine plain, dotted with villages. Soon, a detour (forking left) leads to another ruin, **Giersberg**, once the third castle of the lords of Ribeaupierre. The GR5 continues down, then follows beside

Riquewihr

vines and past a wooden *gloriette* overlooking ⑤ **Ribeauvillé**, a charming town on the wine route. It's worth looking at the town hall and the 13th-century Tour des Bouchers or 'butcher's tower'. There are various hotels from which to choose.

DAY 2: RIBEAUVILLÉ to KAYSERSBERG

A short and pleasant walk with time to explore several delightful Alsatian wine villages and a visit to an otter and stork sanctuary.

Distance 10.25 km (6.5 miles)
Time 2 hours 45

From the Place de la Mairie, walk back up the Grand'Rue and turn left into the Rue de la Fontaine and cross the Strengbach stream. Soon turn right into the Rue du Vignoble and keep straight on along this lane between vineyards for 1.75 km to enter the western end of one of France's most beautiful villages,

⑥ **Hunawihr**. At a T-junction, turn left down Rue de l'Église to visit the 16th-century church and fortified churchyard. Return to the Renaissance *mairie* or town hall and then detour east along Grand'Rue, past the tourist office and along the Route de Ribeauvillé to reach the **stork and otter sanctuary** (entry fee).

Return to Hunawihr's mairie and take the nearby Rue de Riquewihr, a lane marked as a cycle way. This leads between vineyards for about 2 km, steeply up at first and then downhill to the picturesque village of

⑦ **Riquewihr**, another of France's most beautiful. Turn left to walk through the Dolder belfry tower (1291) and enter the main street, lined with geranium-decked houses and shops. Take time to inspect the ramparts and look into courtyards.

Return through the Dolder tower to Place des Charpentiers, turn left along Ave Méquillet and follow blue triangle waymarks towards Kaysersberg. The route rises gently, firstly on a narrow path and then on a broader forest track to reach Chêne de la Chapelle at 602 m. From here, follow the blue-cross path left downhill below the craggy Rocher des Corbeaux.

Descend quite steeply on a broad forest track and, at a junction, go right on a level, narrow footpad signed to Kaysersberg (blue-cross); don't go straight ahead on the alternative blue-cross route. Reach a telecommunication tower where there's a seat and filtered views of the town below. Make a switchback descent from in front of the tower to another, more open, viewpoint with a seat; you can see the village of

Kaysersberg

Hunawihr

Kientzheim below and the Rhine valley beyond.

Continue descending to the 13th-century ⑧ **château ruins**, which you enter from the left. Climb to the top of the tower for excellent views of the Wiess valley.

The path continues down by stone and wooden steps outside the town walls to enter **Kaysersberg** near a compound of religious buildings, including St-Croix church with a 1230 tympanum and, inside, a gilded retable carved in 1518. Next door is the 1463 chapel of St-Michael, with an ossuary in the crypt.

The tourist office, just behind the church, has a brochure with a walking itinerary to guide you around the lovely old lanes of the town in a circuit that starts and ends here. There are several hotels and chambres d'hôtes.

DAY 3:
KAYSERSBERG to Col du CALVAIRE

Today is more demanding: you leave the plain and climb through forest, down into the Val d'Orbey and up onto the long ridge of the Vosges to meet the Route des Crêtes.

Distance	18.5 km (11.5 miles)
Time	6 hours 30
Notes	today's 1250-m ascent could be split up by overnighting at Orbey

Leave Kaysersberg on Rue du Collège, crossing the Wiess stream and continue on, past the 15th-century tower known as the Kesslerturm, which may be topped by a stork's nest. Take the yellow-diamond path, the Rue du 18 Decembre 1944. This crosses the busy N415 and proceeds uphill on a narrow lane.

Soon, a sign leads along a path paralleling the road. Continue quite steeply uphill to reach Chapelle Flieger (446 m). Take a path up right, signed to 'Herrenwassen'. A forest track from the chapel ascends quite steeply for some time then levels. Eventually there is a view over a distant building and back down the valley. Later the path forks and you go left, following yellow-cross waymarks.

Leave the grassy forest track, walking up right on a footpad. Go straight ahead at a path junction and shortly reach the **Col du Herrenwassen** (708 m). At the junction, go right (blue-triangle) through forest to eventually reach the farm of Phimaroche. There are beautiful pastoral views and a seat by rocks, an ideal spot for a break.

Take the green-cross path ahead, soon climbing very steeply through woodland. Detour 50 m from the path to

⑨ **Le Gestion**, an old ruin where there are a pair of glazed ceramic orientation tables and panoramic views, including back to Haut

< The old Franco-Prussian frontier

Lac Blanc >

Konigsberg. Back on the path, descend to reach a four-way path junction and take the second left (green-cross) down to a seat by a paved lane. Pass the farm buildings of Le Léman with lovely views across a stream to the valley and hills beyond.

The path diverges from the track to drop and cross the stream. Soon leave the woods and walk through farmland on an overgrown path through fields and reach a paved farm lane. Ascend this to reach the farm of **Le Bousset**, a gîte d'étape and chambre d'hôte.

Continue descending steeply to reach the D48 on the outskirts of

⑩ **Orbey**, where you can detour right along the D48 to the local supermarket for lunch provisions for the next few days. Return and head up the main road (Rue Charles de Gaulle) to pass through the centre of the long village, where there are hotel-restaurants. At a Y-junction, fork right (blue-rectangle; GR531) on a narrow road uphill and soon after a small war memorial, fork up left on the blue-rectangle path. Reach and cross a road by an old cross and continue on a grassy farm track.

After a time the path joins a farm road and follows it for almost 1 km to **Creux d'Argent**, an attractive Calvary cross, at which point you continue straight ahead on a broad path, partly cobbled with large stones. Eventually, you gain good views back to Orbey. Pass under electricity wires and, at a clearing, keep sharp right on the blue-rectangle path. This climbs steadily and joins a road to reach the

⑪ **Col du Calvaire** at 1144 m. Near the *col* or pass, on the Route des Crêtes, is a Club Vosgien refuge, Le Blancrupt. Another refuge is at Tinfronce, approximately 300 metres north of the col on the GR5.

DAY 4: Col du CALVAIRE to Col de RAINKOPF

After a visit to Lac Blanc, our way climbs high up onto the ridge, to then follow the GR5/E2, known as the Sentier de Trois Pays.

Distance	18.5 km (11.5 miles)
Time	6 hours
Notes	carry lunch supplies

Return along the road and turn right onto the yellow-rectangle GR532 path that drops steeply to the northern tip of **Lac Blanc**. This route is also known as the *Sentier Frennel*. Lac Blanc and nearby Lac Noir were originally glacial; they now comprise a hydro-electric system whereby water is pumped from one to the other and back again.

The path stays near the lake to reach a junction and signboard by a car park. Take the

Erratics from old glaciers

red-white-red stripe footpath to enter the spruce and pine forest of Deux Lacs. Climb steeply to boulders and the rim of the cirque on a path marked as 'difficult', gaining a dramatic view over the lake and a high statue of the Virgin. Reach an excellent viewpoint where there is a short detour left to the

⑫ **Observatoire Belmont Roch**, a memorial with views down to Orbey.

Back at the junction, continue ahead to gain more lake views. At a five-way junction, continue straight on, then turn left onto the GR5 and folow the main ridge. On your right are *hautes chaumes*, open grasslands where for centuries, cows were brought to graze in summer. After 1250 m or so of level, straight walking, reach the Réserve Naturelle de Gazon du Faing at Soultzeren Eck (1302 m). From here, all signposted times to the Col de la Schlucht should be treated with suspicion as they are inconsistent! At a junction here, veer right following the GR5.

Further on, good views open up to the east, down to the intermittent Lac des Truites and across granite outcrops. The path swings south over Taubenklangfelsen (1299 m) and traverses the Gazon de Faîte (*gazon* is a grassy plateau) to reach the high point of Ringelbuhlkopf at 1302 m. About 750 m on, the path touches the Route des Crêtes, the military road built for strategic purposes during WWI. The path proceeds through woodland, obscuring Lac Vert down to the left.

After a short but steep climb, reach

⑬ **Le Tanet** (1292 m) and then descend over boulders, passing the ruins of a military lookout on the left. Cross marshy ground via a wooden bridge and pass the outcrop of Wurzelstein, popular with rock climbers. After a further 1.5 km, reach Haut du Barenbach (1227 m) where there's a junction.

Some 1.5 km further south, you reach

⑭ **Col de la Sclucht**, the principal pass for crossing the ridge, where there are two hotels.

Walk down the main road then veer left on a side road and, very soon, turn left on a broad, stony path, signed GR5/E2. After a steady climb, broken by a short detour to a *belvedere* with views over Munster, pass a turnoff to the CAF refuge and farm of Les Trois Fours. Cross the farm lane to Les Trois Fours (which makes Munster cheese) by a gate. Cross farmland and go through a turnstile gate into forest.

Forest fern

Beyond the forest, the path skirts around the climbers' cliffs, the Rochers de la Martinswand. Soon reach the Col de Falimont, where there are multiple junctions. The GR5 swings southeast for a climb to the summit of

⑮ **Le Hohneck** (1363 m) where there's an orientation table. Here we leave the GR5 for the red-white-red (RWR) path on the ridgeline, just behind the hotel-restaurant on the peak. Descend, with views over the dammed Lac de la Lande, one of the many lakes created to provide power for textile mills, to reach the Collet du Hohneck (1280 m). From here you have a view straight down valley to the village of Munster, famous for its odiferous cheese.

Now follow the fenceline path (rather than veering off left on a variant). Keep uphill and then level to reach an unwaymarked path and turn left; the right-hand path descends to a *ferme-auberge*, Breitsouze. The RWR path leads through meadows of wildflowers, dotted with large granite boulders that were clumped together long ago when the land was cleared.

The path crosses the Kastelberg and swings right, headng down to cross a path and road junction. Soon after, the path joins the GR531 and soon reaches the

⑯ **Col de Rainkopf** where you'll find the Club Vosgien chalet-refuge Louis Herges du Rainkopf, offering accommodation. About 100 m directly north is the ferme-auberge Ferschmuss where you can eat dinner.

DAY 5: Col de RAINKOPF to Le GRAND BALLON

Today you reach the high point of the Vosges after a rambling ridge walk, both through woods and over exposed chaumes.

Distance 22 km (13.5 miles)
Time 6 hours 30

Continue on the RWR path to enter beautiful woodland, traversing a slope above the Route des Crêtes. Reach a seat in a clearing, offering good views of the Lac d'Altenweiher below. After more woodland, the path exits onto pasture and descends gently over the *chaumes* to reach the Col du Rothenberg (1210 m).

Now ascend to a path fork: the recommended route forks right to skirt around the summits of

Wildflowers on the *hautes chaumes*

Rothenbergkopf and Batteriekopf. Contour above the road, with good views down to Lac de Blanchemer and the village of Belle Hutte beyond. Near car access, there is a small

⑰ ***abri*** or shelter, very welcome in wild weather. From here, the path climbs steadily over exposed pasture before dropping over the other side of the **Schweisel** to cross the yellow-cross path. Soon, the route levels through forest on a broad dirt track above the Route des Crêtes. The path reaches the road, passing the Refuge de Hahnenbrunnen; walk along the road to the col of the same name.

Leave up left on a stony path (the GR5) and cross the D27 at Breitfirst. Continue straight on to rejoin a narrow footpad and enter a wood of stunted beech trees. Cross the D430 at a small parking area where there's a sign for a ferme-auberge, Chaume du Steinlebach (1 km detour). Continue uphill on a grassy path (a *piste* or ski run)waymarked to Grand Ballon. This leads to

⑱ **Le Markstein**, with hotel-restaurants and a gîte d'étape in the tourist office. On this section, there are good views to the west.

Walk down to the junction of the D430 and D431 and follow the GR5 above the D431 to

A distant Grand Ballon

a path junction. Now take the GR531 straight ahead, following the road for a while, then parallel but below it through forest. Reach the road again then fork down left on a broad forest path, past a refuge. At a junction, go straight ahead, signed GR532. This passes through beautiful high forest in a reserve.

After a steady ascent, you obtain filtered views of the Lac de la Lauche below left. Soon after, rejoin the Route des Crêtes at the Col du Haag. Here you'll find a ferme-auberge; about 1 km up the road is the Club Vosgien chalet-hotel of Grand Ballon.

Above both of these is the summit of the ⑲ **Grand Ballon**, at 1424 m the highest peak in the Vosges. It is reached by a looping footpath that climbs steadily from the Col du Haag. Just below the summit is a monument to the *Diables Bleus* or Blue Devils, a WWI Alpine regiment that defended these hills. On the top is an aircraft-tracking station in the shape of a giant golf ball; a set of steps leads from it to an orientation table and sweeping views. The *Circuit Versant Ouest* path continues beyond it to reach the road by the chalet-hotel.

DAY 6: GRAND BALLON to St-AMARIN

A short and easy descent through forest to the village of St-Amarin in the Thur valley.

Distance 9.5 km (6 miles)
Time 2 hours 30

Back at the Col du Haag, turn left on the D13-bis, waymarked yellow-rectangle. Soon leave the road at a left-hand switchback and follow a dirt track through a barrier into the Gishouse forest. Descend, then fork right on a level, narrow footpad (yellow-rectangle) that is easy to miss. After 5 minutes, this joins another forest track; keep straight ahead, even though the sign is ambiguous.

Presently reach a junction of tracks where you turn right (yellow-rectangle). After 50 m or so, branch off right downhill, onto a narrow footpad, and continue to weave downhill, crossing various tracks. Continue downhill to cross a paved lane and keep descending, now through the forest of St-Amarin. Leave the wood and descend on a lane to enter

⑳ **St-Amarin** near a church, not far from its rail station. The village has one of the last textile mills in the region, as well as small museums on local military matters and country life. There are two hotels and trains run from here to Mulhouse and the attractive town of Colmar.

View over St-Amarin >

Brightly painted houses, a feature of Alsace villages

LONG DISTANCE STAGES			
km	time	location	acc
		St-Hippolyte	C
10.5	3h45	Thannenkirch	H, C
7	1h45	Ribeauvillé	H, C
2.5	0h45	Hunawihr	H, C
2.25	0h30	Riquewihr	H, C
5.5	1h30	Kaysersberg	H, C
11.75	4h00	Orbey	H, F
6.75	2h30	Col du Calvaire	R
12.5	4h15	Col de la Schlucht	R
6	1h45	Col de Rainkopf	R
4	1h15	Col du Herrenberg	F
6	1h45	Hahnenbrunnen	F
4.5	1h15	Le Markstein	H, G
6	1h45	Col du Haag	F
1.5	0h30	Le Grand Ballon	H, F
9.5	2h30	St-Amarin	H

OTHER WALKS ALONG THE WAY

The Pearls of the Vineyards

This 15-km circuit of footpaths links up six wine-producing villages: Hunawihr, Riquewihr, Bennwihr, Mittelwihr, Beblenheim and Zellenberg. The route has been given the full title of *Le Sentier Viticole des Grands Crus* and is ideal for those with an interest in wine tasting and making. The route is mapped out in a colour brochure while detailed wine notes (in French) are printed in an accompanying booklet; both are freely available from the Riquewihr tourist office. *Allow a full day.*

Cimetière Duchesne

In complete contrast to the walk above, this easy 5-km circuit visits an austere WWI cemetery high on the Vosges ridgeline.

From the Col du Calvaire, pick up the GR532 (waymarked yellow-rectangle) to climb over Petite Tête des Immerlins, descend to a saddle, climb the Tête des Immerlins (1216 m) and descend once more. Some 2.5 km from the col, you reach the cemetery for French soldiers, set among conifers. At a junction just beyond, turn left onto the GR5/E2 (waymarked red-rectangle) and follow this southwest, skirting above the Chaume Thiriet and around the Immerlins peaks. Pass the refuge of Tinfronce and regain the Col du Calvaire. *Allow 2 hours.*

Dijon

Burgundy or Bourgogne is today one of France's most prosperous regions and its capital, Dijon, displays that prosperity. Its cobbled streets are lined with tempting patisseries offering gingerbread or *pain d'épices* and *cassissines* (sweets made from blackcurrants), and yet, you get the sense that this display is not for tourists but rather for its well-heeled citizens.

When Dijon developed, roughly during the 3rd century, it was situated on the great trade route between northern Europe and the Mediterranean, just off the Via Agrippa and along the amber and tin roads. It inevitably prospered and became the capital of the dukes of Burgundy in around 1000. Its medieval centre was all but destroyed by a fire in 1137; the buildings of the old quarter mostly date from after this event.

While the Capetian dynasty were preoccupied with the Hundred Years War against England, the dukes of Burgundy built up a powerful state that included, at its height, Flanders, Holland and much of Belgium. The Valois dynasty made Burgundy a powerful rival to the kingdom of France in the 14th and 15th centuries, as well as a centre for culture by bringing musicians, architects and artists to the court. Philippe le Hardi (the Bold) favoured Flemish artists: the Van Eyck brothers painted for his court and Claus Sluter pioneered realism in sculpture here, contributing to what became known as the golden age of Burgundy.

This glorious period of creative and scientific activity continued under Jean sans Peur (the Fearless) and Philippe le Bon (the Good) who, in a less than noble act, sold Jeanne d'Arc to the English. With the death of Charles le Téméraire in 1477, the duchy's dominions were broken up and incorporated into the kingdom of France.

< Notre-Dame church

NOTES
Getting there: rail from Paris
Tourist Office: Place Darcy, 21022
Dijon ☏ 0380441144
Fax: 0380309002
E: infotourisme@dijon-tourism.com
www.dijon-tourism.com
Markets: Tue, Fri, Sat mornings,
Halles du Marché
Note: museum card available

This decline in status didn't mean the end of Dijon's cultural life. Wealthy men of parliament of the 17th and 18th century had elegant *hôtels particuliers* built for them in the town. The doors and façades of many are decorated by Hugues Sambin, who had been a pupil of Leonardo da Vinci. Another feature of the Dijon townscape are the multi-coloured tiled roofs, typical of this region.

Dijon never became a great industrial power, remaining pleasantly rural. The website of the tourist office proudly points out, however, that the industrial age did not quite pass Dijon by: this was the birthplace of Gustave Eiffel and also of the adjustable spanner.

A tempting shop display

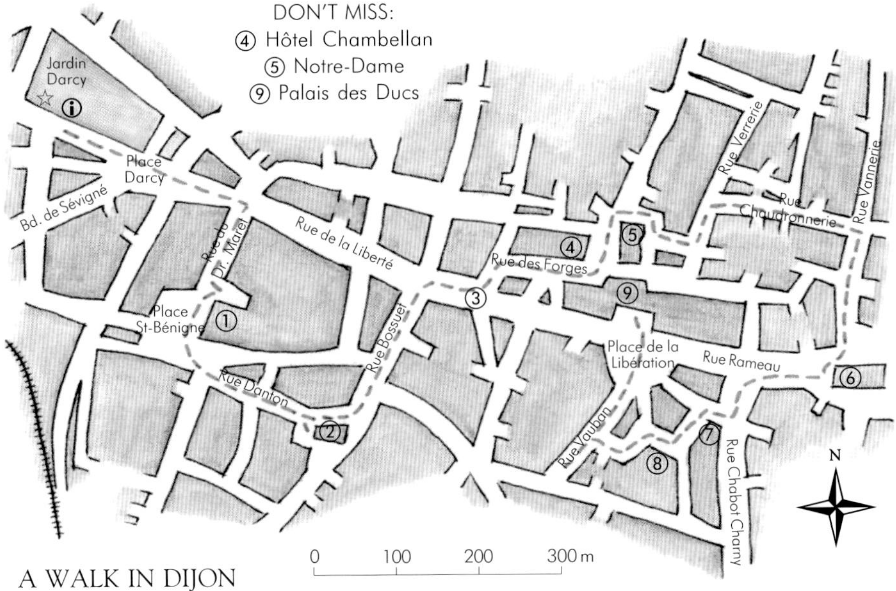

A WALK IN DIJON

Dijon's compact centre has many charms, not the least being its cobbled lanes lined with half-timbered houses and tempting shops.

This walk begins a little way east of Dijon's rail and bus stations in **Jardin Darcy** where you'll find the tourist office. At the other end of Place Darcy stands a 1788 triumphal arch marking **Porte Guillaume**, an old gate to the city. Head south down Rue du Dr-Maret. On the left, under chestnut trees, is the **archaeological museum** occupying the dormitory of a former Benedictine abbey. It boasts a collection of Gallo-Roman sculptures and also the famous head of Christ by Claus Sluter. Next door is the

< Rue des Forges

① **Cathédrale St-Bénigne**. Various churches have stood here atop the possible tomb of St Benignus, said to have brought Christianity to Burgundy as early as the 2nd century. The lower section of a Romanesque rotunda survives from the early 11th century; its evocative crypt (entry fee) is worth visiting. The existing church was built mainly in the late 13th century but the tiled roof and steeple are much more recent additions.

Now walk along Rue Danton to the small Place Bossuet, dominated by the

② **Théâtre St-Jean**, where interesting works of dance and other perforance arts are performed in an unusual space.

Follow Rue Bossuet north and turn left onto Rue de la Liberté to reach

③ **Place François Rude**, named after a Dijon-born sculptor (1784-1855); his bronze of a grape harvester features in this pretty square.

For a visit to the nearby markets (Tuesday, Friday and Saturday) make a short detour from here to Rue Musette.

Now walk along Rue des Forges. This part of the city is filled with beautifully preserved mansions attesting to the wealth of its citizens. At no.34 you'll find the

④ **Hôtel Chambellan**, built in 1490, now housing a branch of the tourist office. Look into the courtyard to admire the open galleries and a spiral staircase topped by a remarkable piece of stone vaulting that grows from the basket of a labourer.

A left turn brings you to the church of

⑤ **Notre-Dame**, built in Burgundian-Gothic style between 1220 and 1240. The gargoyles, arranged in tiers on the façade, are replicas of the originals. On the top right is the Jacquemart clock, seized from the Belgians in 1382 by Philip the Bold. Time is struck by the figure of Jacquemart and by various relations who were added over the centuries. Inside the church is a cherished 11th-century black Madonna.

Follow the winding Rue de la Chouette, named for the carved owl on the side of the church, thought to give luck to those who rub it, and look left to admire **Hôtel de Vogüé** at no.12, decorated with Burgundian cabbages

Hôtel Chambellan

Cathédrale St-Bénigne

Place Darcy

and fruit garlands carved by Hugues Sambin.

Turn left up the medieval Rue Verrerie, then right into Rue Chaudronnerie, noting the 17th-century mansion known as the **Maison des Cariatides**, on the right. Turn right into Rue Vannerie to reach the church of

⑥ **St-Michel**. This was begun in the 15th century in Flamboyant Gothic style but when the west front was due to be built tastes had shifted, and it was completed in ornate Renaissance style to great effect. The towers were added in 1667. The interior is an anti-climax and you could safely walk on.

Nearby is **Musée Rude**, a collection of the sculptor's work displayed in a deconsecrated church. From here, weave around into Rue des Bons Enfants. This district holds many elegant 17th and 18th-century mansions and one of these is at no.4, which houses the

⑦ **Musée Magnin**, a collection of artworks collected by a brother and sister and displayed in their family home, complete with furnishings.

A short way south, in Rue du Palais, is the

⑧ **Palais de Justice**. Built in the 16th century to house the Burgundian Parliament, this building, now the law courts, still has its 1572 façade. You can still view inside the 1522 **Chambre Dorée** on weekdays when the court is not in session.

Weave around into Rue Vauban, where it is worth detouring briefly left to view the courtyard of no.21, the **Hôtel Legouz de Gerland**, and the façade of no.23. From here you enter the grand **Place de la Libération**, laid out by one of the architects of Versailles in 1686. It faces the much remodelled

⑨ **Palais des Ducs**, once the seat of the dukes of Burgundy and now serving multiple functions, including that of the town hall. The oldest parts of the building are the 15th-century **Tour Philippe-le-Bon**, that can be climbed for excellent views, and the 14th-century Tour de Bar. This houses the **Musée des Beaux-Arts**, which includes an excellent collection of paintings as well as wonderful carvings and sculptures rescued from around Dijon. One small room is dedicated to the carvings of Hugues Sambin.

Visiting the museum also allows you to view the tapestry-hung Salle des Gardes containing the sculpted and painted tombs of Philippe le Hardi, Jean sans Peur and his wife Marguerite de Bavière. The palace also features a marble staircase known as the **Escalier Gabriel**.

Escalier Gabriel

Gypsy musicians in Rue des Forges

FURTHER AFIELD

Jardin de l'Arquebuse

Dijon's botanic gardens are a pleasant green space, popular with ducks, children and boules players. The natural history museum here has an exquisite collection of butterflies. To reach the gardens from Place Darcy, walk southwest along Boulevard de Sévigné, under the rail line and across Avenue Albert 1er.

Chartreuse de Champmol

This former charterhouse or Carthusian monastery was founded in 1383 by Phillipe le Hardi as a final resting place for him and his successors. It was almost completely destroyed during the Revolution and several pieces that survived – such as the ducal tombs – are now in the Beaux-Arts museum. One masterpiece that remains is the *Puits de Moïse* (Well of Moses, although it is not a well) crafted by Claus Sluter between 1395 and 1405.

To reach the chartreuse, continue west along Avenue Albert 1er for a further 500 m beyond the botanic gardens to the grounds of Champmol. Although this now houses a psychiatric hospital, you can still freely visit the remains of the chapel.

The Morvan

About 60 km west of Dijon is the Parc du Morvan, a hilly, wooded region with a series of nature trails. A 4-km waymarked path leads to Lac Chamboux from the D26 just out of Saulieu, on the edge of the park (a bus runs daily from Dijon to Saulieu).

OPENING HOURS

Musée Archéologique	daily except Tue 9-12, 2-6 (9.30-6.30 Jun to Sep)
Musée Rude	daily except Tue 10-12, 2-5.45 Jun to Oct
Musée Magnin	daily except Mon 10-12, 2-6 (10-6 in summer)
Tour Philippe-le-Bon	daily 9-12, 1.45-5.30 (reduced hours Dec-Mar)
Musée des Beaux-Arts	daily except Tue 10-6
Musée d'Histoire Naturelle	Mon, Wed-Sat 9-12, 2-6
Chartreuse de Champmol	daily 8-6

Annecy

The town of Annecy is a delightful melding of water, mountains and human settlement. Nestled at the northern tip of Lac d'Annecy, it is constrained between the peak of Mont Veyrier and the long ridge of Le Semnoz. It is saved from Alpine perfection by the number of other visitors who want to share it with you.

The setting has been a drawcard for a long time: neolithic people lived where the town's harbour now lies and its name derives from a local Gallo-Roman mansion, Villa Aniciaca. The town as we know it developed around its massive castle from the 12th century. Annecy's moment of glory came in the early 16th century when it replaced Geneva as the region's capital. When the Reformation claimed Geneva for the Calvinists, Annecy also became a centre of Catholic power.

An intellectual elite soon gathered in the town: the outstanding figure was François de Sales, a lawyer turned bishop who was later canonised. In the early 17th century he co-founded the *Académie Florimontane*, a literary institution with liberal aims that still meets in Annecy to this day. Another local literary character is Jean-Jacques Rousseau who arrived here as a youth in 1728 and was converted to Catholicism by an attractive mentor, Madame de Warens.

NOTES
Getting there: rail from Paris, Lyon, Geneva or bus from Geneva
Tourist Office: Centre Bonlieu,
1 Rue Jean Jaurès, 74000 Annecy
☏ 0450450033 Fax: 0450518720
E: ancytour@noos.fr
www.lac-annecy.com
Markets: Tue, Fri & Sun am, Rue Ste-Claire

The town's charming medieval quarter straddles the river Thiou, which drains Lac d'Annecy and joins the Fier only 5 km away, making it one of the shortest rivers in France. Nonetheless, its power helped make Annecy a manufacturing success story in the early 19th century, with mills dedicated to cotton spinning and weaving along its banks. These days, Annecy augments its tourism income with various high-technology industries.

Fortunately its markets, held in the narrow streets several mornings a week, haven't changed a great deal and you can sample a wide range of Savoyard *saucissons* and cheeses. Annecy is also famed for its cream-filled chocolates. There are plenty of restaurants along the *quais* of the old town but, if the day is fine, a picnic on the lake edge, admiring the mountain scenery, would be hard to surpass.

If you have a couple of days in Annecy, there are good hiking trails through woods on Semnoz and there is a level bicycle track all along the west side of the lake.

Lac d'Annecy & Mont Veyrier

Pont de l'Évêché on market day >

Captain
Pub
RESTAURANT

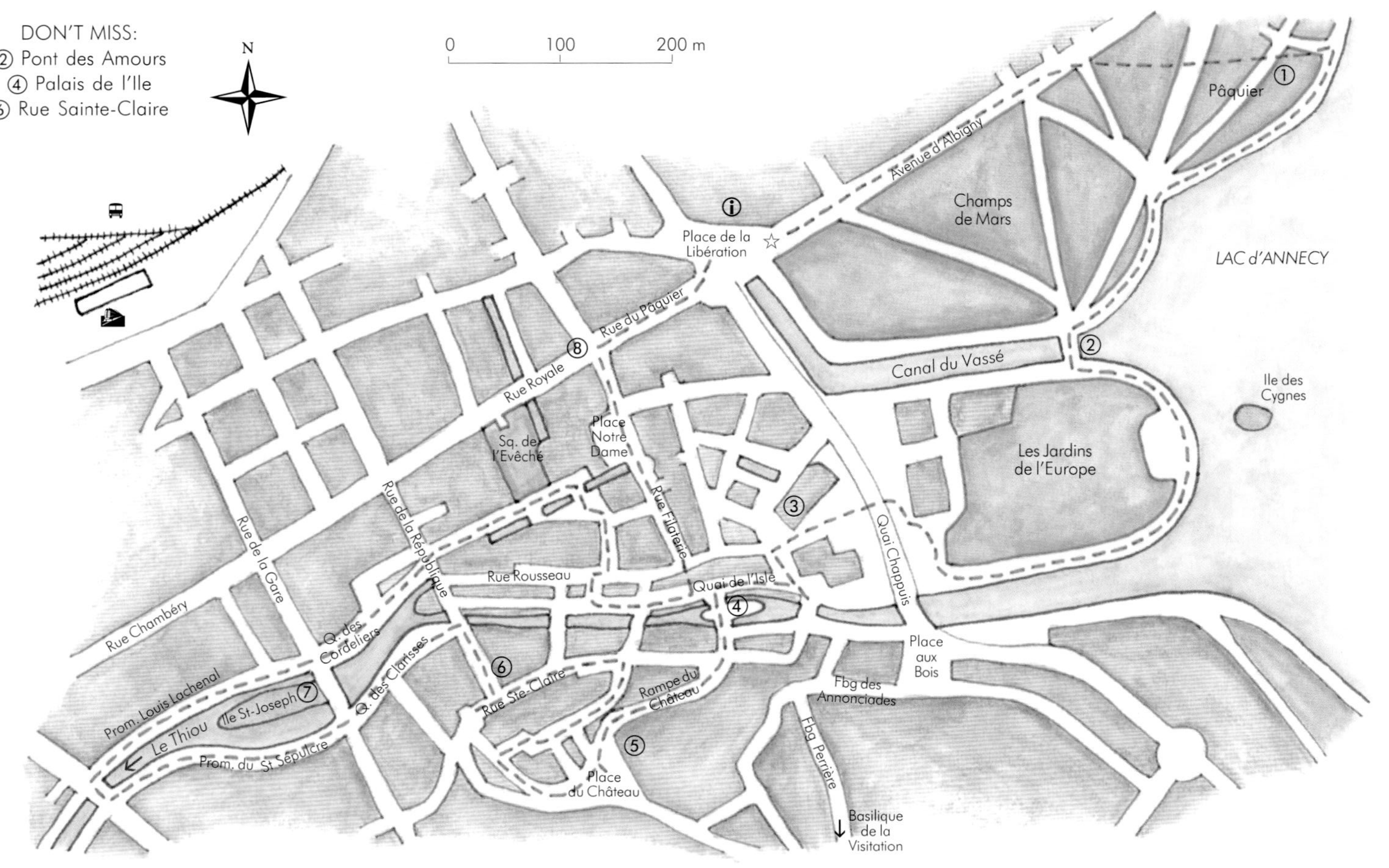
DON'T MISS:
② Pont des Amours
④ Palais de l'Ile
⑥ Rue Sainte-Claire
N
0
100
200 m
LAC d'ANNECY
Pâquier
Ile des Cygnes
Avenue d'Albigny
Champs de Mars
Place de la Libération
Canal du Vassé
Les Jardins de l'Europe
Rue du Pâquier
Rue Royale
Place Notre Dame
Sq. de l'Evêché
Rue Filaterie
Quai Chappuis
Quai de l'Isle
Rue Rousseau
Rue de la République
Rue de la Gare
Rue Chambéry
Q. des Cordeliers
Q. des Clarisses
Rue Ste-Claire
Rampe du Château
Place du Château
Place aux Bois
Fbg des Annonciades
Fbg Perrière
Basilique de la Visitation
Prom. Louis Lachenal
Ile St-Joseph
Le Thiou
Prom. du St-Sepulcre

A WALK IN ANNECY

This circuit never strays too far from Annecy's chief delights: its canals, river and lake.

Start at Centre Bonlieu, housing the tourist office. Walk along Avenue d'Albigny, lined with ancient plane trees, past the 19th-century **Préfecture**, then stroll across the
① **Pâquier**, once the communal grazing area, to an orientation table on the lake's edge. The view here is dominated by Mont Veyrier to the east and by the Crête du Maure to the west. **Lac d'Annecy** is made up of two depressions once separated by a saddle at Duingt; you are looking at the Grand Lac. The lake is fed by several streams, and by an underground spring, the Boubiaz.

Walk along the lake edge, where rowboats and pedal boats can be hired, to the ironwork ② **Pont des Amours**, spanning the shady Canal du Vassé. Continue around the edge of the **Jardins de l'Europe**, gardens planted in 1863. This area has been changed over time: the gardens were once an island and the nearby Ile des Cygnes is artificial. The statue near here is of Berthollet, a chemist from Talloires who invented bleach.

At the back of the gardens is the neo-Classical **Hôtel de Ville** and, across Quais Chappuis, is the church of
③ **St-Maurice**, a former Dominican church built in the 15th century. Its overhanging roof is typical of the regional style. Inside are several interesting examples of 15th-century artwork.

Walk toward the river and pause on the Pont Perriere to enjoy the delightful view of the
④ **Palais de l'Ile**, seemingly floating in the Thiou, before walking along the Quai de l'Isle and turning onto the island to the entrance. This 12th-century stronghold was a palace, the mint, the courthouse and a prison; today it houses a museum of Annecy's history, with access to the prison cells.

Leave the island by the other side and ascend the Rampe du Château which leads to the entrance of the
⑤ **Château et Musée d'Annecy**. To the right of the entrance is the 12th-century **Tour la Reine**, a massive tower with walls up to 4.5 metres thick. The château dates from the 12th to the 16th centuries and was built by the counts of Geneva and then bought as a residence by the house of Savoie. It served as a barracks from the late 17th century and now houses a museum of archeological finds and an interesting exhibition on Alpine geography.

From Place du Château, walk down Chemin des Remparts and look for an opening on the right for access to the **Jardin des Senteurs**, a small garden among densely-packed houses.

Canal du Vassé & Pont des Amours

Palais de l'Ile

Continue down the *chemin* and turn right into a lane running alongside the hill, which becomes the Rue Basse. The small houses on the left are in fact the top level of houses in the street below. After a turn you descend steps to exit through a passageway into

⑥ **Rue Sainte-Claire**, the high street of old Annecy. This arcaded street is at its most charming during the outdoor markets held each Tuesday, Friday and Saturday morning. In 1606 the *Académie Florimontane*, a group of literary intellectuals, began meeting at **Hôtel Favre**, at no.18. At the west end of the street is the medieval gateway, **Porte Ste-Claire**.

Walk up Rue de la République and then turn left along Quai des Clarisses, where there is a pleasant park by the river Thiou. The nearby ⑦ **Ile St-Joseph** was once a textile mill; today it is a quiet garden with a small aviary. Continue along Promenade du St-Sepulcre and cross the river at one of the bridges; downstream the banks become more rustic, with the occasional lock or dyke as a reminder of the industrial uses to which the waterway was put.

The Promenade Louis Lachenal is named after a famous local mountaineer. Further along, on the Quai des Cordeliers, is a covered wash-house once used by the town's washerwomen. The Quai Madame de Warens, which runs along the Canal Notre-Dame, commemorates the woman who converted Jean-Jacques Rousseau hereabouts in 1728. Cross the footbridge to skirt the **Ancien Palais Episcopal**, built in 1784 on the site of Madame de Warens' house.

Beyond this is the **Cathédrale St-Pierre**, a 16th-century edifice with a Renaissance façade on Rue Rousseau and a Gothic interior. Head to the river to view **Pont Morens**, the town's first stone bridge, then turn left into the Passage de l'Ile and along the arcaded Rue Filaterie. This leads to a quaint square with an obelisk fountain and **Notre-Dame-de-Liesse**, with its leaning 16th-century bell-tower. The original town hall, with an elegant 1771 iron staircase, is also in the square.

Turn left from the church and soon reach Rue Royale, which becomes Rue du Pâquier. Nearby is the massive

⑧ **Saint-John's well**, all that remains of a Knights of Malta church that once stood here. Walk along Rue du Pâquier. On the left at no.12 stands the 17th-century **Hôtel de Sales**; its sculptures depict the Seasons, as well as Night. The walk ends at Place de la Libération, near the starting point.

Market stalls in Rue Ste-Claire

OTHER EXCURSIONS

Basilique de la Visitation and Semnoz

The basilica is a steep climb up from the old town and can be reached by bus. From the Pont de la Halle, cross the Place aux Bois, once the marketplace for firewood and other timber, to walk along the Faubourg des Annonciades. Turn left up Faubourg Perrière and continue straight on to Place du Paradis, where an art museum is housed in a 17th-century building.

A statue of Joan of Arc marks the start of the Avenue de la Visitation. A short way up, take steps to the right that will bring you to the early 20th-century basilica-monastery, home to the sisters of the Visitation and a shrine to the founders of the order. The tower boasts a set of 38 bells with a concert performed each Saturday afternoon in summer; a pre-performance tour is run at 4pm. From the esplanade there is a fine view over Annecy and beyond to the western Préalpes.

Just above the basilica, at La Tambourne, you reach the forest of **Semnoz**. A marked path leads up to the **Belvédère de la Grande Jeanne** for a view over the lake.

Lake Circuit

A good way to enjoy Annecy's setting is to hire a bicycle from the excellent service beside the railway station and spend a day in the saddle, cycling around Lac d'Annecy. (Alternatively, you could catch a ferry to Menthon-St-Bernard and walk through the Roc de la Chère reserve to Talloires, then catch a ferry back to Annecy.)

Circle the lake clockwise, so that the hard work is done in the morning. From the Bonlieu tourist office, take the cycle path along the avenue of plane trees and then follow the road around the lake, through the district of Chavoire to the village of Veyrier-du-Lac. Keep right on the D909a and then on a minor road through Menthon-St-Bernard.

Cycling around the lake

If you don't mind a rough path, you can now follow a track through the wooded reserve of Roc de la Chère and push your bicycle up to a dramatic viewpoint across the lake. From here, descend steeply to the village of Talloires, where there is a lovely lakeside park. The D909a now cuts through the district of Angon, and then hugs the lake and stays quite level. Watch out for paragliders wafting down from the hillside to your left.

At the southern end of the lake, the D909a road skirts the marshland of a nature reserve. Turn left on a minor road and cross the N508 road to reach the *piste cyclable* or cycle path, an old rail line put to excellent use. Turn right and follow this north. You might want to detour off to visit the village of Duingt or to seek refreshments at Sevrier. The path ends near Annecy, requiring a brief road ride around a spur where springwater is harnessed. You can ride quayside, negotiating pedestrians, right up to the Pont de la Halle. *Allow a full day.*

OPENING HOURS

Palais de l'Ile	Jun-Sept daily 10.30-6; Oct-May Wed-Mon 10-12, 2-5
Musée-Château	Jun-Sept daily 10.30-6; Oct-May Wed-Mon 10-12, 2-5
Basilique de la Visitation	daily 7-12, 2-6

THE VANOISE

The Parc National de la Vanoise, with its magnificent mountain landscapes and its rich flora and fauna, is a walker's paradise. The park was France's first, established in 1963 to protect reintroduced herds of ibex that had survived in Italy's bordering Gran Paradiso national park. Together these parks constitute the largest nature reserve in western Europe.

NOTES
Type: day walks & a 4-day circuit
Base for day walks: Bonneval-sur-Arc
Getting there: rail to Modane; bus to Bonneval (www.altibus.com)
Tourist Office: 73480 Bonneval-sur-Arc
☏ 0479059595 Fax: 0479058687
E: info@bonneval-sur-arc.com
www.bonneval-sur-arc.com
Map: Didier Richard 1:50000 Vanoise 11
Best timing: mid-June to mid-September

The Vanoise massif – the core of the park – consists mainly of schist and metamorphic crystalline rocks. It has over a hundred summits above 3,000 metres, with many glaciers suspended on their slopes. The valleys of the Arc and Isère rivers, confusingly known as the Maurienne and Tarentaise valleys, form the natural southern and northern boundaries of the Vanoise. Valleys here are deep, their slopes dotted with stone huts and covered with verdant pasture that feeds tawny Tarine cows, prized for their milk and cheese. The climate is relatively dry and sunny but high ground is subject to the usual vagaries of mountain weather.

Criss-crossing the park is a network of 500 km of marked trails, including the GR5 and GR55 paths. Most are accessible from early June to late October but the many refuges tend to open only from mid-June to mid-September. Spoilt for choice, we've described two superb day circuits starting at the charming village of Bonneval-sur-Arc, the highest in the Maurienne. Here stone houses with *lauze* roofing and flower-decked wooden balconies huddle around an old church. It also has a range of hotels and, unusually, a CAF refuge. Both day walks are to refuges where you get a taste of the high mountains and their glaciers.

Walk 3 is a multi-day circuit around the Glaciers de la Vanoise, a huge ice cap slung between Col de la Vanoise and Col d'Aussois. The refuges *en route* provide meals and are all sited amid spectacular scenery, with abundant opportunities for wildlife watching. In season the park's wildflowers grow in profusion, making the walk even more memorable.

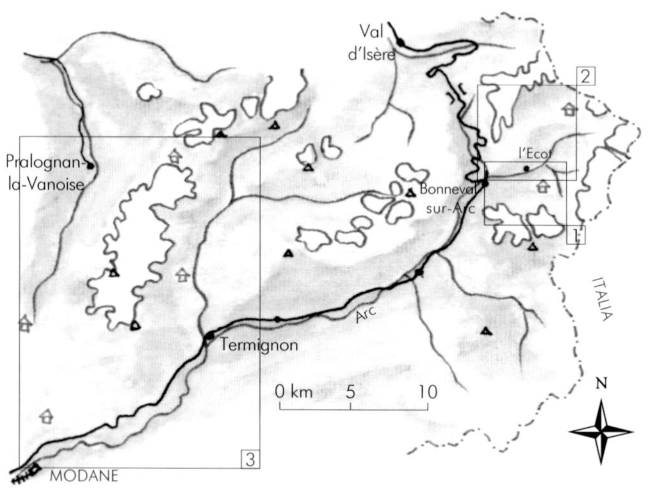

High in the Maurienne >

< Myrtilles below Ouille Mouta

WALK 1: Les EVETTES

A high balcony path leads to the beautiful Cirque des Evettes, from where you can return via a dramatic gorge descent and the ancient hamlet of l'Ecot.

Distance	14 km (8.7 miles)
Time	6 to 7 hours
Difficulty	medium with rough descent
Notes	There is the option of an easier return route from the cirque.

From the centre of Bonneval, cross the Arc river on the Pont du Pautas and follow the path that climbs steeply up a ski-slope to the ① **Refuge du Criou**, where you can recover while enjoying the view up the valley.

Continue uphill, staying on the same side of the Vallonnet stream, to a junction where you fork left and cross a minor stream and then the Vallonnet via grassy embankments. Look out for marmots hereabouts. Ascend a short distance on the other side, then veer left off the track and look for red-and-yellow GRP waymarks. These lead you up to the rocky spur where you'll find a footpath marked with red and yellow stripes.

This zigzags uphill and becomes a balcony path heading up valley with views down over Bonneval and then the hamlet of l'Ecot. The pathside vegetation is varied and features

Lacs des Pareis

myrtille, the low shrub that turns red in autumn and bears fruit used in the local cuisine.

After a pleasant level walk, you arrive at a junction giving you a choice of a *facile* (easy) route or a steeper *raccourci* (short-cut), both of which bring you, after 40 minutes or so, to ② **Refuge des Evettes** (☏ 0479059664). The refuge, guarded in summer months, sits at 2590 m on a rocky spur near the lakes of Pareis, surrounded by dramatic glaciers and peaks. Detour further along the path to fully appreciate the glacial cirque, a classified site that contains a wealth of alpine flowers.

Now take the path in front of the refuge, signed to the cascade. The rocky path descends to a junction, where you detour right, following cairns, to a pretty stone bridge near where the ③ **cascade of la Reculaz** plunges into its narrow gorge. A rocky ledge before the bridge gives a vertiginous view, but great care should be taken!

Return to the path junction and take the downhill path signed 'Sentier a John'. (In wet weather this can be slippery and dangerous; in this case you should return via the refuge and then descend to l'Ecot via the Plan des Roches.) The *Sentier a John* makes a very steep descent through rocky clefts; at the second of these, watch for a fixed chain on your right to assist you. At the open area below this, there is an amazing view of the cascade and a dramatic finger of rock, jutting out over the gorge.

Follow cairns over the rocky landscape, at times over smooth sheets of stone that can be slippery, down to the valley floor. The now grassy path stays on the same side of the river and climbs over a low spur. Cross meadow to pick up the riverside gravel track that continues in th same direction.

At a signpost, cross the Pont St-Clair to reach the hamlet of

④ **l'Ecot**. This collection of lovingly-restored stone cottages was once permanently inhabited; it is now a classifed site.

Beyond l'Ecot, follow the charming *Chemin des Agneaux* down the valley. On your left are the boulders of the Clapier de Fodan, which, according to legend, swallowed up a village in the 10th century. The path brings you to the road at Tralenta, the eastern end of Bonneval-sur-Arc.

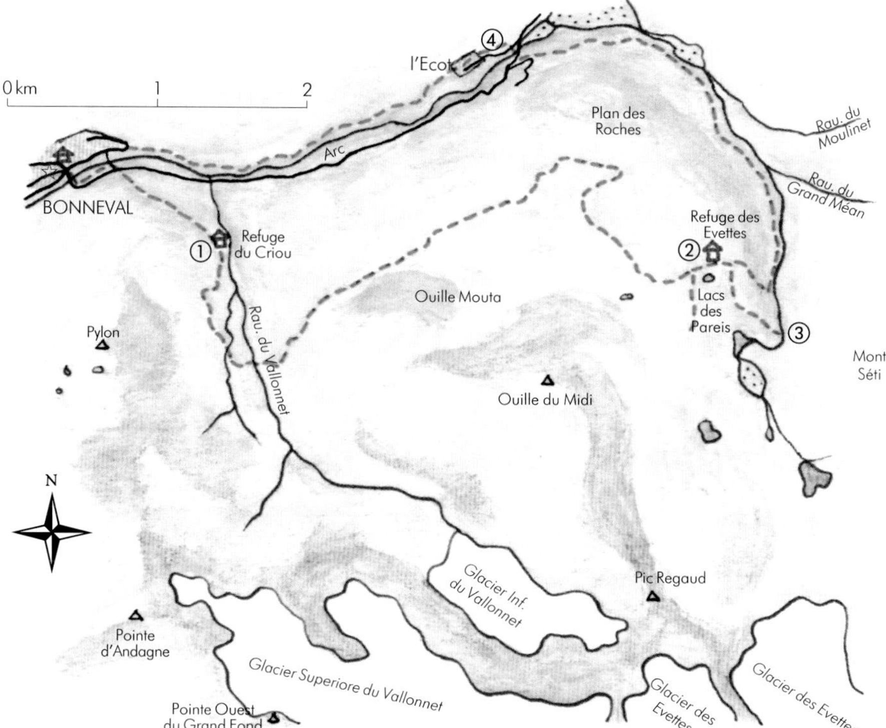

Refuge du Carro on Lac Noir

WALK 2: Le CARRO

An ascent to one of the highest refuges in the Vanoise and a return via an easy balcony path provides stunning panoramas of surrounding glaciers and peaks.

Distance	20 km (12.5 miles)
Time	7 to 8 hours
Difficulty	medium but long
Notes	This walk finishes at Pont de l'Oulietta; check shuttle schedule or face a long downhill walk!

From Bonneval, walk up to the hamlet of l'Ecot along the *Chemin des Agneaux*; this takes 1 hr 15 minutes (see page 153 for more detail). Alternatively, catch a shuttle to l'Ecot.

Continue in the same direction beyond the hamlet, passing a telephone box. Nearby is a yellow signpost indicating Refuge du Carro. Enter the national park and soon, at Les Vaillettes, the road forks; turn left uphill.

About 50 m beyond the houses of ① **Duis d'en Bas**, pick up a footpad veering left uphill, leading past a house; the path marked on the map has been closed due to rockfall. A fairly steep climb brings you to

Sheep graze on the Ouille des Reys

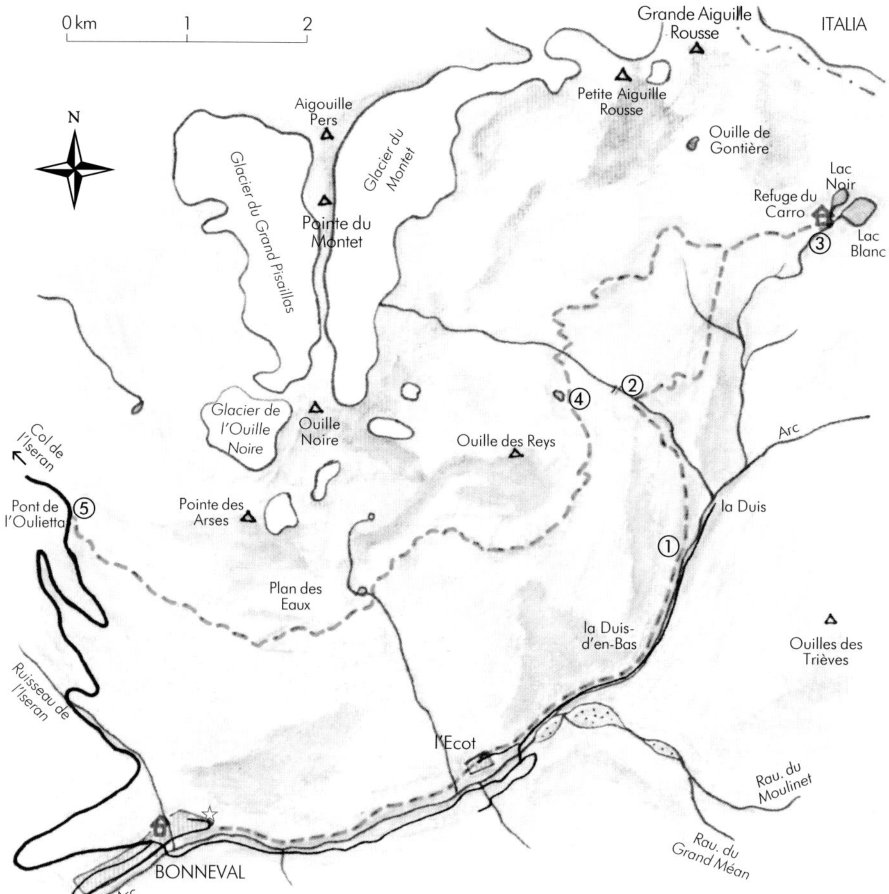

② **le Montet** (2405 m) at the foot of an attractive cascade. Take a rest before crossing the Montet stream on a footbridge and then climb to a path junction at Plan Sec (2700 m). Turn right to contour the rocky spur of Gontière and to soon reach, at 2760 m, the

③ **Refuge du Carro** (☏ 0479059579). The refuge (open in summer) is perched by Lac Noir and Lac Blanc, contrasting lakes which live up to their names. Behind them rises the Grande Aiguille Rousse (3482 m) on the Italian border.

Return from the refuge to Plan Sec and then take the right-forking path signed to l'Oulietta. Watch out for *bouquetin* (ibex) on the slopes north of the path. The gentle descent over high parture then allows you stunning views across valley to the chain of glaciers at the source of the Arc.

Zigzag down to cross the Montet stream and then, just before a rockfall, watch out on the right for the concealed

④ **Lac de Pys**. The path now contours around the Ouille des Reys and reaches a junction at Les Reys (2650 m). Continue ahead on the balcony path, enjoying a panorama across valley to the glaciers of Evettes and Vallonnet and the peak of Albaron.

On the Plan des Eaux you pass a small lake ringed by white *linaigrettes* in season. The balcony path eventually descends the slopes of Pointe des Arses to reach the D902 road at the

⑤ **Pont de l'Oulietta carpark**. If you have no transport from here, follow the road downhill to Pied-Montet, the 'roadmender's house' on a hairpin bend, where you can pick up the GR5 and then its variant path that leads directly down to Bonneval.

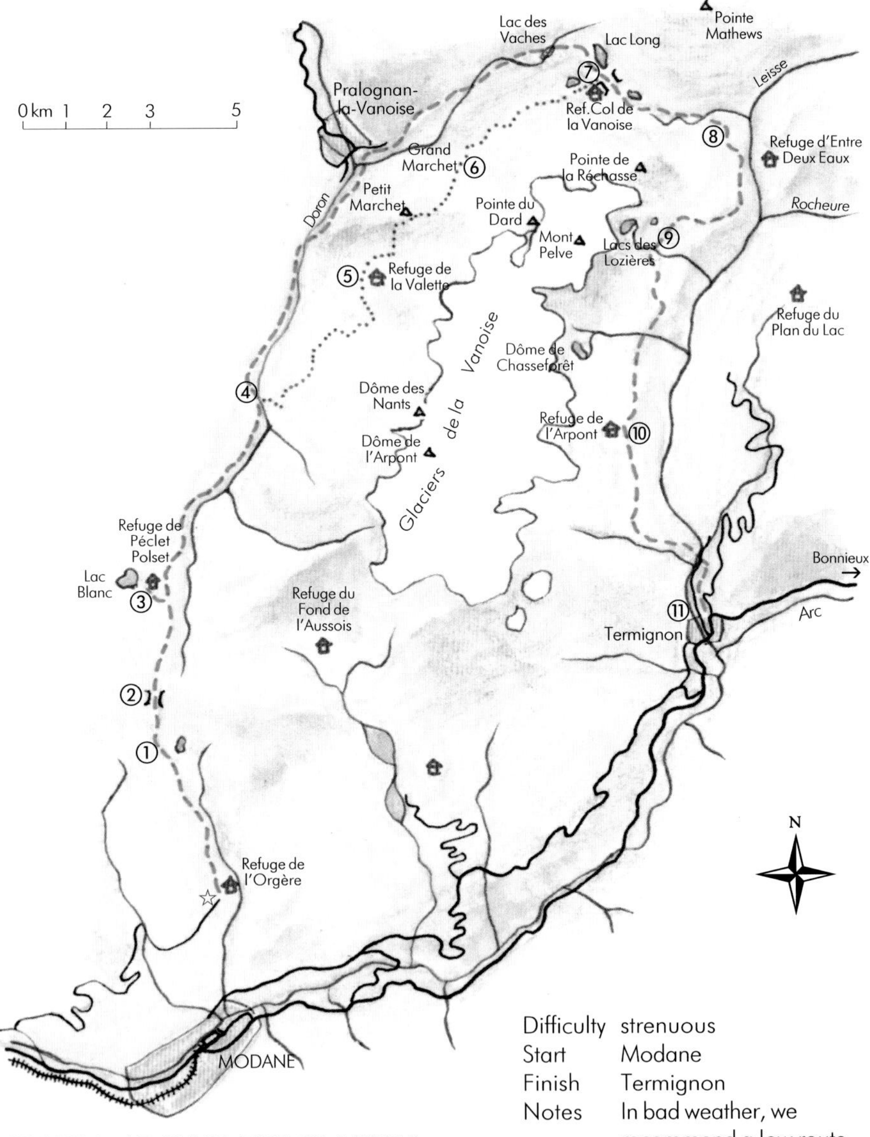

WALK 3: AROUND THE GLACIERS

This abbreviated version of the classic Vanoise circuit allows easy access from the Maurienne valley. The first and last stages are half-days, allowing time for travel.

Distance	50.5 km (31.5 miles)
Time	4 h: l'Orgère to Péclet-Polset
	5 h: Péclet-Polset to la Valette
	6 h: la Valette to Col de la Vanoise
	6 h: Col de la Vanoise to l'Arpont
	3 h: l'Arpont to Termignon

Difficulty	strenuous
Start	Modane
Finish	Termignon
Notes	In bad weather, we recommend a low route that bypasses la Valette.

The starting point, Refuge Porte de l'Orgère, sits 850 m above Modane, an industrial town at the end of a rail line. While you could pick up the GR5 footpath from its district of Loutraz, a taxi to the refuge saves a long haul uphill.

From the refuge, cross the road and take the path signed to Col de Chavière. This climbs, cruelly steeply at first,through an *arolla* pine forest, and then traverses the slope of Tête Noire, offering an excellent view east of the

Male *bouquetin* or ibex >

Rateau d'Aussois and, northeast, of the Aiguille Doran. At the head of the valley, by a large erratic, reach ① **a path junction** where you join the GR55. Enjoy the sight here of a nearby waterfall from glacial melt.

Continue north, but detour a few steps off the path to enjoy Lac de la Partie on the right. A short way on, on a spur above the lake you might see *bouquetin* or ibex grazing.

The final climb to the 2796-metre ② **Col de Chavière** is steep but your efforts are rewarded by a wonderful view back. This *col* or pass is the highest climbed by any GR in France. Descend with care on a stony path, following cairns. When you see the modern refuge in the distance, take the unmarked footpath which forks left and leads directly to the national park's refuge of Péclet-Polset (☏ 0479087213). An essential detour is to take the footpath from the front of the refuge for a ten-minute ascent to a spur where you can view ③ **Lac Blanc**, named for its milky hue.

Descend from Péclet-Polset to rejoin the GR55. The path becomes a farm lane and descends along the Doran de Chavière river to reach the Alpage des Ritort, where Beaufort cheese is made in summer and refreshments might be purchased. A further 1.5 km of easy walking brings you to the hamlet of ④ **La Motte**, where there's a very cosy private chalet-refuge Roc de la Pêche (☏ 0479087975).

From here, you have a choice of route to Col de la Vanoise; the high route has several sections where snow can still lie in summer and is more challenging. The lower route, which could be achieved in a long day (7 hrs), is outlined in italics.

Continue along the valley floor, passing Pont de la Pêche where there are toilets beyond the bin shelter. Further down valley, cross the river to walk through the hamlet of les Prioux (where there is a private refuge Repoju). Stay on the left bank of the river, passing Pont du Diable, until the Pont de Gerlon and then follow the GR55 through the Isertan forest to the edge of Pralognan-la-Vanoise, which has a gîte d'étape and hotels.

When you leave the town, walk through the villages of Barioz and Bieux and follow the GR55 to the hamlet of les Fontanettes. The path follows a piste *(ski run) that climbs steeply to the privately operated Refuge des Barmettes (open in summer). Cross the Pont de la Glière and follow the walled mule track. Further up valley, you cross the river on the Pont du Chanton and ascend to the lovely Lac des Vaches, so shallow it can usually be*

< Lac Blanc, above Péclet-Polset

< Lac des Vaches

crossed on lauzes *or flat stones. The path climbs the lower moraine of La Grande Casse and then swings around beneath the Aiguille de la Vanoise and alongside Lac Long to reach the Refuge of Col de la Vanoise.*

The high-level 2-day route, via Refuge de la Vallette, is as follows. Just after la Motte, watch for a right-forking path that drops to cross the river and climb to the nearby hamlet of Montaimont. From there, take the path that climbs over the Plan des Bos and heads northeast across the lower slopes of Dôme des Nants to the Chalet des Nants. Here you turn east, then climb steeply north up the Pic de la Vielle Femme to reach the national park's
⑤ **Refuge de la Vallette** (☏ 0479229638).

From the refuge, the path continues north to pass left of the Roc du Tambour. You pass near a cirque and then climb around the summit of Petit Marchet, where snow can lie quite late. A short, exposed section is equipped with a cable for assistance. The path now enters the cirque of Grand Marchet and then climbs steeply to the
⑥ **Col du Grand Marchet** at 2490 m. From here you descend steeply into the Cirque de Dard, following cairns, to cross a bridge and descend further to a path junction at 1881 m. Fork right and climb up by the stream of Arcelin. This passes the ruins of chalets and then skirts the Lac des Assiettes to arrive at
⑦ **Col de la Vanoise** (2516 m), a grand location for the CAF refuge (☏ 0479082523).

The path from the refuge is gentle descent along the Vanoise stream between la Grande Casse and Pointe de la Réchasse, passing by Lac Rond, Lac du Col de la Vanoise and a third, intermittent lake. The valley opens and you gain a dramatic view northeast up the Leisse valley, dominated here by the ridge between la Grande Casse and la Grande Motte.

The path drops to a nearby
⑧ **blockhouse**, and then to a memorial to Alpine regiments. Shortly, the GR55 forks off left to the private refuge of Entre-Deux-Eaux across valley, but your route continues south, crossing the Vôute de Clapier Blanc, or Vault of White Boulders, following cairns. The view now extends east up the more verdant

Vallon de la Leisse

Rocheure valley. You should also watch out for chamois on the slopes on your left.

At the Roc de la Para junction, continue ahead, now on the GR5 heading southwest in a series of hairpin bends. On one of the last of these, look for a huge stone table, about 10 m off the path to the left: this is an example of an 'acorn-cup' shaped by neolithic residents of the Haute-Maurienne.

Beneath the dramatic Roche Ferran are the
⑨ **Lacs des Lozières**, a chain of three lakes surrounded by glacier-polished rocks offering a selection of lunch spots. From here the path crosses streams and climbs over scree, then traverses the grassy slopes of the Pelve plateau, with a good view of the peaks to the east.

As the valley below narrows into a gorge, watch out for ibex and also for Lac Blanc, perched high across the valley. The path then swings around to reveal the picturesque buildings of the national park's
⑩ **Refuge de l'Arpont** (☏ 0479205151) at the base of the hanging glacier of l'Arpont and with fine views over the Doron valley.

Descend from the refuge, passing the chapel of St-Laurent, summer *alpes* and several ruins. At the junction of Le Mont (2090 m), leave

The Vanoise Glaciers, above the Lacs des Lozières

the GR5 and take the hairpin footpath steeply downhill. This passes the ruined chalets of l'Esseillon and gives you glimpses north to the craggy Gorge-dessous.

The footpath descends eventually to the Pont du Châtelard where it reaches the D83 road. Pick up a footpath that runs between the road and the Doron de Termignon and follow this downstream to the village of

⑪ **Termignon**, which has a gîte d'étape, hotels and a bus service back to Modane.

LONG DISTANCE STAGES

km	time	location
		Refuge de l'Orgere
8.5	4h00	Refuge de Péclet-Polset
5.5	2h30	La Motte (Roc de la Pêche)
6	2h30	Refuge de la Valette
9.5	6h00	Ref. du Col de la Vanoise
14	6h00	Refuge de l'Arpont
7	3h00	Termignon
alternative low route:		
		La Motte (Roc de la Pêche)
2.5	0h45	Prioux (Repoju)
4.5	1h15	Pralognan-la-Vanoise
3	1h45	Refuge des Barmettes
4	2h15	Ref. du Col de la Vanoise

Across the Doron to Grand Roc Noir

The hamlet of l'Ecot

OTHER WALKS IN THE REGION

L'Ecot

If you don't have the time or the inclination to take on the walks described earlier in this chapter, make sure you walk from Bonneval to the hamlet of l'Ecot along the *Chemin des Agneaux*. This leaves from Tralenta (the upper village)and heads up valley, traversing the rockfall known as the Clapier de Fodan, which, according to legend, destroyed a village of ill-repute in the 10th century.

Make a short detour off the path to stand on the nearby Pont de la Lame and enjoy the views up and down the Arc river. Continue up the right bank of the Arc as the path gently rises to l'Ecot. Until recently, this was France's highest inhabited village at 2027 m. Now, the classifed and restored hamlet has summer residents but in winter months is deserted. The path meanders between stone cottages to the 12th-century Romanesque chapel of Ste-Marguerite.

Return to Bonneval by the same route. *Allow 2 hours 30 minutes.*

Tarine cows below Bonneval >

Le Villaron circuit

This circuit from Bonneval takes pretty *Chemin du Petit Bonheur* down valley to the hamlet of Villaron and returns via a balcony path.

Walk down through the lower village and, 50 m further on, by an oratory, take the gravel track right, along the Arc river. This route (which is also the GR5E) leads you past large erratics, rocks embedded in the valley floor by the retreating glacier. Pass by a bridge and then the huts of the hamlet of Evasset. Just over the grassy spur, fork left down to river level and cross the Vallon side stream on a footbridge.

A huge block of serpentine known as the Rocher du Château dominates the next section of path, and a sign alerts you to ochre paintings of deer which adorn it; they are faintly visible just beyond the sign. The path goes on through larch forest to reach a minor road near the entrance to Villaron, a pleasant hamlet of stone houses roofed with shingles and a picturesque chapel of St-Bernard.

Walk up through the village and follow the GR5E as it climbs steeply to a junction with the GR5 on the boundary of the national park. Turn right and climb to the hamlet of Mollard. The balcony path now heads north, crosses the Vallon in a cirque, and traverses the alpine meadows of Bufettes, giving wonderful views over the Arc valley to the Vallonnet glaciers.

Just before the Rocher stream, at a path junction, fork right to descend steeply towards Bonneval. This path crosses the D902 and drops down to the old village, by the 17th-century church. *Allow 5 to 6 hours.*

Lyon

France's second city lies at the confluence of two major rivers. You can easily ignore the frenetic activity on the east bank of the Rhône, as there is plenty to see on the Presqu'île (the tongue of land between the rivers), in Vieux-Lyon on the west bank of the Saône, and on the Fourvière hill. Lyon's large historic centre has been a UNESCO World Heritage Site since 1998.

Celtic legend has it that two princes laid the foundations of the town where the Saône joined the Rhône. More certainly, the Romans made this site, known as Lugdunum, their base camp in 43 BC and, shortly afterwards, the capital of Gaul. Roads were built radiating out of the city and trade made it an important business centre, as it still is today.

Early in the 15th century, Lyon began holding great commercial fairs. These, together with the establishment of banks brought great prosperity to Lyon. Newly invented moveable type arrived here in 1473 and Lyon quickly became one of Europe's major publishing centres, with over 400 printeries here by 1548.

In 1536, François I authorised silk-weaving in the city so as to reduce the amount imported, particularly from Italy. A canny Italian merchant brought weavers from Genova and set up a workshop in Lyon. However, it was not until the invention of the Jacquard loom that the silk industry really developed here. Precious bolts of silk were carried safely through the town by means of *traboules*, a word that probably comes from the Latin *trans ambulare* meaning 'to walk through'. More than 300 of these passages still exist in Lyon, and some are opened for viewing. Silk workers were known as *canuts* and were generally poorly paid. In 1831 the canuts called a strike; in the ensuing fighting between workers and soldiers, some 600 people were killed before the strike collapsed.

The Roman theatre

NOTES
Getting there: shuttle from Lyon-Saint Exupery airport (25 km); rail from Paris
Tourist Office: Place Bellecour, 69214
☎ 0472776969 Fax:0478420432
E: info@lyon-france.com
www.lyon-france.com
Markets: Quais Saint-Antoine & Célestins Tue-Sun 7-1

Resistance is a repeated theme in Lyon's history. The city resisted the Convention during the Revolution and paid a terrible price in loss of life. During WWII, Lyon was a centre of the French resistance; a museum here bears witness to this.

It also has its lighter side. Around 1800, an unemployed canut named Mourguet resorted to tooth-pulling to earn his keep. To attract customers he used puppets, a ploy that led him to create the cheeky character of Guignol, his wife Madelon, and his drinking partner Gnafron. Puppetry is a great popular tradition in the city.

Another enjoyable tradition is that of fine cuisine: Lyon is considered the gastronomic capital of France. There are restaurants of every variety but a local peculiarity is the *bouchon*, an unpretentious and inexpensive restaurant that serves Lyonnais dishes.

A traboule >

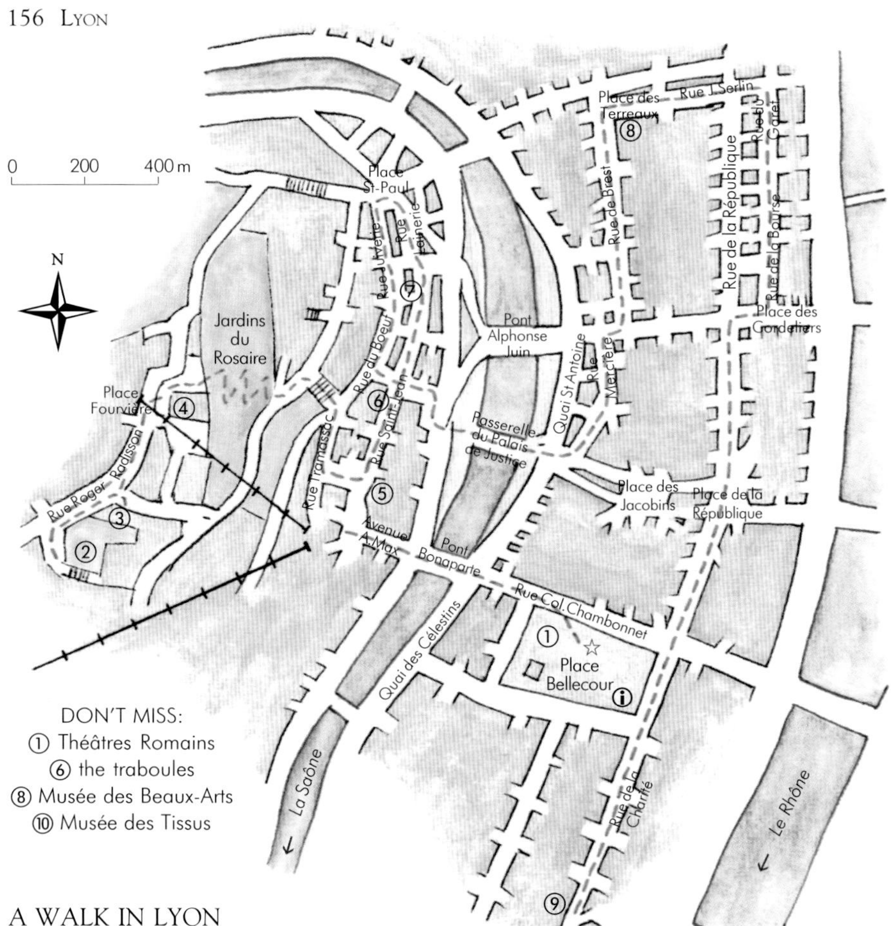

A WALK IN LYON

Visit Lyon's Roman heritage and gain a panorama over the city before walking down into Old Lyon and back onto the Presqu'île.

Our walk begins in the grand ① **Place Bellecour**, one of the largest in France, on the site of a Roman stockade. It is lined on the east and west by symmetrical buildings that were restored in 1802. The statue of Louis XIV, known simply by locals as 'the bronze horse' stands above allegorical figures of the Rhône and Saône, each facing their river. You'll also find the **tourist office** here.

Leave the square at its northeast corner and walk along Rue Chambonnet to cross the Saône on Pont Bonaparte. Ahead, in Ave Adolphe-Max, you'll find the lower station for the Fourvière funicular, known locally as La Ficelle or 'the String'. Catch this up to the Fourvière district then turn right and walk along Rue Roger Radisson, named after a Lyon journalist executed by the Nazis. This leads to the ② **Théâtres Romains**, free to enter. Nuns, digging on their land in 1930, discovered this archaeological site. It contains a 1st-century theatre with seating for 10,000 spectators, a smaller, 2nd-century odeon designed for music and poetry recitals, and a group of shops.

Around the corner, on Rue Cléberg, you'll find the discreet entrance to the fascinating ③ **Gallo-Roman museum**. Inside, a ramp leads you deeper into the hillside past exibits from Lugdunum, many uncovered during excavations for métro tunnels and funiculars.

Return to Place Fourvière, dominated (as is the whole of Lyon) by the ④ **Fourvière basilica**. This mixture of Byzantine and medieval features was begun in 1872 after the Franco-Prussian war to fulfil a vow made by Lyon's archbishop. It is heavily ornamented throughout. The northeast tower, **Tour de l'Observatoire**, can be climbed in season for a full panorama and a small fee.

There is also a fine panorama to be had from the terrace on the right-hand side of the basilica; on a fine day it extends as far as Mont Blanc. Walk around the basilica to the other terrace to descend into the **Jardins du Rosaire**, weaving down on a series of steps.

Exit the park, cross the road and head left down the 228 steps of Montée des Chazeaux. Its original name – Montée du Tire-Cul (or 'arse-drag steps') – indicates its steepness. At the bottom, turn right along Rue Tramassac, passing below a garden that now lies where houses were destroyed by a landslide in 1930. Turn left into Place St-Jean to visit the

⑤ **Cathédrale Saint-Jean** built from the 12th to 14th centuries in mostly Gothic style. Its statuary was torn down by the Huguenots in 1562 and further damage was wrought during the Revolution but the façade still bears 368 stone medallions depicting an array of scenes. The cathedral, which hosted major historic events, also features a fascinating 14th-century astronomical clock. To the right of the cathedral

Hôtel Bullioud's courtyard

Cathédrale Saint-Jean

is the choir school: the building dates from 1200, but the institution goes back to Charlemagne.

Walk down Rue Saint-Jean where some doors conceal the passages known as

⑥ **traboules**. At no.27, right, a traboule leads through two courtyards, one with elegant galleries and a splendid spiral staircase. No.28, on the left, is late 15th-century; note the *cave* or cellar door in one of its courtyards. The courtyard of no.24 has a spiral staircase encased in an octagonal tower.

Walk through Place du Change, once a centre for money-changing and keep on along Rue Lainerie. No.14 was the house of Claude de Bourg, an alderman whose face appears in a sculpted medallion above the door. No.2 Place St-Paul was home to the puppeteer Mourguet.

At Place St-Paul, turn sharp left to return south along Rue Juiverie; Jewish merchants were expelled from the street in 1394. The 17th-century mansion at no.23 is known as the 'House of Lions'. On the right, between nos.16 and 18, the passage known as Ruelle Punaise or 'Stinking Alley' was a medieval sewer. Look into no.8, Hôtel Bullioud; the second courtyard features a famous gallery that is a gem of Renaissance architecture.

Turn left and then right into Rue de Gadagne

Bartholdi's fountain

to reach Place de Petit College, where the Renaissance Hôtel de Gadagne houses the ⑦ **Musée de la Marionette**, with puppets from around the world, and also a museum of Lyon. Continue straight ahead on Rue du Boeuf; more traboules can be visited at nos.27 and 31. The courtyard in the traboule of no.16 is overlooked by a lovely tower known as the **Tour Rose**.

Turn left into Place Neuve St-Jean to walk down Rue du Palais de Justice, along the side of the courthouse, and down through Marché de la Creation, scene of art markets on Sunday morning. Cross the footbridge over the Saône and walk up through the outdoor food market. Veer left up Rue de la Monnaie, then left up **Rue Mercière**, lined with Renaissance houses.

Turn right along Rue Grenette and then left into Rue de Brest to pass the Gothic church of **St Nizier**, said to stand on the site of first Christian sanctuary. Continue on to **Place de Terreaux**, once the site of public executions. Today it features a fountain sculpted by Bartholdi and 69 jets of water that are illuminated at night. Edging the square are the 17th-century Hôtel de Ville and a former convent which now houses the ⑧ **Musée des Beaux-Arts**, one of France's richest collections of fine art. The whole of European art history is well represented, but a recent gift has made the Impressionist section particularly magnificent.

Leave the square on Rue Joseph-Serlin to view Lyon's Neoclassical **opera house**. Turn right down Rue du Garet, which becomes Rue de la Bourse. (It's possible to walk through the ancient school of Lycée Ampère to Passerelle du Collège, a footbridge over the Rhône). Beyond Place des Cordeliers is the solemn church of **St-Bonaventure**. From here head west to pick up the pedestrian-only Rue de la République (known as La Ré to locals), lined with 19th-century buildings.

Pass (if you can) the shop of Voisin on the right, the best *chocolatier* in Lyon. Cross Place de la République and continue south to regain the Place Bellecour. With luck, you still have sufficient time and energy to continue on Rue de la Charité for 500 m to the Hôtel de Villeroy, housing one of Lyon's best museums, the ⑨ **Musée des Tissus**. It follows the history of fabrics, with an emphasis on the use of silk.

FURTHER AFIELD

La Croix-Rousse

This district, covering the steep slope of the Presqu'île, derives its name from a stone cross

View from the Fourvière hill

that stood at a crossroads here until the Revolution. From Place des Terraux, weave up to the **Amphithéâtre des Trois Gaules**, where delegates from sixty cities of the Three Gauls – Celtic, Belgium and Aquitaine – assembled annually from 12 AD to the 3rd century in France's first 'parliament'. In 177 AD, Christians were thrown to lions here.

Head east and turn left up Montée Saint-Sébastien, passing an ex-convent, **Résidence Villemanzy**, with a fine view from the terrace. The hillside was covered with religious estates until the clergy were driven out during the Revolution. The slope was quickly covered with tall buildings that could accommodate Jacquard looms for making silk.

At Boulevard de la Croix -Rousse, detour right to view the **Gros Caillou**, a boulder transported from the Jura mountains by a glacier during the Ice Age. Now climb Rue de Belfort and turn left into Rue d'Ivry to visit **Maison des Canuts**, a museum and working co-operative where silk is made using traditional techniques. At the end of the street, turn left to reach métro *Croix-Rousse*.

Parc de la Tête d'Or

This extensive park on the Rhône is so named because a golden head of Christ is said to lie buried here. The English-style gardens include a rose garden that blooms lavishly between June and October, and a garden of Alpine plants. An underground passage leads onto Île du Souvenir, one of three islands in the large lake.

To reach the park, catch bus #4 from Part-Dieu rail station or catch the métro to *Masséna* and then walk north up Rue Masséna.

OPENING HOURS

Théâtres Romains	daily 9-dusk
Musée Gallo-Romaine	daily except Mon 10-6
Basilique N-D de Fourvière	daily 6-7; tower Wed-Sun in Apr-Sep
Cathédrale Saint-Jean	Mon-Fri 7.30-12, 2-7.30; S-S until 5
Musée de la Marionette	daily except Tue 10.45-6.00
Musée des Beaux-Arts	daily except Tue 10-6; Fri from 10.30
Musée des Tissus	daily except Mon 10-5.30
La Maison des Canuts	daily except Sun 8.30-12, 2-6.30

< Evening in Vieux-Lyon

Monts Dore

NOTES
Type: day walks
Suggested base: Le Mont-Dore
Getting there: rail from Clermont-Ferrand
Tourist Office: 96 ave de la Libération, 63240 Le Mont-Dore,
☏ 0473652021 Fax: 0473650571
E: ot.info@mont-dore.com
www.sancy.com
Map: Chamina *Massif du Sancy* 1:30000
Best timing: May-June; Sep-Oct

The distinctive landscape of the Auvergne in central France has been shaped by the volcanic activity of three great chains – all now extinct – that developed over different periods. The oldest of these is the Cantal range, the youngest is the Monts Dômes. The Monts Dore is the middle sibling: its volcanoes bubbled away several million years ago.

Today, the landscape is shaped by eroded cones and plugs while the mineral-rich mantle covers this skeleton with fertile farmland. The green, rolling hills are home to the red-coated Salers breed of cattle and local dairy farmers contribute various fine cheeses – St-Nectaire, Bleu d'Auvergne, Cantal – to the cheeseboards of France.

Water is a major feature of the region. The sources of the Dordogne – the streams of the Dore and the Dogne – begin high on the slopes of Puy de Sancy. From the peak you can see some of the lovely crater lakes that lie dotted around. Volcanic activity has also produced numerous hot springs and many towns such as St-Nectaire-le-Bas and Le Mont-Dore offer spa cures. The Gauls and then the Romans made use of these in their swimming pools.

Le Mont-Dore, a good base for walking in the region, developed in the 18th century when a road was built to reach the narrow valley that ends at the Puy de Sancy. The town stretches along the Dordogne river, hemmed in at the sides by the Capucin and the Puy de l'Angle. The railway brought more visitors to 'take the waters' in the 19th century and the town boomed in a genteel way. Today it is a strange melting pot of people seeking cures and more robust walkers or, in winter, snow enthusiasts.

There are many well-marked trails around the town, catering to walkers of all levels of endurance. Our first two walks are in the Grande Vallée, east of the Sancy massif, and are pleasant circuits from historic villages into the surrounding hills. Walk 3 is the classic ascent of Puy de Sancy, a peak that affords a panorama of the Auvergne. During the summer holidays, the summit is awash with people who have made the ascent by *téléphérique* or cable-car. At other times of the year, you may see wild *mouflon*, introduced from Corsica, on nearby spurs of rock.

Puy de Sancy >

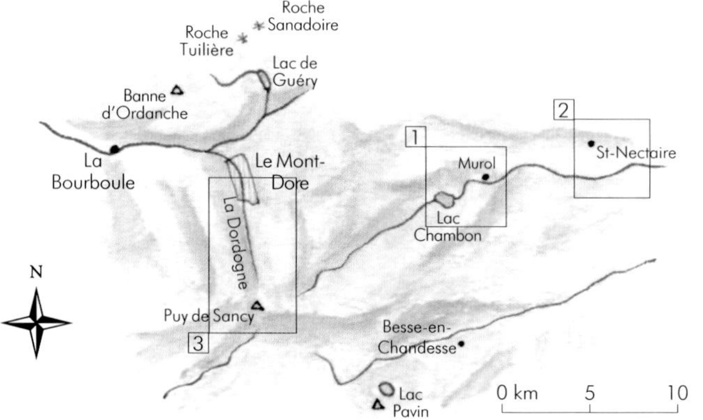

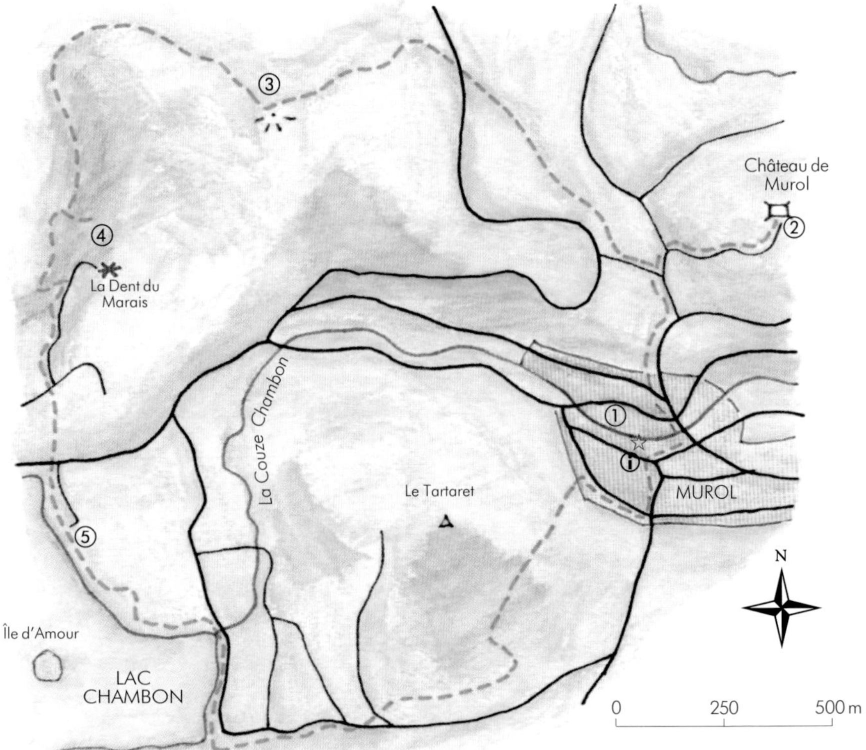

WALK 1: LAC CHAMBON

East of the Sancy massif runs the Grand Vallée, featuring the landmark castle of Murol and the lovely Lac Chambon.

Distance	6.5 km (4 miles)
Time	3 hours 30 (with castle visit)
Difficulty	easy
Start/Finish	Murol, on the D996

The walk starts at the tourist office in ① **the village of Murol**. At the onset of the 20th century, this quiet village was home to various landscape artists who made up the 'school of Murol'; the Maison des Peintres exhibits a collection of their works.

Cross the river and follow the many yellow waymarks and signs up the steep hill to the ② **Château du Murol**. The inner fortress was built by one of the lords of Murol in the 12th century but it passed into the hands of the Estaing family in the 15th century and was extended and richly decorated. During the Revolution the castle was used as a hideout for brigands and it fell into ruin until being classified. Now restored, it is the site of guided tours and colourful pageantry. Even if restored castles leave you cold, the battlements are worth climbing for the stunning views of the surrounding countryside, including the Massif du Sancy.

From the public toilets below the castle, pick up the GR30 and the yellow PR that lead up a track signed to Le Fougère. After an excellent patch of blackberries, fork left at Fougère, uphill on a GR path signed to Lac Chambon. The narrow path climbs up through woods and crosses several stiles to gain the ridge of a cirque, with a fine panorama and ③ **an observation board** that points out la Dent du Marais and other landmarks. A nearby bench makes this a wonderful spot for a picnic.

Continue uphill and soon join a track veering left. Shortly, fork left on the GR marked path signed to the lake. The path skirts pasture and then descends, following GR waymarks. A short detour left takes you up onto the rocky tooth of the

Lac Chambon >

④ **Saut de la Pucelle**, all that remains of the Dent du Marais volcano. Local legend relates that a shepherdess once leapt from the jagged rock to avoid the attentions of a nobleman.

Retrace your steps and then make a steep descent through woods (the path is slippery after rain) to a signpost at Le Marais. Turn right onto a lane and then left directly after an electricity station, following the GR30. Eventually, steps lead you down to the D996 road, at the northeast corner of Lac Chambon. Yellow waymarks lead down steps by the lake's edge to then wend south, passing near the pretty Île d'Amour. You soon cross a bridge over La Couze Chambon to arrive at
⑤ **la Plage**, or the beach of Lac Chambon, often carpeted with sunbathers in summer. Walk along this and turn left at a signpost to Murol on a track that climbs the wooded volcanic hill of Le Tartaret. Zigzag uphill following the yellow PR, eventually following it left where it parts from GR waymarks; a few metres to the left of this junction is a basalt monument that commemorates the painter Charreton.

At a path junction, follow the yellow spots down wooden steps to the right. The path crosses a road and continues down steps to the road, back in Murol. Turn right onto the road and then left by the post office to regain the tourist office.

La Dent du Marais

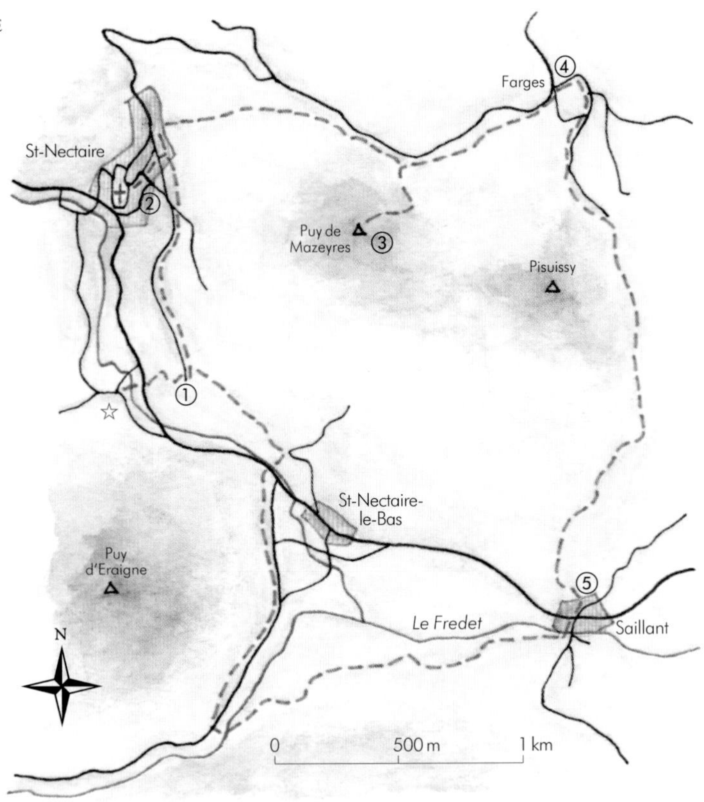

WALK 2: PUY de MAZEYRES

The village of St-Nectaire sits in the heart of the Auvergne's cheese-producing farmland and features a magnificent Romanesque church.

Distance	8 km (5 miles)
Time	3 hours 30
Difficulty	easy
Start/Finish	St-Nectaire

Start at the casino, near the tourist office, located midway between upper and lower St-Nectaire. Cross the footbridge above the road and climb on steps, following a PR waymarked with yellow dots, to the *raison d'être* of the ① **Parc du Dolmen**, an impressive dolmen. From the nearby tower, turn left onto a track, the Chemin de la Parre, that passes a cross and heads towards the old village of St-Nectaire-le-Haut. Detour left along a lane past the *boulangerie* to visit a masterpiece of Romanesque art, the 12th-century ② **Église de Saint-Nectaire**. The church was badly damaged during the Revolution but restored in 1875. Inside, it has a marvellous unity of style and is decorated with 103 wonderful capitals, many of them still in polychrome. It still has a collection of fine medieval treasures on display.

Return to where you left the PR and follow the yellow waymarks through the edge of the old village, then veer right to follow a lane as it rises to eventually join the D150 at L'Homme.

Dolmen, St-Nectaire >

Église de Saint-Nectaire

Enjoy the view WSW to the castle of Murol (visited in Walk 1). Turn right onto this road and take the first road right to continue uphill to the top of

③ **Puy de Mazeyres** (914 m), where there is an orientation table and a bench to enjoy the sweeping views of the Monts Dore.

A farm building near Farges

Retrace your steps and turn right along the D150. About 150 m on, veer left onto a grassy lane and descend to the quiet hamlet of

④ **Farges**, that features a *lavoir*-fountain of lava stone. The route passes something that boasts the name of Les Mystères de Farges (open July-August); look into the charming courtyard as you pass. Turn right, following waymarks, and soon pass the dairy farm of Bellonte, where the *fermier* version of Saint-Nectaire cheese can be tasted and bought.

Continue straight ahead on the lane, that winds downhill for 2.5 km to enter the village of Saillant. Turn right at the road to reach the main square with its fountain and bread oven. Cross the D996 and take the Chemin de Chastrilles (with a yellow signpost to St-Nectaire). Pass by the

⑤ **Cascade de Saillant**, where the stream of le Fredet cascades down a broad lava rock face, and follow it upstream. After 100 m or so, fork left on a path skirting pasture to wind uphill through woodland. Continue following the yellow spots through several junctions and pass below the crags of Puy d'Eraigne. Cross la Couze Chambon on a cement footbridge and turn right onto the D642 to reach the spa town of St Nectaire-le-Bas.

Turn left onto the D996 and soon right (at La Cabrette) up to touch a minor road at a bend. Leave this left on a path for 500 m back to the Parc du Dolmen.

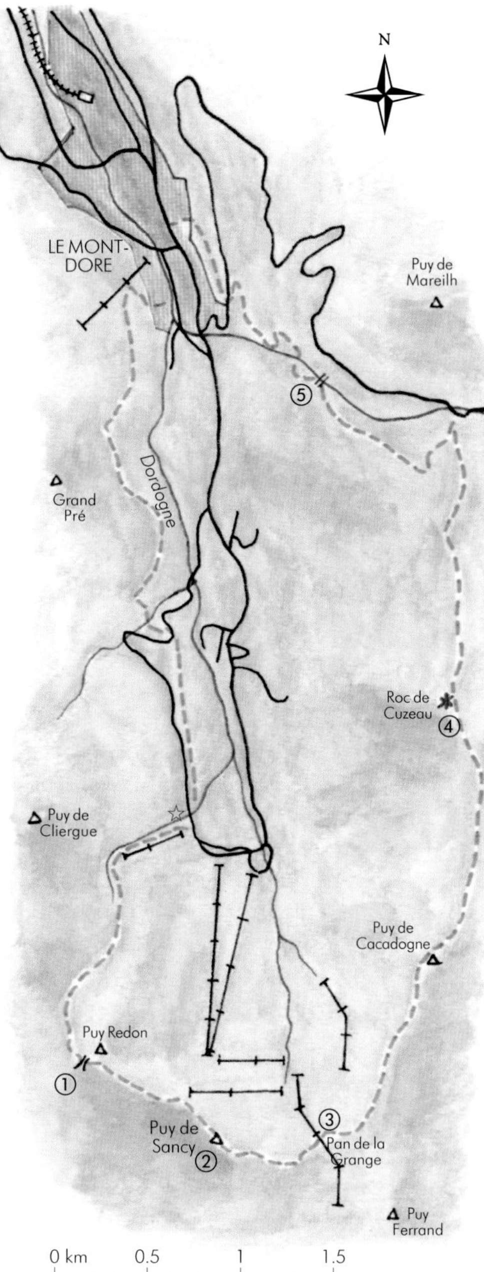

WALK 3: PUY de SANCY

This ascent of the highest peak in the Massif Central begins with a steep climb and then a dramatic ridge walk to a high waterfall.

Distance	10.7 km (6.6 miles)
Time	6 hours
Difficulty	moderate
Start	Station du Mont-Dore
Finish	Le Mont-Dore

To reach the starting point, you could catch a shuttle or a taxi from the centre of Le Mont-Dore, or you could walk along the **Chemin des Artistes**, a pleasant route described overleaf. Take a picnic lunch.

From the western end of the car park area at Station du Mont-Dore, pick up the PR path (waymarked yellow) that passes a ruined *buron*. In 1944, three resistance fighters were executed here by the Gestapo who then torched the hut; its ruins remain as a memorial. Head uphill by a ski-lift and follow a stream up through the meadows of the Val de Courre.

Continue uphill, following yellow spots on rocks, and watching the crags and spurs above for mouflon and chamois. The path steepens and zigzags up by crags to the
① **Col de Courre** (1722 m) from where you have a wonderful view back down valley and over into the Vallée de la Fontaine Salée. Once you've enjoyed the views, turn left and follow the GR30 footpath that traverses Puy Redon and gives stunning views of the jagged Aiguilles du Diable, or 'devil's needles'. There is a balcony with tables and an information board, then wooden steps lead up to a panoramic viewing table on the peak of
② **Puy de Sancy** at 1885 m. On a clear day, views can stretch as far as the Dauphiné Alps. The three volcanic ranges of the Auvergne lie closer: the Dômes range to the northeast, the Cantal range to the south and, of course, the Monts Dore immediately around you.

Continue downhill in much the same direction, descending to the Col de la Cabane where you keep left on a broad track marked with a green arrow. At a sign that says 'montée interdite' veer left and then down to the right (erosion is a serious problem on the massif, so follow current signs carefully). The broad track descends through a barrier to the
③ **Pan de la Grange** (1720 m). Here you follow the GR4 steeply uphill (signed to Col

The Sancy massif from Cuzeau >

Croix St-Robert) and then contour right of a minor peak, heading for a GR post. Follow yellow spots over the Pic Intermediaire: to your right lies the Vallée de Chaudefour and the sharp Dent de la Rancune. Skirt left (west) of the next peak, Puy de Cacadogne, gaining a view of Le Mont-Dore and the high balcony above it.

From the *téléski* winches on the Puy des Crebasses, descend to the next yellow waymark, veering left towards the ridgeline. You now gain a good view northwest of Lac Chambon and the Château du Murol. You cross a col and climb to the dramatic

④ **Roc de Cuzeau**, a fractured wall of rock perched above the valley. From above it you have extensive views, including north beyond the Plateau de Durbise to Lac de Guéry. The path then zigzags downhill in broad sweeps. At a junction below the Roc, leave the GR and veer left on a path signed to the cascade.

Soon, you must climb a stile and descend on a grassy sheep track that heads towards Le Mont-Dore but then veers sharply right downhill to a yellow pointer directing you down steps to the top of the pretty

⑤ **Grande Cascade**. Cross the bridge below the waterfall and then descend on the pleasant woodland path. When you reach the D36, cross the road and pick up the Chemin de Melchirose heading downhill. Soon, turn sharp left on the steps of Chemin de la Bane, reaching Les Thermes at Place Chazeret in the centre of the town.

Roc de Cuzeau

Grande Cascade

OTHER WALKS IN THE REGION

Chemin des Artistes

This pleasant walk leads you up-valley on a balcony through woodland. It can also serve as the first stage of the Puy de Sancy route described in Walk 3.

Cross the bridge over the Dordogne near the tourist office and follow Avenue de la Liberation for 50 m, then turn left into Chemin des Mille Gouttes, that climbs steeply. Turn left after 200 m and cross a bridge above a funicular railway, then keep right at a fork. The Chemin des Artistes now leads gently up valley and, after 2.5 km or so, arrives at a T-junction where you turn left. Some 200 m on, remain on the main path as it swings left.

Just before you reach the road, turn right onto a track that leads past a car park and grassy area with excellent views ahead. This is a good place to pause and enjoy the surrounding mountains before returning to Le Mont-Dore. If you plan to climb Puy de Sancy, continue along the grassy track that follows *téléski* pylons to the Station du Mont-Dore. *Allow 1 hour 30 one-way; 2 hours 30 return.*

La Banne d'Ordanche

Catch a train to the nearby spa town of La Bourboule. From the station, walk east on the D130 along the Dordogne river to pick up GR waymarks. Follow these over the river and across the railway line, then up to the hamlet of Les Planches. Cross the D996 and walk up through the village of L'Usclade then start a steep climb. At a path junction at Le Vieux Loup, keep north on the PR10.

At Col de St-Laurent, a detour left brings you to the viewpoint of La Banne d'Ordanche at 1512 m. In the Auvergne dialect, *banne* means a horn; this basalt outcrop is the remains of a volcanic chimney. Return to the col and continue east, passing the old Puy May farm after 1.6 km. After another 2.5 km of open pasture, tracks lead you to the Col de Guéry, with its magnificent view of the Roche Tuilière and Roche Sanadoire. Walk around Lac de Guéry on the D983 and, at the lake's southern tip, keep right on a track to pick up the GR30. At the far edge of a pine forest, veer west on the GR30 to a saddle, where you

Many paths can be walked under snow >

leave the GR and turn south on the PR11.

A long descent brings you to the buildings of Pailloux, where you follow the PR11 right to the hamlet of La Fougère. Here you turn left onto a road for 400 m then left again on the D996 that leads you through the district of Le Queureuilh and up through Le Mont-Dore. *Allow 6-7 hours.*

Two Rocks ring walk

North of Le Mont-Dore, just beyond Lac de Guéry, stand the Roche Tuilière and Roche Sanadoire, two amazing volcanic formations divided by a glacier-carved valley. Transport is needed to reach the start of the walk, a lay-by on the D983, 1.5 km north of the Col de Guéry parking area.

A small platform here allows a close look of the looming Roche Sanadoire, all that remains of a volcanic cone. Until the 15th century, the rock was topped by a fortress; it was used as a stronghold for mercenaries in the Hundred Years War.

Take the PR15 (waymarked with a blue stripe) downhill through the beech woods of the Chausse Corrie. The path descends to cross the road, forks right and then crosses the road again below. Continue descending alongside the stream of Fontsalade to reach a large clearing with a stunning view of the prismatic columns of the Roche Tuilière, the chimney of an ancient volcano.

Staying east of the stream, veer right onto a track. Follow this north for 1.5 km to reach the end of a road, where you climb to the hamlet of Douharesse. Pass through the hamlet and take the track left to reach the D27 where you turn right. After 250 m, behind the farm of Chez le Poutou, turn right. Follow this track south for 1 km, passing to the right of Le Montagne du Cros farm.

At the entrance to the woods, leave the main track and pick up a path to the left, that then climbs. After 250 m, turn right on a path to then rejoin a track. Continue following blue stripe waymarks to regain the D983 and the parking area. *Allow 2 hours.*

Roche Tuilière

A farmhouse above Le Mont-Dore

Grenoble & the Vercors

Even if it had nothing else to offer, the site of Grenoble – at the confluence of the rivers Drac and Isère and wedged between the massifs of the Chartreuse, Vercors and the Belledonne – makes it a destination for any lover of mountain landscapes. As luck would have it, this surprising city has much else to please the traveller.

The town was founded by Gauls and then fortified by Romans. The surrounding region was later named Dauphiné (after one of the names of its owner, the count of Albon) and was sold to the king of France in 1349. Thereafter, the title Dauphin was conferred, with the land, on the heir to the French throne. The city became renowned for its glove-making, but in the 19th century it diversified and prospered from cement production, coal mining and hydro-electric power. Today it is a high-tech centre for electronics, chemical and nuclear research.

As you might expect from a place that relies on technological developments, Grenoble is a forward-looking city. New buildings, such as the art gallery, reflect a bold sense of architecture and offer an interesting counterpoint to the buildings of the old quarter. Old Grenoble is a lively place, with an outdoor market and plenty of sidewalk cafés. The banks of the Isère are lined with restaurants catering to the 35,000 plus students of the city's science-oriented university.

Mont Aiguille

NOTES

Getting there: rail from Lyon or Marseille

Tourist Office: 14 Rue de la République, 38019 Grenoble
☏ 0476424141 Fax: 0476001898
E: info@grenoble-isere.info
www.grenoble-isere.info

Markets: Place Ste-Claire Wed-Mon; Les Halles Tue-Sun 6-1

Note: Multipass Grenoble available

Immediately southwest rises the Vercors, a horseshoe-shaped citadel of limestone ridges, cut through by the action of water to create deep gorges and natural amphitheatres. Its cliffs and plateaux form a natural fortress: wildlife still finds refuge here and, during WWII it was a stronghold for the French Resistance. The Germans, unable to breach the difficult terrain, eventually parachuted in three SS divisions to defeat the guerilla fighters in 1944. Various memorials bear witness to the tragic loss of life here.

Atop the Vercors, you'll find rolling farmland and wooded hillsides, but the high plateaux are a dry stretch of limestone fissures and sinkholes. The eastern edge of the massif – punctuated only by passes known locally as *pas* – is particularly dramatic, and includes the high summits of Moucherotte, Grand Veymont and Mont Aiguille. This last, a free-standing tower of rock east of the escarpment, saw the beginnings of mountaineering in 1492.

Included in this chapter are three walks that take in these landscapes, plus a long-distance route that links them.

Grenoble's Isère river >

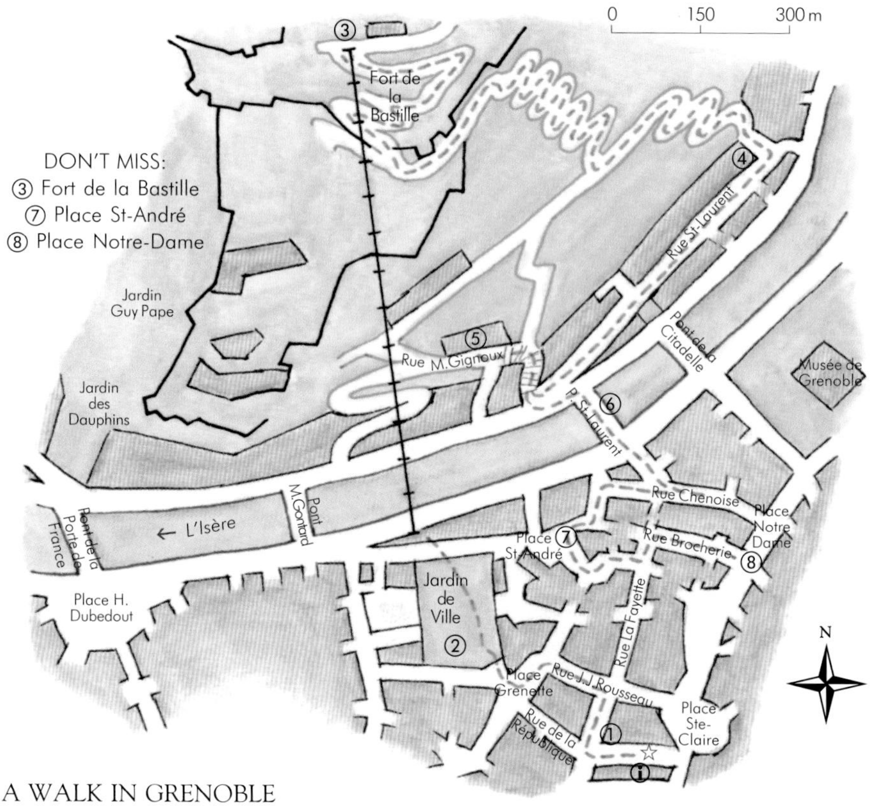

A WALK IN GRENOBLE

Grenoble may be counted as France's flattest city, but a detour up to its perched Bastille is essential, simply for the stunning views.

Though the core of Grenoble lies at some distance from its rail station and bus terminal, it is a quick ride on the tram. From the tourist office near Place Ste-Claire, turn left along Rue de la République, and then right into Rue Lafayette, by a remnant of the eight-metre-high ① **Roman wall** that was built late in the 3rd century. Bronze studs in the ground mark the outline of the elliptical wall.

Rue Jean-Jacques Rousseau was given its name because the philosopher once stayed for a month at no.2. Number 14 has a greater claim to fame: it was the birthplace in 1783 of Marie-Henri Beyle, who became the writer Stendhal and left his middle-class upbringing for Paris when he was 17. The mansions at nos. 15 and 16 are worth viewing closely for their architectural details.

At the end of the street, turn left along Grande Rue, former Roman way, to reach the end of **Place Grenette**, the site of livestock markets in the Middle Ages. When it was integrated into the city in the late 16th century, it hosted the corn exchange and any public executions.

Walk through the nearby passage to enter ② **Jardin de Ville**, a pretty green space containing ancient plane trees and a charming 1878 sculpture-fountain known as *Le Torrent*.

At the park's end, by Quai Stephane Jay, is the station for the **Bulles**, Grenoble's unusual cable car that will transport you 263 m aloft. If this is not operating, cross the Isère river by the M.Gontard bridge and walk downstream. By a statue of Philis, pick up a path to climb through the Jardin des Dauphins and then continue up through the Jardin Guy Pape to reach the ③ **Fort de la Bastille**. This bastion, built in the 16th century to control approach routes to the city, was enlarged in the 19th century and while its warren of galleries is interesting, the main attraction is the stunning view it affords. The rooftop beside the cable car station has orientation tables showing the peaks of the Chartreuse, the Vercors and, on clear days, the Alps including Mont Blanc. For the curious, a path through an arch near toilets leads to a tunnel in the hillside; the path soon exits higher up Mont Jalla at a grassy spot near a kiosk.

From the fort, follow the *Circuit Léon-Moret* which leads you downhill to the 17th-century Porte St-Laurent, near the

④ **Église St-Laurent** and its archaeological museum. Excavations in this former church reveal an early necropolis, the lovely St-Oyand crypt of the 6th century, and a medieval cloister.

Walking along Rue Saint-Laurent, you traverse the 'Italian quarter' where tanneries and workshops produced some of Europe's finest gloves in the 17th-19th centuries. The raised square midway along commemorates Xavier Jouvin, a glovemaker who invented the 'iron hand' method.

The 1843 *Fontaine au Lion* that dominates **Place de la Cimaise** represents the tenuous control that Grenoble holds over the serpentine Isère river. Climb steps to the right of the

A courtyard off Rue Chenoise

Le Torrent

fountain and detour a short way to the

⑤ **Musée Dauphinois**, set in a 17th-century convent. It has an interesting exhibition on traditional mountain life, but is also worth visiting for its cloister and Baroque chapel.

Back by the fountain, cross the

⑥ **Passerelle St-Laurent**. This footbridge dates from 1837 and is in much the same location as the one the Romans first raised in 43 BC. In between, many wooden and stone bridges have been swept away by the river, swollen with snow-melt.

Back on the Left Bank, fork left for a look down **Rue Chenoise**. There are attractive courtyards behind the façades of nos.8 and 10. Turn and walk along Rue Madeleine to reach

⑦ **Place St-André**, the centre of local power in the Middle Ages. The **Palais de Justice**, on the north side, once housed the Dauphiné parliament; it open to the public. The octagonal spire of the 13th-century chapel of St-André dominates the square, along with a statue of the knight Bayard. Also here, you'll find France's second oldest café, **Café de la Table Ronde**, dating to 1739.

Indeed, you pass quite a few cafés as you

Cathédrale Notre-Dame

wander through Place Claveyson to **Place aux Herbes**, which is thought to be where the first local settlement was located.

Now walk along Rue Brocherie to arrive at ⑧ **Place Notre-Dame**, where a cathedral has stood since the 4th century. The present cathedral has been remodelled many times but retains some pre-Romanesque features. The adjoining former Bishop's Palace is now the museum of **L'Ancien Évêché**, offering a further historical perspective of the city.

From Place Notre-Dame, you can choose to walk south to Place Ste-Claire or north towards the river where you'll find the **Musée de Grenoble**, one of France's most prestigious regional art collections, housed in a striking modern building.

OPENING HOURS

Musée Archeol.	Mon, Wed-Sun 9-6
Musée Dauphinois	Mon, Wed-Sun 10-6 (10-7 Jun-Sep)
Musée de l'Évêché	M, W-Sa 9-6; Su 10-7
Musée de Grenoble	M, Th-Su 11-7; W 11-10

WALKS IN THE VERCORS

The limestone cliffs of the Vercors' eastern edge rise like ramparts above the Drac valley. These three day-walks take in various high points along this dramatic escarpment.

Map: IGN 1:60000 Vercors 3615
Timing: May to mid-Nov

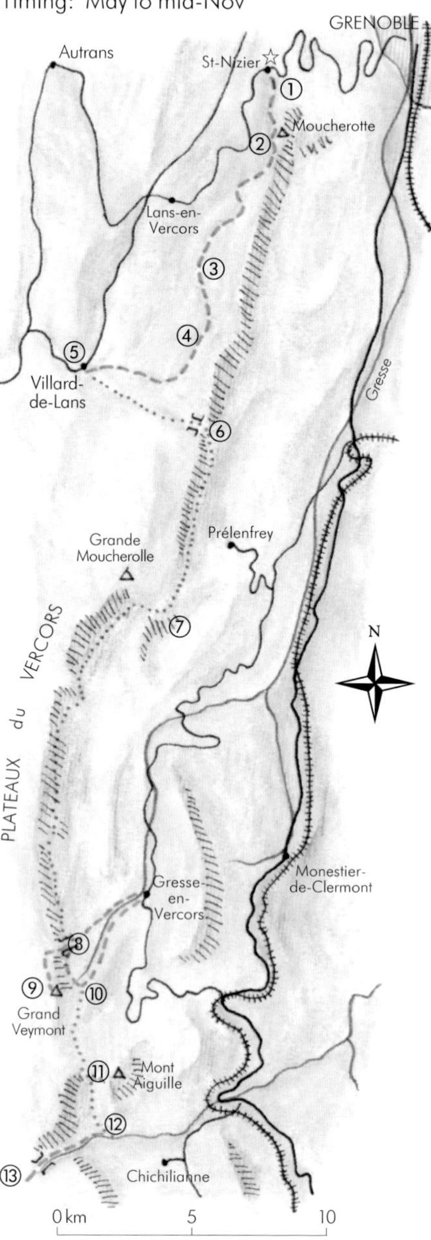

WALK 1: Le MOUCHEROTTE

You may wish to break this rewarding hike along the GR91 into two easy days by stopping overnight at Lans-en-Vercors.

Difficulty	medium
Start	St-Nizier-du-Moucherotte
Finish	Villard-de-Lans
Transport	bus #510 from Grenoble
Distance	19.5 km (12 miles)
Time	7 hours 30

High on the plateau above Grenoble, overlooked by the rock needles of Les Trois Pucelles or 'Three Virgins' is

① **St-Nizier-du-Moucherotte**. The village was restored after it had been burnt to the ground by the Germans in 1944; the cemetery by its restored church contains the graves of 96 Resistance members who died in the attack. A lane left of the church leads to an orientation table and superb views of the Chartreuse, Mont-Blanc, Belledonne and Ecrins massifs.

From the viewpoint, follow a lane uphill to a gate to pick up the GR91. After a steady climb, reach the **Roc de Bataillon** (1440 m). The track now becomes a ski *piste*, rising steeply with views opening up of the Vercors plateau. At a cairn and sign, turn right steeply up through forest to a junction at **les Forges** (1630 m). The forest track levels with views west and south. Pass a stream and then wend uphill more steeply to an *abri* or shelter. Just beyond is a side path up to an orientation table on top of

② **le Moucherotte** (1901 m). An expensive hotel, catering to the rich and famous operated here in the 1950s. The views, over Grenoble and beyond, are remarkable.

Return to the GR91 and continue down on a farm track to the Combe de St-Nizier. Lower down, a path forks left to an *abri* but you keep straight ahead on the GR91. At

③ **la Ramme** path junction you could fork right on the GRP to Lans-en-Vercors in the valley below. Otherwise, keep high on the GR91, passing below ski-lifts to reach a *stade de neige* or ski centre. Meet and follow the road downhill. At a sharp bend, the GR leaves it and follows a stony path up to the auberge of

④ **les Allières** offering accommodation (check if open) and a possible lunch stop.

The Vercors from le Moucherotte

Soon after, the route becomes a stony forest path rising to cross a ski *piste* before reaching the spring of Font Froide. From here, it becomes a wonderful balcony path, the *Sentier Gobert*, that passes calciferous rocks shaped by erosion; the result is known as *lapiaz*. To the right are excellent views over the fertile plateau.

Leave the GR path at Combe Chaulange, at a sign pointing right to La Conversarie. Descend steeply on a footpad, then on a farm track to La Ya. Turn left and watch for signs to L'Essendole if you want to overnight in a rustic gîte d'étape (☏ 0476950571). If not, follow lanes into

⑤ **Villard-de-Lans**, a lively town with hotels and restaurants and a bus stop for Grenoble.

WALK 2: LE GRAND VEYMONT

This rewarding circuit involves a climb of over 1000 metres, but offers stunning views and the chance to see chamois and ibex.

Difficulty	medium-hard (steep & rocky)
Start/Finish	Gresse-en-Vercors
Transport	bus from Monestier-de-Clermont
Distance	16 km (10 miles)
Time	6 hours
Notes	carry lunch supplies

Mont Aiguille from Grand Veymont

From the village of **Gresse-en-Vercors**, follow the road up through the hamlet of La Ville and on to the ski-base at Plan de l'Herse (driving to here would take 4 km off the total distance of the walk.)

Take the *Sentier Central* (signed to Pas de la Ville) to climb southwest, gradually at first and then steeply through woodland. It leaves the woods and climbs to

⑧ **Sous le Pas** (1710 m) where you cross the *Sentier du Balcon Est*. Continue, now zigzagging steeply up the scree slope to reach **Pas de la Ville**, a narrow and dramatic pass. Branch off left to follow the ridge line, with some dramatic glimpses down east. Cairns mark the summit of

⑨ **le Grand Veymont**, at 2341 metres the highest peak in the Vercors. Here you gain a sudden and thrilling view over Mont Aiguille, plus a panoramic vista.

Retrace your steps to the junction of Sous le Pas and turn right onto the balcony path. Pass a resurgent spring and, after some woodland, pass just above the forest shelter of

⑩ **Baraque du Veymont**. Just after the *baraque*, leave the balcony path to descend left through woods to regain Plan de l'Herse and then, some 30 minutes on, Gresse-en-Vercors.

Pas de l'Aiguille >

WALK 3: PAS de L'AIGUILLE

A short ascent to a historic site on the plateau, overlooking the extraordinary Mont Aiguille.

Difficulty	medium
Start/Finish	Richardière
Transport	taxi from Clelles rail station
Distance	9 km (6 miles)
Time	4 hours
Notes	carry lunch supplies

From the hamlet of

⑫ **Richardière** take the lane following the Donnière upstream to a large clearing with a memorial to the *maquisards*, resistance fighters.

At the back of this, a path enters woodland and climbs steadily. Eventually, the path leaves the trees and zigzags up over stony scree to the

⑬ **Pas de l'Aiguille**, some 500 m above the valley floor. This pass brings you onto the high plateau in a lovely wide valley. Here you'll find a massive monument to the eight maquisards who died in a nearby cave in July 1944. You can enter the cave above the pass, where 23 men held out against German attack for over 30 hours before the survivors escaped. Further up valley, past a herder's *cabane* is an unmanned and basic refuge. Once you have explored the plateau, retrace your steps to Richardière.

Grand Veymont

WALK 4: ALONG THE EASTERN RIM

The three previous walks can be linked up in a challenging hike that makes use of a dramatic balcony path.

Type: a 4 or 5-day walk - 70 km (43.5 miles)
Difficulty: medium-hard; steep inclines
Start/Finish: St-Nizier (bus from Grenoble)
Finish: Richardière (taxi to Clelles)
Notes: carry lunch supplies

Walk from ① **St-Nizier** as described in Walk 1. Next day, leave ⑤ **Villard-de-Lans** southeast, via the Cochettes district. From a parking area at the foot of a *téléski* (ski-tow) pick up the footpath signed to Col Vert. The path, an old one for herding animals down to market, eventually passes the Plâtres cross and then the Royban refuge to reach ⑥ **Col Vert** on the lip of the plateau. It then descends the steep slope, heading south to connect with the *Sentier du Balcon Est*. Fork right on this amazing balcony footpath and follow it for 5.5 km, passing the Rochers des Deux Soeurs to a major spur. Make your way down to the top of the *télésiège* or chairlift, to the gîte d'étape (☏ 0476723881) above ⑦ **Col de l'Arzelier**.

On day 3, return to the *Sentier du Balcon Est* and continue as it contours the escarpment. After almost 7 km, pass a left-branching path that descends to the hamlet of St-Andeol. Keep on and, after another 11.5 km of excellent walking, reach a junction known as ⑧ **Sous le Pas** (see Walk 2). A left turn leads down to **Gresse-en-Vercors** and accommodation. (Alternatively, less than 2 km straight ahead is the unguarded forestry hut of Baraque du Veymont; you'll need food and sleeping gear.)

On day 4, return to Sous le Pas and climb to the **Pas de la Ville** and then up to the peak of ⑨ **le Grand Veymont**, following notes in Walk 2. Return via the same route to the path junction and continue south once more on the *Sentier du Balcon Est*. It passes a spring and then the *baraque*, then wends through woods to eventually reach a path junction. Turn right to follow the *Tour du Mont Aiguille* south to ⑪ **Col de l'Aupet**, very close to the huge tower of Mont Aiguille.

Carefully descend the steep, rocky gully and then follow a well-graded path down through woods to reach a lane that leads into the hamlet of ⑫ **Richardière**, where there is a hotel/gîte d'étape. On the last day, you could follow notes in Walk 3 for a short climb to ⑬ **Pas de l'Aiguille** and back to Richardière.

LONG DISTANCE STAGES

km	time	location	acc
		St-Nizier	C
12.5	5h	Les Allières	H/R
7	2h30	Villard-de-Lans	H,C,G
12	5h	Col de l'Arzelier	G
22.5	7h	Gresse-en-Vercors	G,C
16	6	Richardière	H,G

Le Puy

Few towns of 20,000 people have such a remarkable setting as Le Puy. It lies in the *département* of the Haute Loire – not a great distance from that long river's source – in a region shaped by volcanic activity. Le Puy itself features three plugs of laval rock that the inhabitants have put to dramatic use.

The word *puy* is one of the terms used locally for a volcanic peak and, so as to distinguish it from other *puys*, the town's full name is Le Puy-en-Velay. The Velay is an old name for this part of the Massif Central, and it is characterised by rolling, fertile land with eruptions of rocky outcrops and steep wooded hills.

A religious centre from the 5th century, the town's fortunes soared when, in the 10th century, bishop Gothescalc of Le Puy made the first recorded pilgrimage to the Spanish town of Santiago de Compostela. He returned to build a chapel on one of the fingers of lava and Le Puy became the starting point on the pilgrimage route known as the *Via Podiensis*.

The thousands who followed his example over the centuries gathered in Le Puy, visited the cathedral to be blessed and then set out on their 1600-kilometre *grand randonnée*. Today, that route is roughly followed by the GR65, a section of which is described in the next chapter of this book, and many walkers still set out from Le Puy.

Stone detail, cathedral cloisters

NOTES

Getting there: rail from Lyon (via St Etienne) or Clermont-Ferrand

Tourist Office: Place du Breuil, 43000
☏ 0471093841
Fax: 0471052262
E: info@ot-lepuyenvelay.fr

www.ot-lepuyenvelay.fr

Market: Saturday, Place du Plot

Pilgrims, like modern tourists, gave the town an income, and Le Puy's architecture reflects a wealth beyond that of most towns its size. The Cathédrale Notre-Dame-de-France and surrounding ecclecsiastical buildings, all informed by Moorish architecture, form a unique ensemble, made all the more remarkable because of their position atop a volcanic plug.

Fortunately for its preservation, the town avoided becoming heavily embroiled in the Wars of Religion that ravaged other local populations. Its local industries included tanning and lacemaking, both of which are in little demand these days, though the latter is enjoying a small revival as a traditional craft.

Le Puy, of course, is also famous for its green lentils, known as the 'poor people's caviar', grown for 2000 years in the Velay. Le Puy even appears in the generic name for the pulse, *Lens esculenta puyensis,* and a plate of salt-cured pork served on a bed of lentils is a great local delicacy. You'll need this kind of sustenance if you're to climb Le Puy's three major monuments and its steep alleys.

Chapelle St-Michel, perched on its rock needle >

0
100
200
300 m
N
DON'T MISS:
③ Cathédrale de Notre-Dame
④ Rocher St-Michel
⑥ Rocher Corneille
St-Clair
Monument aux Morts
Sentier du Faron
Rue Gouteyron
Rue du Cloître
Rue Grasmanent
Rue des Farges
Rue St-George
Place des Tables
Rue des Tables
Évêché
Rue Cardinal de Polignac
Rue Raphaël
Rue Roche Taillade
Rue Chamarlenc
Rue du Bouillon
Rue Meymard
Place du Marché Couvert
Rue Pannessac
Rue Courrerie
Place du Clauzel
Place du Plot
Place du Martouret
Rue Chaussade
Rue Porte Aiguière
Rue Crozatier
Boulevard Maréchal Fayolle
Place aux Laines
Place du Breuil
Musée Crozatier

A WALK IN LE PUY

You could spend much time wandering Le Puy's delightful maze of medieval alleys but it's obligatory to climb at least one of the town's rocky spurs!

Find your way to the tourist office on Place du Breuil, 600 m west of the rail station and just south of the old town. Walk towards the Crozatier fountain, then cross Boulevard Maréchal Fayolle (named for the WWI general who was a native of Le Puy) and walk up Rue Porte Aiguière to enter

① **Place du Martouret**, the site of some 41 executions during the French Revolution. In 1794 Le Puy's famous statue of the Black Virgin was burnt here; it's said it was then revealed to have been a statue of the Egyptian goddess Isis.

On the left of the square is the 1766 Hôtel de Ville or town hall, also the victim of many fires. Take Rue Courrerie, behind this, and take a close look at the restored Renaissance house at no.6. Its vaulted passage leads to a courtyard with a 1571 turret. Further along is the site of the old pillory,

② **Place du Plot**, where lively Saturday markets are now held. It is also the starting point for the Saint-Jacques pilgrimage or GR65;

Start of the GR65

The cathedral from Rocher Corneille

note the signboard on the wall. The Bidoire fountain, Le Puy's oldest, dates from 1246; its decoration was added in the 15th century.

Continue a short way up Rue Pannessac and turn right into Rue Chamarlenc. No.16-18 was the headquarters of the Cornards, a company of licensed satirists; hence the cheeky *mascarons* or masks on the façade. At the end, turn left into Rue Raphaël, home to Le Puy's leading citizens in the 18th century. Walk through Place des Tables, which features a 15th-century fountain dedicated to a young chorister who sang in these streets.

Continue along Rue des Farges, once filled with workshops of farriers and ironmongers. Turn right to weave back along Rue Boucherie Haute and then turn left up the picturesque Rue des Tables, so named because religious souvenirs were displayed here to catch the eye of passing pilgrims. At the end are steps up to the west front of

③ **Cathédrale de Notre-Dame**. Begun in the 11th century, with a clear Byzantine and Moorish influence, this cathedral stands partly on the rock of Mont Anis and partly on a platform supported by pillars. Inside are various wonders, including a copy of the Black Virgin – still revered and paraded around the streets

A cobbled lane in the old town

during festivals – and a wonderful fresco from the late 15th century, depicting the liberal arts in a charming tableau. In a passageway in the cathedral is the Fever Stone – perhaps once a prehistoric dolmen – which was reputed to have healing properties; it was routinely touched by those departing on a pilgrimage.

Return down the main staircase and turn right into Rue Becdelièvre then zigzag left then right into Rue Gouteyron to reach Porte Gouteyron, dating back to 1295. Keep right along Sentier du Faron and continue past the war memorial and the 12th-century, octagonal Chapelle Saint-Clair to the base of the extraordinary

④ **Rocher St-Michel**, also known as Mont d'Aiguilhe and once the site of a Roman temple to Mercury. This 80-metre-high basalt plug poses a steep climb, rewarded by magnificent views, but also by the close inspection of

⑤ **Chapelle St-Michel**. This Romanesque church, built on Bishop Gothescalc's return from Spain and consecrated in 962, shows a strong Moorish influence in its beautifully decorated façade. Its original bell-tower was destroyed in 1245 by lightning.

Retrace your steps to Porte Gouteyron and turn left along Rue Grasmanent. If you feel up to another climb, turn left into Rue du Cloître, passing the 1584 Penitents' Chapel, now a small museum of paintings and sculptures. During the Revolution, the chapel was saved from damage by the guild of butchers; the White Penitents make a spectacular annual procession through the streets.

It's now time to ascend the

⑥ **Rocher Corneille** – another volcanic finger – surmounted by an immense, ugly statue of the Virgin, cast from 213 cannons captured at Sebastopol during the Crimean war. You can actually climb inside the statue as high as the neck for a fine view over the old town.

Back in Rue du Cloître, you'll find the entrance (there's a fee) to the

⑦ **cathedral cloisters**, well worth visiting if you haven't already. They date from the 11th

A lace shop >

Le Puy from the GR65

to 12th centuries and feature sculpted columns supporting unusual polychrome arches. Entry to the cloisters also lets you visit a museum of 13th- to 18th-century sacred art.

Across the street from the cloisters is the ⑧ **Baptistère Saint-Jean**, dating back to the 10th or 11th centuries, which functioned as a baptistry during the Revolution.

Follow Rue St-Georges as it bends around, then turn right to walk the length of Rue Cardinal de Polignac. No.8 on the left is the Hôtel de Polignac, featuring a 15th-century, polygonal tower. Turn the corner, marked by the 15th-century Hôtel du Lac de Fugères, and descend Rue Roche Taillade. Turn left into Rue du Bouillon and then right along Rue Meymard, skirting **Place de Clauzel**, where paupers were buried until the mid-17th century.

At Place du Martouret turn left into Rue Chaussade and then right into Rue Crozatier to return to your starting point.

OTHER EXCURSIONS

Musée Crozatier

This museum, which stands outside the old town, has a display of bobbin and needlework lace from the 16th century to the present, along with a good collection of medieval artefects and 15th-century paintings.

From the tourist office, walk south through the extensive Vinay gardens. The museum stands on its southern edge in a purpose-built 1868 building.

GR65/Chemin de Saint-Jaques

The first stage of the famous pilgrimage route is decribed in the next chapter of this book. For a little taste of it, you could follow the waymarks from Place du Plot as the route heads southwest out of the town.

OPENING HOURS

Chapelle Saint-Michel	daily 9-6.30 May-Sep; check other months (closed mid-Nov-Jan)
Rocher Corneille	daily 9-6 or later Apr-Sep; 10-5 Oct-Mar (closed Dec-Jan)
Cloisters & museum	daily 9.30-6.30 Jul-Sep; closes at lunchtime other months
Musée Crozatier	daily 10-12, 2-6 June-Sep; Wed-Mon10-12, 2-4 Oct-May

A Pilgrimage

In medieval Christendom, the shrine of Santiago de Compostela (St Jacques to the French; St James in English) in northwest Spain was a pilgrimage centre ranked third in importance behind Jerusalem and Rome's St Peters. Pilgrimages to Santiago (where St James is supposedly buried) reached their apogee in the 12th century when over half a million pilgrims flocked there each year from all over Europe. Four great pilgrim routes (beginning in Paris, Vezelay, Le Puy and Arles respectively) were used to cross France and enter Spain over the Pyrénées. The first recorded pilgrimage to Santiago was made in 951 by Bishop Gothescalc from Le Puy, along a route that became known as the *Via Podiensis*. Churches, shrines and hospices sprang up and some of the greatest examples of Romanesque architecture can be found in small villages through which the routes pass.

One of the longest *grandes randonnées*, the GR65 Chemin de St Jacques, now follows the ancient Via Podiensis fairly faithfully. Its entire 800-km length from Le Puy in the Auvergne to Roncesvalles in the Spanish Pyrénées can be walked with minimal incursion from urban sprawl. Some stretches have more to offer than others and our six-day itinerary between Aumont-Aubrac and Conques provides a superb meld of quiet countryside and historic interest. If time is available, you could start from the spectacular town of Le Puy-en-Velay, from where it is a four-day walk to Aumont-Aubrac (see end of chapter).

Our route is through the southern part of the Massif Central, France's huge central upland. It passes through two *départements*: Lozère (France's least populous) and Aveyron. Topographically, our route begins on the Aubrac plateau: sparsely populated country now given over to pasture. The rolling hills, once forested, are now almost treeless and life in this isolated area is no doubt hard. The route then descends to the valley of the river Lot which we cross at St-Côme-d'Olt (the Lot was called the Olt in the local Occitan language). This marks the change to a far more fertile landscape, pastureland giving way to crop farming and a noticeable increase in prosperity. The way follows the Lot for several days before parting company with it just past Estaing and heading towards Conques.

Signs of the Via Podiensis are frequently seen along the way, whether they be perfect Romanesque chapels, carved stone crosses, or simply the scallop shell which was the badge of the St James pilgrim. Reaching the jewel of Conques is a wonderful reward for all who tread this path.

NOTES

Type: a 6-day walk - 114 km (72 miles)
Difficulty: medium with two long days
Start: Aumont-Aubrac (rail from Clermont-Ferrand)
Finish: Conques (bus to Rodez)
Tourist Offices:
Lozère - ☎ 0466656000
Aveyron - ☎ 0565755575
Map: IGN 1:100000 #58 *Rodez-Mende*
Best timing: May-Jun and Sep-Nov

A pilgrim's prayer

Crossing the Aubrac >

< A waymark near Aumont-Aubrac

DAY 1: AUMONT to NASBINALS

A lengthy walk leads from a market town, through several hamlets, and onto the strange, open plateau of the Aubrac.

Distance	26 km (16 miles)
Time	7 hours
Notes	take lunch

Our pilgrimage route begins in ① **Aumont-Aubrac**, a small town – probably of Roman origin – lying on the Agrippan Way (now part of the D987) that linked Lyon and Toulouse. St Etienne church is a remnant of a 12th-century priory and the old town boasts some fine 16th and 17th-century houses.

Leave Aumont-Aubrac west on the D987, pass under the rail line and turn left. A signpost points the way to Nasbinals; the GR65 is well marked with such signs and red-and-white waymarks. For the next few km, the GR65 coincides with the GRP Tour de l'Aubrac.

Turn right up through woods, then follow a minor road right for 400 m. A tunnel passes under the A75 motorway; it may not appear on old maps. Branch left off the road and walk through woods for 2 km. Fork right and, in 500 m, join a minor road (diverging from the GR Tour de l'Aubrac). Continue for 1 km to the hamlet of **La Chaze-de-Peyre**, its church steeple visible from afar. From here, follow a minor road for 1 km to join the D987 at the Chapelle de Bastide and walk through **Lasbros** after a further kilometre. Soon after, branch left from the D987, descend over a stream, bear right for 300 m and then left. In 2.5 km, having crossed the Riou Frech, a typical Aubrac granite stream, climb to **Le Quatre Chemins** where there's a café. Rejoin the D987 briefly before again forking left through pine forest. Cross the boggy Ruisseau de la Planette and continue over open country, crossing a minor road after 2 km. A short diversion down this leads to a bridge and the derelict ② **Moulin de la Folle** (watermill of the mad woman); here is a tranquil picnic spot by the brook.

Back on the path, note the old *buron* up on the left, typical of rural Aubrac architecture. Burons are huts built of lava and granite, roofed with *lauzes* (stone slabs), usually built into the slope with a single opening. They are

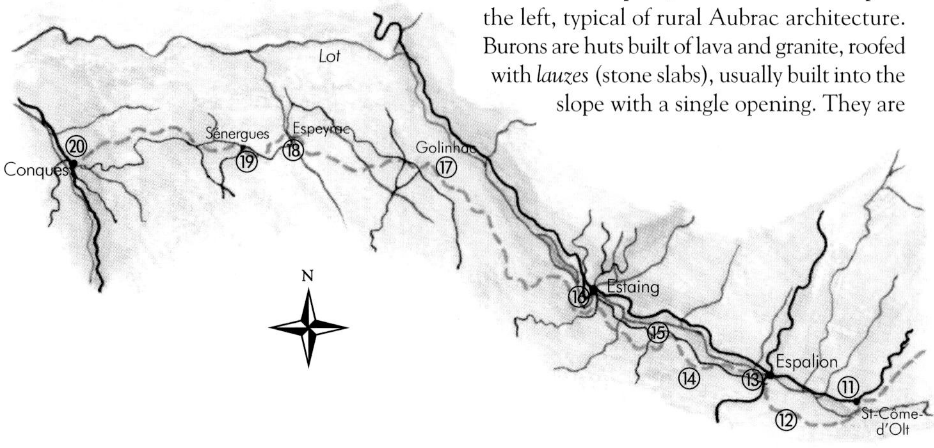

found in pasture near a stream and were used (some still are) by cowherds as summer quarters where they could make and mature cheese. The track follows the course of the river Rimeize, crosses a tributary on a granite slab bridge and passes a cross at Ferluc before crossing the D73. Here the route becomes a minor road to the hamlet of **Fineyrols** (note the beautiful barn) from where it forks right and crosses a treeless plateau, the Montagnes d'Aubrac, where dry-stone walls divide fields strewn with granite boulders. The views here of rolling hills are vast and strangely beautiful. Join a minor road that bridges the stream of La Peyrade, and shortly reach the hamlet of

③ **Rieutort-d'Aubrac**. Look out for two old fountain troughs and a communal oven before leaving the hamlet by the more westerly of the two lanes (ignore the GR65A that takes a more southerly route to the town of Aubrac).

Our route continues SW on a minor road with views down to the river Bès on the right. A ruined watermill here is named on the map as Bouquincan, a corruption of Buckingham, and this location may mark the defeat of the famous English captain in the 14th century. Turn right onto the D900, crossing

④ **a bridge** over the Bès and take an uphill path right to reach Montgros hamlet after 1.5 km. For the next 2 km, you follow a wide, stony *draille*. Drailles are ancient drove trails used for the *transhumance*, the annual movement of cattle between the valleys and high summer pasture. The draille descends to rejoin the D900 into the market town of

The river Bès

⑤ **Nasbinals**. Be sure to visit its magnificent 11th-century Romanesque church. Built of local brown basalt and roofed with schist, it has an octagonal bell-tower and its porch is supported by four fine capitals, one of which depicts a battle between archer and lancer.

DAY 2: NASBINALS to ST-CHÉLY

Today's journey is short but exhilarating as you continue over the wild Aubrac.

Distance 17 km (10.5 miles)
Time 4 hours 30

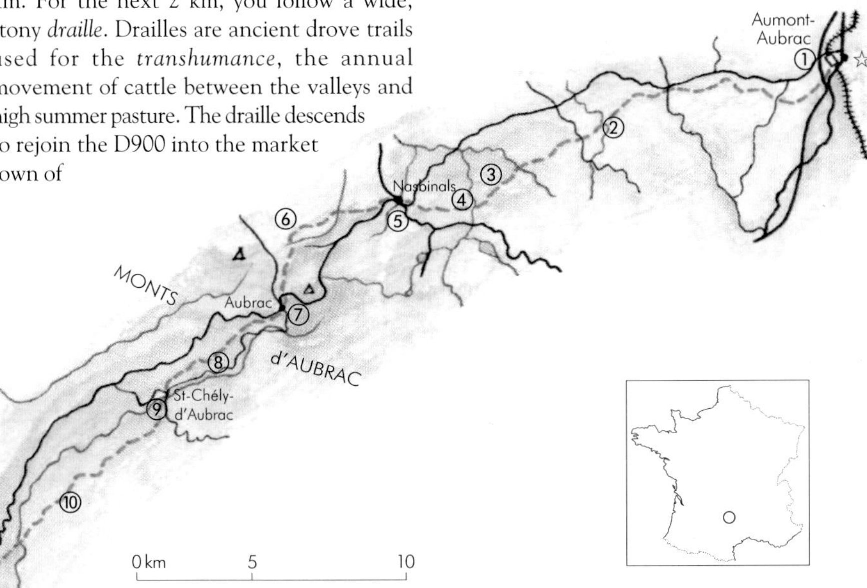

A *buron* on the Aubrac

Follow the GR65 southwest out of Nasbinals on the D987 and after 500 m, at Le Coustat, bear off right. After 2 km, cross the Chamboulies stream. Beyond this, bear right over open pasture, by which time the route has become a *draille*. It can be difficult to follow the waymarking in this area. The draille climbs gently towards

⑥ **Ginestouse Bas Buron** and after a further 1 km it skirts north of some woodland, passing beneath the buron of Ginestouse Haut, and swings SE to the west of Ginestouse farm. Hereabouts, the path leaves the department of Lozère and enters Aveyron. Near buildings of the Royal Ancient Sanatorium, the draille descends to the D987 and into the village of

⑦ **Aubrac**. This is the location of the annual *Fête de Transhumance* held on the last Sunday of May; at this time the Salers cattle are collected from the Lot valley, garlanded and moved up to mountain meadows on the drailles. Aubrac herders hire the cows from their owners for the summer to make cheese.

The town is overlooked by the Tour des Anglais, constructed in 1353 as a defence against the English during the Hundred Years War; it now houses the gîte d'étape. Aubrac's church, built in 1220, reflects a transition between Romanesque and Gothic. All these buildings and a forester's lodge once belonged to the Brothers Hospitaller of Aubrac, monastic knights who offered escort and refuge to pilgrims. The church bell was rung in stormy weather to guide lost travellers.

Leave Aubrac by the D987. After 500 m turn left and descend through woods. Cross a fast stream and pick up a wider draille that continues down. Before reaching Belvezet, diverge left to follow a path around a basalt

Nasbinals' church >

outcrop on which is perched ruins of
⑧ **a Templars castle** dominating the hamlet below. From Belvezet, descend on woodland paths then turn left onto a lane near ruins. Follow this down to the charming village of
⑨ **St-Chély-d'Aubrac**, snug in its picturesque valley setting.

DAY 3: ST-CHÉLY to ST-CÔME-d'OLT

Today, you descend from the Aubrac plateau, through a succession of beautiful landscapes down to the fertile and picturesque Lot valley.

Distance	16 km (10 miles)
Time	4 hours
Notes	take lunch or eat at St-Côme

The route leaves St-Chély to the south, crossing the Boralde de St-Chély over an old bridge bearing a 16th-century Calvary cross, decorated with a pilgrim holding his staff and rosary. At this point the GR6, which entered St-Chély from another direction, diverges left. Your GR65 route climbs to the right, behind the cemetery, joins the D19 and veers right onto a lane passing through the hamlet of Le Recours. Descend right on a path through oak forest and after 2 km reach
⑩ **Les Cambrassats**. Turn left onto a lane contouring around a hill. Pass Foyt and ignore the Bessiere turn-off at 1.5 km, but then turn right towards L'Estrade.

The route diverges right just before entering L'Estrade and follows a path west through chestnut woods before crossing a road and descending to ford a stream. Ascend to a minor road that soon joins the D557. Cross this and take a path along the left bank of the Boralde stream. Cross an old bridge and follow the D557 for 2 km to Martillergues hamlet. Turn left after the last house and continue through fields. At a T-junction turn left then right on a farm road into **La Rigaldie**. At the communal bread oven (now a henhouse) turn left onto a path and then right, following a minor road into
⑪ **St-Côme-d'Olt**. A classified 'beautiful village', St-Côme-d'Olt is superbly set above the river Lot. Its fortified walls contain alleys lined with 15th and 16th-century houses. The Gothic-Flamboyant church was built in 1522;

Near St-Chély-d'Aubrac

it is famed for its unusual twisted bell-tower and studded Renaissance doors. The town hall is an 11th-century château, once home to the lords of Calmont and Castenau. Outside the town walls are elegant Renaissance houses and the 11th-century Chapelle des Pénitents, a beautifully proportioned Romanesque chapel that was St-Côme's first church.

DAY 4: ST-CÔME-d'OLT to ESTAING

The route runs above the south bank of the Lot, descending to the bustling river town of Espalion before climbing and following the Lot to the beautiful village of Estaing.

Distance	17 km (10.5 miles)
Time	5 hours
Notes	allow time to visit Espalion

Today's journey, though not overly long, is so full of interesting diversions that an early start should be made. There are plenty of lunch options in Espalion.

The GR6 rejoins the GR65 at St-Côme and both routes leave by the bridge at the SE edge of the town. Cross the Lot, marking the boundary between the Aubrac and the ancient province of Rouergue. Turn right on a riverside road for 1.5 km where the GR6 and GR65 again diverge. Branch left on a path steeply uphill and pass through beech, oak and chestnut woods. After climbing to a ridge, the path veers NW, passing through private property. After about 2.5 km, views across the Lot valley open up. For even better views, watch carefully for a right-branching path in a few hundred metres. This leads, after less than 500 m, to a rock outcrop bearing a 19th-century statue of the Virgin, known as

⑫ **the Vierge du Pic de Vermus**. From here there are commanding views of the valley back to St-Côme and downstream to Espalion. Back on the main path, descend to the superb **Église de Perse**, deserving of close inspection. Built in the 11th-12th centuries and dedicated to Charlemagne's confessor, St Hilarian, this red-sandstone Romanesque church was one of the daughter-houses of Conques abbey. The austere interior houses capitals sculpted with scenes such as a lion hunt. A tympanum over the main entrance depicts Pentecost above the Last Judgement. Note also the charming, naive carvings of the Magi in adoration, high to the left of the portal.

Espalion's bridge in morning mist

St-Côme-d'Olt

The GR6 rejoins the GR65 to follow roads for 1 km into Espalion.

⑬ **Espalion** is full of interest. From the Lot's south bank, beautiful views are gained of the turreted Vieux Palais (dating from 1572 and once the residence of Espalion's governors), the 11th-century Pont Vieux and the old tanneries, timber-balconied buildings that line the north bank. Animals are still herded over the bridge during the transhumance. The folkloric Musée Joseph-Vaylet is housed in the restored 1472 church of St Jean. The Musée du Rouergue (local life and customs) occupies the nearby cells of the old prison. High above Espalion (3.5 km by road) on a basalt outcrop, stands a ruined medieval fortress, the **Château de Calmont d'Olt**, that houses a siege museum (open in summer). The steep walk is worthwhile if time permits and there are fine views from the ruins.

Leave Espalion by the Rue Camille Violand along the southern bank of the Lot. After a somewhat suburban and dull 1.5 km, join the D556 and follow it for 1 km. Take a path left that leads, after 500 m, to the church of

⑭ **St Pierre-de-Bessuéjouls**, nestled at the foot of a wooded hillside. Unpretentious on the outside and at first sight inside, this 16th-century church hides an extraordinary little Romanesque chapel beneath its 11th-century belltower (a vestige from an earlier church), reached by a worn and narrow stone staircase that ascends from a rear corner. This chapel of pink sandstone is exquisitely decorated with archaic motifs including knotwork and Maltese crosses on sculpted capitals inspired by those at Conques abbey. Note also the 9th-century altar, carved with Archangels and St Michael slaying the dragon.

Continue on a minor road, cross a stream and then climb NW on a steep path to a plateau before joining another lane through a hamlet, Griffoul. Soon, the route diverges right on a track and descends to pass
⑮ the **Château of Beauregard** and the church of Trédou. From here, backroads are followed for 3 km into the beautiful and well-preserved village of **Verrières**. Take the D556 and then the D100 along the bank of the Lot. 500 m on, veer left up through forest, then descend and rejoin the road to cross the Gothic bridge into the classified village of Estaing.
⑯ **Estaing** is a delightfully picturesque medieval village. The houses of the old town huddle around the 15th-century château and church of St Fleuret. Notice the magnificent sculpted cross outside the church's south doorway depicting a kneeling pilgrim. The château was once the home of the Comtes d'Estaing but is now a convent that may be visited: the views over the town from the high dungeon tower are dramatic. If time permits, visit the **Chapelle de l'Ouradou** (1.5 km north on the D97); this small chapel dating from 1529 is now surrounded by farm buildings.

DAY 5: ESTAING to SÉNERGUES

A long day's walk, leading you above the gorges of the Lot and then over to the next river valley.

Distance 26 km (16 miles)
Time 7 hours 30

Golinhac is the only village where lunch may be purchased. Note that the GR65 has been rerouted to pass through Sénergues; the map may show it passing to the north. Cross the bridge and turn right onto a lane that is followed for 3 km, where the GR65 diverges left before

Estaing and the Lot river

the hamlet of La Rouquette. After 750 m, cross a bridge over the Ruisseau de Luzane and take a forest path that short-cuts the bends of a climbing road and reaches Montegut. The route continues to climb as a forest path, then as a lane through woodland then farmland to the hamlet of **Le Mas**.

After bends in the road, you follow a path left before the hamlet of Falguières. Massip is reached after 2 km of woods and, after a further 1.5 km of paths and minor roads, you arrive at
⑰ **Golinhac**, commanding fine views of the surrounding countryside. The church of St Martin has a beautiful altar and the village boasts an ancient stone cross, its base decorated with a pilgrim bearing a staff.

A path from behind the church leads west through fields to Le Poteau and at a junction continues west on the D42 then WNW on a path to Les Albusquiès. You then follow minor roads and farm paths into the hamlet of **Campagnac** where the GR6 rejoins the GR65. A winding road descends through farmland, woods, and the hamlets of Le Soulie and Carboniès and into the village of
⑱ **Espeyrac** on the river Daze. Note the old stone cross at the entrance to the village. Espeyrac has a hotel-restaurant and a shop

Conques' abbey-church

and offers an alternative overnight stop to nearby Sénergues. From Espeyrac, cross a footbridge by the cemetery and take a minor road. After about 500 m, watch for a road branching left; the GR65 has been rerouted from this point for several kms. Join the D42 briefly before branching left on a lane to ⑲ **Sénergues**. This pretty village, with its old château, has hotels that may be closed out of season. It is serviced by buses to Conques.

DAY 6: SÉNERGUES to CONQUES

Today's short journey allows you to reach Conques by midday, leaving maximum time to explore the village and its exquisite church.

Distance 10 km (6 miles)
Time 3 hours

From Sénergues, follow the D42 briefly SW then fork right uphill to skirt a forest. The path glances the D42, then rejoins it in 2 km, just before a junction with the D137 where you take a lane through farmland. After 500 m, turn west into Fontromieu. Take a lane to the hamlet of **St-Marcel** and, 1.5 km further on, pick up a stony path that branches left and descends with views of your destination, ⑳ **Conques**. Built above the confluence of two rivers, Conques is an unashamedly lovely medieval village. Golden stone houses range up the hillside, clustering around the magnificent former abbey-church of Ste Foy. Conques is full of hotels, restaurants and shops with artisans and artists at work. A good point for viewing the village and church is Chapelle St-Roch, reached from Rue Charlemagne.

Once simply a halt on the pilgrimage route, Conques became a pilgrimage destination in its own right in the 9th century when it acquired the relics of the 4th-century child martyr, Ste Foy (or St Faith). Legend has it that a monk from the poor abbey of Conques insinuated himself into the wealthy abbey at Agen and was eventually entrusted with guarding the relics which he promptly purloined. As a result of this 'holy theft', Conques' treasury now holds arguably the most important collection of medieval and Renaissance goldwork in Western Europe. The Romanesque church, built in the 12th century on the site of an earlier church, fell into disuse when pilgrim numbers dwindled. It was reduced to ruins during the Wars of Religion but was saved from destruction in the 19th century when the towers were rebuilt.

The tympanum at Conques

The simple, elegant interior soars to a height of 22 metres with a nave comprised of three tiers of arches topped by over 200 decorated capitals (binoculars are useful). The wide chancel allowed numerous pilgrims to file past the saint's relics once displayed there; these are now exhibited in the Treasury. The tympanum above the west doorway depicting the Last Judgement is one of the glories of Romanesque sculpture. Once polychrome, it is remarkably preserved, having been resited from the church's interior in the 16th century. Ideally it should be viewed in the late afternoon when the crowds have thinned and the sunlight works its magic on the stone.

A farm building in the Lot valley

LONG DISTANCE STAGES

km	time	location	acc
		Aumont-Aubrac	H,G
23	6h00	Montgros	G
3	0h45	Nasbinals	H,G
9	2h30	Aubrac	G
8	2h00	St-Chély d'Aubrac	G
16	4h00	St-Côme-d'Olt	H,G
6	1h45	Espalion	H,G
11	3h15	Estaing	H,G
14	4h15	Golinhac	G
8	2h15	Espeyrac	H,G
3	1h00	Sénergues	H,G
10	3h00	Conques	H,G

EXTENDING THE WALK

Le Puy to Aumont-Aubrac

If time is plentiful, you could extend your walk along the GR65 by starting at the pilgrimage centre of Le Puy. The route is waymarked.

DAY 1: From Le Puy's Place du Plot, take Rue St Jacques, Rue des Capucins, then Rue de Compostelle to climb out of the town. Tracks lead SW, between the volcanic plug of Le Croustet and the Dolaizon river gully, through the basalt hamlet of La Roche, then SW to Ramourouscle. After the chapel of **St-Roch**, pass the hillside hamlet of Montbonnet and then walk through forest to gain Le Chier. The route then heads W to cross the gully of the Rouchoux stream and climbs to the village of **St-Privat-d'Allier**, perched on a rocky spur above the Allier gorge. *22km; allow 6 hours.*

DAY 2: The GR65 heads W to **Rochgude** with dramatic ruins of a tower and chapel. Descend through pine forest to Pratclaux and thence to **Monistrol-d'Allier**, a mining town on the Allier river. A steep climb out of the gorge takes you past the rock-chapel of **Madeleine** and up to Escluzels, then W through woods to Montaure, on the edge of the Gevaudan plateau. From here, the GR65 heads S to Roziers, then to Le Vernet, Rognac and finally to **Saugues**, home to some fine medieval buildings. *17.5km; allow 5 hours.*

DAY 3: The GR65 heads SW over farmland and through the hamlet of Le Pinet. After pine forest, you reach **La Clauze** which boasts a tower built on a slab of granite. A lane leads S to Villeret d'Apchier and you cross the Virlange river before continuing S, past a mill, to Chazeaux. Further south, pick up the D587; keep on until the fountain and chapel of **St-Roch** (another one), then follow the GR SW to Le Rouget, then SSW to **St-Alban-sur-Limagnole**. *28km; allow 7 to 8 hours.*

DAY 4: Leave St-Alban (with lunch supplies) from the town hall square, along a road which joins the D987 for a while. Turn right and climb to a tall cross and descend, via Grazieres-Mages, to cross the Limagnole river. Cross the D987 and head S through **Chabanes-Planes** to Les Estrets. Just beyond the village, cross the Truyère river, and take a path up to tiny Bigose, then continue climbing SW. Head W on a lane through woods, then follow the D7 W, past a lovely *pigeonnier*, and into **Aumont-Aubrac**. *20km; allow 5 hours 30.*

ALBI

Albi is one of the most beautiful cities in France. It's a highlight for anyone visiting the southwest of the country, though it is far from overrun by tourists. Old Albi, on the south side of the Tarn, is mostly built of red brick from river clay and its fine medieval and Renaissance buildings have been preserved largely intact, making its narrow streets a delight to explore.

Albi's provenance stretches back to the Gallo-Roman period, its name a contraction of Civitas Albigensium. It was already a sizeable market town by the 4th century but nothing remains from this period. Also missing are the city's outer ramparts, constructed in the Middle Ages. These served to limit the damage caused when Albi endured the Pope's crusade against the Albigensians, the Hundred Years War and the Wars of Religion.

'Albigensians' was the name given in the 12th century to followers of Catharism, a heretical doctrine that spread within the Languedoc Roman Catholic church, partly in response to the decadence of the church hierarchy. Cathars held that the material world was governed by Satan, while God's world was a purely spiritual one. The Bishop of Albi became one of four who headed the Cathar church, against which two crusades were instigated, in 1209 and 1226.

Albi's awesome fortress-like cathedral was built not long after the heresy was quelled, its huge proportions embodying the power and grandeur of the church that had conquered the city. The new bishops ruled from the adjoining Palais de la Berbie, an imposing palace overlooking the Tarn.

NOTES
Getting there: rail from Toulouse or Brive-la-Gaillarde
Tourist Office: Place Ste-Cécile, 81000
☏ 0563494880
Fax: 0563494898
E: otsi.albi.info@wanadoo.fr
www.tourisme.fr/albi
Markets: Tue-Sun am, Place du Marché

Albi prospered in the 15th and 16th centuries due to the rapid boom in the production and trade of *pastel* or dyer's woad, the plant used to obtain blue dye until the introduction of the indigo dye from the Indies. From this period are to be found many beautiful Renaissance mansions, including the Hôtel de Ville, Hôtel de Reynès and Maison du Vieil Alby, with its woad drying room. These lovely buildings evidence the wealth created by the textiles and dyeing industries.

Natives of Albi are remembered in its various museums. Admiral de Lapérouse, one of France's great scientific explorers – he arrived on the east coast of Australia within weeks of Captain Cook – was born on the outskirts of Albi in 1741. In 1864, Henri de Toulouse-Lautrec was born, the victim of a congenital disorder, in a mansion in the old quarter and spent his childhood here before gaining a reputation as an artist and libertine.

< Albi's fortress-cathedral

The cathedral's rood screen >

A WALK IN ALBI

This route takes in a circuit of the old town and crosses the Tarn, essential for the best view of Albi's astonishing buildings.

It would be impossible to ignore Albi's giant structure for very long, so start in Place Sainte-Cécile and make straight for the ① **Cathédrale Sainte-Cécile**, entered through the elaborate porch on the south. Imposing and austere, this red-brick fortress-cathedral is a masterpiece of Southern Gothic style. It was built over two centuries in the

Saint-Salvi cloisters >

aftermath of the Albigensian crusades and consecrated in 1480. The cathedral, dedicated to the patron saint of music, has an elaborate entrance or porch. Inside is a wealth of decoration: frescoes on the vaulting by Italian artists, an intricately-carved limestone rood screen, magnificent polychrome statues of thirty Old and New Testament figures, and a vast painting of the Last Judgement.

Next to the cathedral, on the banks of the Tarn, stands the 13th-century fortified **Palais de la Berbie**, the Bishop's palace. Today it houses both the tourist office and the

② **Musée Toulouse-Lautrec**. This museum is among the finest in regional France. The extensive collection of over a thousand works follows the artist's evolution from his early drawings to his final pieces. It includes the famous Parisian brothel scenes, as well as his lithographs and his 31 ground-breaking posters. One floor displays works by his contemporaries.

Do not leave the palace without visiting

③ **the Palais Gardens**. This former parade ground was laid out as a flower garden in the formal French style during the late 17th century.

From Place Sainte-Cécile, walk east along Rue Mariès. On the right is the Norman church ④ **Saint-Salvi**, built between the 11th and 15th centuries. It is surmounted by a lookout turret characteristic of the Norman style. Its pretty cloisters contain beautiful Norman and Gothic capitals.

Turn left towards the *marché couvert* or covered market, a good place to buy fresh produce, and continue up Rue des Foissants, in one of the city's oldest districts. Turn briefly right and then left to reach the 11th-century

⑤ **Pont-Vieux**, one of France's oldest bridges.

Turn right on the other bank and walk along Rue Porta to visit the

⑥ **Musée Lapérouse**, a well-planned museum dedicated to the 18th-century explorer, who was born in Albi. The museum, displaying models of the two frigates – the *Astrolabe* and the *Boussole* – from his 1785 Pacific expedition, is housed in a section of **les Moulins Albigeois**, 19th-century mills which have been cleverly restored. Walk through to the pleasant Square Botany Bay (a name familiar to many Australian visitors)

Cathédrale Sainte-Cécile

Hôtel de Rèynes

which offers an excellent viewpoint back over the Pont-Vieux to the cathedral and palace.

Leave via the Rue de la Visitation and turn right onto the major Boulevard de Strasbourg to cross the Tarn, this time on the graceful 19th-century **Pont-Neuf.** At the Esplanade des Partisans, veer southwest down Rue Emile Grand; the buildings on your left form the **Lycée Lapérouse**. Now turn left to head south along Rue St-Afric and Rue Ste-Claire. Note the interesting 15th-century brick-and-timber building on the corner of Rue Mariès, but turn left and veer along Rue Timbal. On the left is the Hôtel de la Prefecture. The timber-framed chemist on the right is the **Pharmacie des Pénitents**, housed in the 16th-century Maison Enjalbert. At no.14, you'll find the

⑦ **Hôtel de Reynès**. The Reynès family prospered from the pastel trade, as their 16th-century mansion attests. It now houses the Chamber of Commerce and is closed to public viewing but you can take a look in the courtyard, endowed with a double gallery and a 14th-century tower.

A short way along is the lively Place du Vigan. Midway along the square, turn right along Rue de l'Hôtel de Ville, which indeed features the town hall, housed in two 17th-century mansions

The river Tarn

< Cordes-sur-Ciel

bought by the city in the 18th century. At the Hôtel de Saunal (another pastel merchant's home) veer left and left again into Rue de Verdusse, then soon right along Rue Toulouse-Lautrec. At the end is the Hôtel du Bosc, the birthplace of the painter. Around the bend is a house bought by Lapérouse in 1780, now the **Musée de Cire** displaying waxwork tableaux of historic moments in Albi's history.

At the junction you'll find the restored ⑧ **Maison du Vieil Alby**, a half-timbered medieval house which features a *solelhièr*, a room for drying pastel, and an exhibition on the town's history.

From here, it is a short walk north along Rue St-Clair (named for Albi's first bishop) and along the shop-lined Rue Ste-Cécile to return to your starting point.

FURTHER AFIELD

Along the Tarn

On the left bank of the Tarn is a 1-km path known as the Pastel Route, punctuated by six information panels on the dyestuff and its role in Albi's history.

Upstream from Albi, a waymarked route heads, for 200 km, through the Gorges du Tarn (see our chapter on this section) and beyond. Enquire for details at the tourist office in the Palais de la Berbie.

Parc Rochegude

In the 19th century, a keen collector of plants, Admiral Rochegude, gave three hectares of garden to the people of Albi. There are two sections: one is laid out in the English style with a maze, ponds and tree-lined alleys, all in contrast with the terrace laid out *à la Française*. The admiral's 17th-century mansion, **Hôtel Rochegude**, now houses the town library.

From Place Vigan, walk south on Lices Jean Moulin. Cross Place Jean-Jaurès and follow Ave Gambetta to its junction with Rue Rochegude. *Allow 2 hours.*

Cordes-sur-Ciel

Some 25-km by road northwest of Albi lies a picturesque bastide town built atop a steep hill. With its narrow lanes closed to car traffic, this is a pleasant place to wander, admiring the medieval buildings and the many small galleries that exhibit the artistic community's works.

The tourist office in Cordes should have copies of *Guide des Visites* to help you explore. Infrequent buses run to Cordes from Albi's bus station. *Allow most of a day.*

OPENING HOURS

Cathédrale Sainte-Cécile	daily 9-12, 2.30-6.30 (8.30-6.45 Jun-Sept)
Musée Toulouse-Lautrec	vary greatly, often closed 12-2; closed Tue Oct-Mar
Saint-Salvi	daily; cloisters 7am-8pm; church 8.30-12, 2.30-6
Musée Lapérouse	daily 10-12, 2-5 (9-12, 2-6 Apr-Sep)
Maison du Vieil Alby	Mon-Sat 3-7
Musée de Cire (Wax)	Tue-Sun 10-12; 2.30-5 (till 6 in summer)

THE CÉVENNES

The southern area of the Massif Central is a region of hills known as the Cévennes: high ground formed of rounded peaks of schist and granite. Two major rivers – the Lot and the Tarn – rise in these uplands, amid pasture and forest. It is, without being spectacular, quite beautiful countryside, and ideal for walking.

The Cévennes is an isolated region, populated with only small towns and villages, and life here can be hard. It was harder still in the 18th century when this was a bastion of Protestantism. Following the revocation of the Edict of Nantes, Louis XIV sent clergy into the area to rout the Protestants. When the king's man was assassinated in Le Pont-de-Montvert there was a vicious reprisal by the crown, with nearly 12,000 Protestants executed. This, in turn, provoked a bloody guerrilla war against the state. Rebels became known as Camisards as they had no uniforms but fought in ordinary shirts, or *camiso* in the local dialect of the *langue d'Oc*.

Woodland mushrooms

NOTES
Type: a 3-day walk - 67 km (42 miles)
Difficulty: medium with long stages
Start: La Bastide (rail from Alès)
Finish: Florac (bus to Alès)
Tourist Office: Ave J.Monestier, 48400 Florac, ☏ 0466450114
Fax: 0466452580
E: otsi@ville-florac.fr
www.chemin-stevenson.org
Maps: IGN 1:25000 #2738E & 2739OT
Best timing: Apr-June; Sep-Nov

Today it is difficult to imagine such scenes of violence and turmoil. Tourism is not well-developed, but the settlements cater well for walkers, with gîtes d'étape scattered along the way. Thanks for this are in part due to Robert Louis Stevenson who, in 1878, made his famous literary hike with Modestine the donkey and wrote *Travels with a Donkey*.

His route through the Cévennes is now the basis for the GR70 that we take for three days, following red-and-white waymarks. From La Bastide Puylaurent, situated on the rail line, we cross over Mont Lozère, the highest non-volcanic peak in the Massif Central. The exposed peak is not a difficult climb, but in bad weather the traverse can be grim: note the absence of any summit photos in this book! Fortunately, fingers of granite known as *montjoies* guide you over the mountain, as they have guided past travellers during bad weather. From Mont Lozère, the route descends to Le Pont-de-Montvert on the banks of the Tarn. The third day leads up onto the massif of Bougès and then down a long ridge to the town of Florac, once a stronghold of the Camisards.

At Florac, the landscape takes a dramatic turn, with limestone plateaux known as causses, rearing up. Should you want to explore this area you could continue on into the gorges of the Tarn, following the route in the next chapter.

A granite menhir >

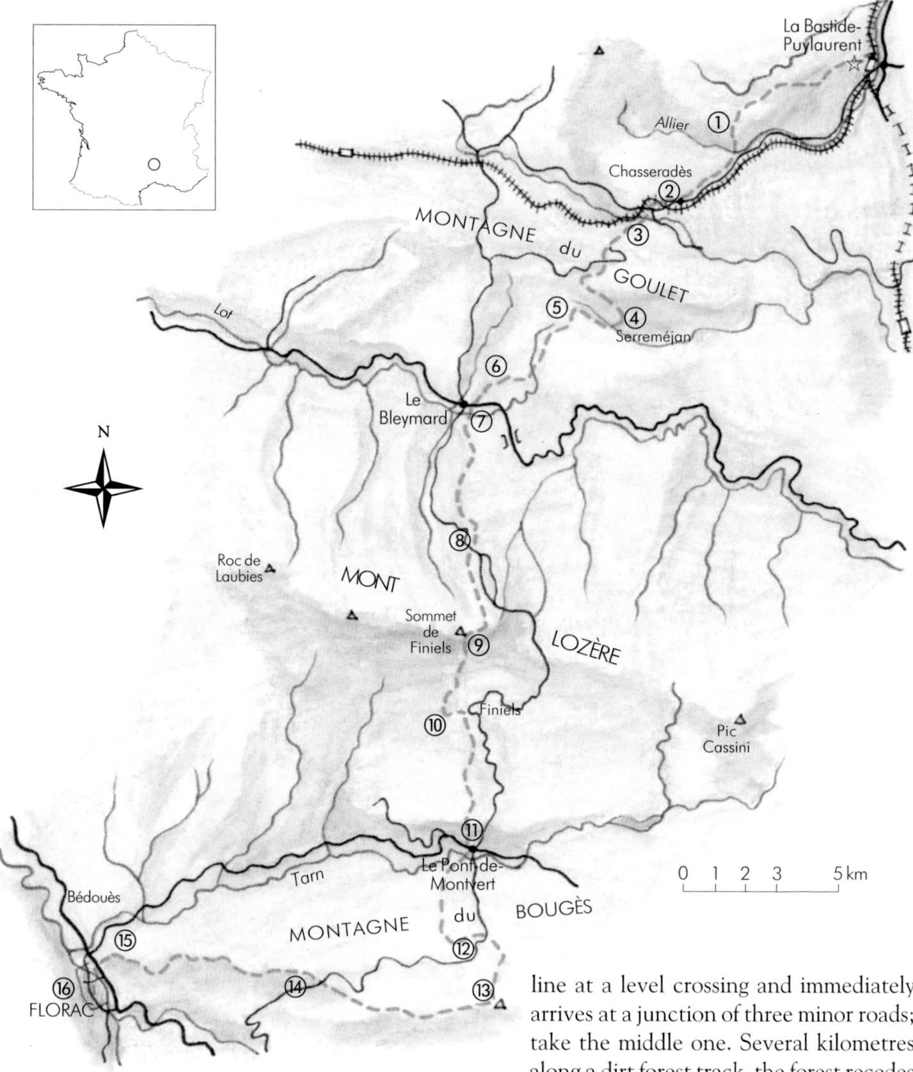

DAY 1: La BASTIDE to Le BLEYMARD

Forest, woods and moorland lead to the pretty village of Chasseradès, from where we cross the Montagne du Goulet ridge to reach the night's destination.

Distance 26 km (16 miles)
Time 6 hours 30

The GR7A/70 leaves (along with the GR7) from the northern end of the rail station, signposted as the *Chemin de Stevenson* to Chasseradès. The minor road crosses the rail line at a level crossing and immediately arrives at a junction of three minor roads; take the middle one. Several kilometres along a dirt forest track, the forest recedes to give good views back over La Bastide and beyond it to the monastery of Notre-Dame-des-Neiges.

On the top of **La Mourade**, you reach a forest clearing with picnic tables and benches, offering sweeping hill views. The path levels on moorland of the Plateau du Chambonnet. Descending from the plateau, the track becomes stony. Follow the red-and-white waymarks to fork left. At a junction near the

① **Rocher de la Réchaubo**, turn left and descend to the hamlet of **Chabalier**. The road becomes paved and you immediately turn right onto another paved road.

This minor road soon crosses the Allier river on a bridge. Minutes later, veer right downhill on an old stony path that fords the stream of Fontaleyres and then crosses pasture. Turn left onto a paved road to reach a rail platform and then right on the D6, following it over the river and up into the village of

② **Chasseradès**. There are a couple of hotel-restaurants to be found; if you've brought a picnic lunch, head for the beautiful 12th-century church of Saint-Blaise and enjoy the bench by nearby trees.

From the church, take the level paved road past the cemetery, where a stone records the death of four workers on the Mirandol viaduct. The road then makes a steep, winding descent of the narrow valley to the hamlet of **Mirandol**. It features a gîte d'étape and a

③ **rail viaduct** that was under construction when Stevenson walked by. Walk under the viaduct and uphill briefly before following waymarks right uphill. This rocky path climbs steadily for a few minutes and then you turn right onto a sometimes boggy farm track.

Cross over two stiles and then descend into the hamlet of **L'Estampe**, where you turn left onto the D120 and follow it uphill. At a point where L'Estampe and Chasseradès are aligned in your view back, waymarks direct you right on an unpaved track that cuts off a long loop of road. Clear waymarks lead through various forks and up through pretty woodland, then left onto a level dirt track. When you regain the paved road, turn right to continue climbing and reach the ridgetop of the **Montagne du Goulet**.

Chasseradès

The Lot, near its source

At a junction by a monument to a forester, waymarks lead down the second track on the left, through a barrier and down an unpaved track through forest. After gaining views south, fork right downhill into woodland. Waymarks direct you to turn sharply, passing the ruined hamlet of

④ **Serreméjan**. From here, the grassy path crosses the gully floor and an intermittent stream. Follow waymarks through various junctions as you zigzag up the other side to a wide track known as the *Draille des Mulets*. Turn right and, after only 20 m, turn left onto a grassy footpath signed to Le Bleymard. This descends steeply to follow GR70/7a waymarks through several junctions to the official

⑤ **source of the Lot river** as it spills down

Le Bleymard's town hall

a delightful valley. Walk down to merge with a paved road; a gîte d'étape is signed to the right. Follow the road downhill to

⑥ **Les Alpiers**. Before the end of the hamlet, fork right onto a gravel track. The route descends between pastures and then becomes a stony path through gorse, dropping steeply onto the road at the entrance to

⑦ **Le Bleymard**. The sole hotel, La Remise (☏ 0466486580), is just before a bridge over the Lot. The village centre, which includes a boulangerie and épicerie, is beyond the bridge.

DAY 2: Le BLEYMARD to Le PONT-de-MONTVERT

An old drove road brings you onto the moors of Mont Lozère, where granite shards lead to the peak of this 'bald mountain' before a descent to a historic village on the Tarn.

Distance	18 km (11 miles)
Time	7 hours
Notes	a lengthy exposed section

Just after the *bar/tabac* in the village centre, turn left uphill and zigzag up between the houses, following GR waymarks. Turn right off the paved road at a cross and seat. Soon, keep right at a fork; the track levels then climbs. At a path junction on the **Col Santel** follow the GR70/7a signs straight ahead to then climb through pretty woodland.

About an hour from the start, you reach exposed moorland with young fir trees; much work has been done to remedy the serious deforestation of the 18th and 19th centuries. The track then levels and descends a little to the chalet-hotels and ski complex of

⑧ **Mont Lozère station**. A park information centre is also here and a UCPA (outdoor sports association) building welcomes walkers.

Keep on, past the National Park centre and, 700 m up the road, at a communication tower, follow the GR70 sign onto a footpad forking right uphill. Follow a chain of granite fingers or *montjoies* that indicate the route of this ancient *draille* in bad weather; there are no GR waymarks here. Eventually you reach a yellow *balise* or signpost. (If the weather is bad, continue straight ahead here, through the next junction still following granite markers, onto a bridle path that descends through dense forest, crosses a track and continues down to the road about 1 km above Finiels.)

Le Pont-de-Montvert >

Cham de l'Hermet plateau

Otherwise, turn right, for the final 1 km to ⑨ **Sommet de Finiels**, at 1699 m, the highest summit of the Lozère massif. The peak offers good views south over the Cévennes.

From the summit, the GR70 heads due south and then left onto a track at the edge of forest. About 100 m along, turn right to descend through forest to the Nègres forest track. Turn right onto this and, in 50 m, turn left, passing a forest bivouac. This track contours around the curiously named hill, L'Travers de l'Homme. Turn left onto a fire break and descend to a junction; turn left onto an old mining road that leads to the hamlet of

⑩ **Finiels**. At its entrance, fork right on an old path, leading below the telephone box and past a small cemetery. The grassy track becomes a narrow footpath, descending between granite boulders. Pass through a gate and continue down to cross the pretty stream of Rieumalet on a log bridge.

Soon after, you reach a junction: the main path for the GR70 heads left to soon ford the stream and then pick up the D20 road. In times of *crue* or spate, a sign points you right to pick up a minor road that descends to cross the stream by a bridge and then join the D20. About 100 m down the road from this point, fork right onto a footpath that descends by the municipal gîte d'étape to enter

⑪ **Le Pont-de-Montvert**. This charming village straddles the Tarn, by its confluence with the Rieumalet and Martinet. Its 17th-century humpbacked bridge is topped with a toll-house tower. In 1702 the Abbé du Chayla, appointed to quell the Protestant fervour in the region, held and tortured prisoners in the tower. A group of rebel Protestants killed the abbot and threw his body from the bridge.

DAY 3: PONT-de-MONTVERT to FLORAC

After a climb out of the beautiful Martinet valley, you ascend the ridge of the Montagne du Bougès before dropping to the spectacularly-sited town of Florac.

Distance	24 km (15 miles)
Time	7 hours
Notes	start early; take lunch

Cross the bridge over the Tarn and turn left. Opposite the boulangerie, turn right and weave up between buildings. Pass through a well-secured gate and walk straight ahead, then zigzag up to a board depicting wildlife in times past. Climb steadily above the Martinet, gaining excellent views over the village.

Florac and the Causse Méjean

The path then levels on the plateau of **Cham de l'Hermet**; on the right you pass near a traditional *bergerie*, or herder's hut, set among pasture. The road comes into view but, before you reach it, waymarks direct you left onto a footpath and through a wire gate. This leads through patches of bracken (overgrown in places) and down into beech woods in the valley of Fiarouse. Cross a couple of streams and turn left onto the D20, heading downhill. About 200 m along, just before an old stone bridge, fork right up on a gravel track. This becomes concreted and climbs steadily to

⑫ **Champlong-de-Bougès**, passing by a traditional Cévenol farmhouse. The GR72 joins in from the left, and you proceed straight ahead, following a sign to Florac. This broad, schist track climbs through mixed woodland and continues south to reach

⑬ **Col de la Planette**, where the GR68 joins in from the east. A plaque here pays homage to Raymond Senn, a pioneer of the GR system in the Cévennes.

Head west along the ridge of **Montagne du Bougès**, following waymarks through several junctions and then climb steadily to a group of tall schist stacks, where the track curves right. You reach open moorland and make a short, sharp ascent over sheep pasture, then descend between woods and moor. At the entrance to woods, waymarks direct you sharp left down through a corridor of beech trees.

Descend over moor to pass the Bonnal hut, an unguarded shelter for herders and walkers. The now narrow track of salmon-pink granite crosses a heather-covered slope with views left to the valley below. A junction at the

⑭ **Col du Sapet** is marked by a pink granite stone. Cross the D20 and continue straight ahead, watching for a menhir in the field up to your left. The broad gravel track veers over a small *col* or pass and turns to schist, with forest views down to the left. A gentle descent follows, and you keep straight on at a junction of many tracks. Pass a stone shelter with a bench inside. At

⑮ **a junction**, where the GR70 curves sharply right, signed to Bédouès, turn left to follow the GR68, signed to Florac.

The track contours around the peak of La Chaumette; at the next junction, keep left. The GR68 rises to a pass where a yellow *balise* directs you onto a narrow footpath down through forest. The route skirts pasture and winds steeply down with dramatic views over Florac and across to the Causse Méjean, before dropping into chestnut woods. Waymarks direct you left onto a narrower footpath which drops to the main road. Cross the bridge over the Tarnon river and enter

⑯ **Florac**, via its long main street. This small town, set at the foot of dolomitic cliffs, has a reputation for good food. The Cévennes national park has its headquarters here, in a 17th-century château.

LONG DISTANCE STAGES

km	time	location	acc
		La Bastide	H,G,C
12	3h00	Chasseradès	H
2	0h30	Mirandol	G
10	2h30	Les Alpiers	G,C
2	0h30	Le Bleymard	H,C
5	2h	Mont Lozère	H,G
8	3h	Finiels	C
5	2h	Pont-de-Montvert	H,G,C
24	7h	Florac	H,G,C

OTHER WALKS ALONG THE WAY

Notre-Dame-des-Neiges

If you arrive early in La Bastide-Puylaurent, you might walk north to visit this abbey-monastery where Stevenson spent three days.

At the north end of the station, cross by a level crossing and pick up GR7/70 waymarks leading north. The path climbs the Serre de la Bastide and descends to a road near Le Fraisse; turn right and follow the road over the rail line to the D906 at **Rogleton**. Turn left then soon right and, about 150 m on, turn right at a junction. This track heads east, alongside the stream of Bois de Serres. After 3 km it switches back to climb the **Coulet de Pecoyol**. At a path junction, turn right onto the GR7 to the Pal cross, where the GR7/72 turns right onto a lane, passing La Felgere to reach the abbey of **Notre-Dame-des-Neiges**.

At the far end of the complex, continue on the GR7/72. At Le Bories farm, keep straight ahead to La Courege and then take a lane which descends into La Bastide. *Allow 4 hours.*

Château du Tournel

This day walk from Le Bleymard takes in the river Lot, stunning castle ruins and beautiful Cévenol countryside. Take lunch supplies.

From the hotel in Le Bleymard, walk along the D901 road towards St-Julien-du-Tournel, soon passing a Romanesque church (note the carving of a devil by the road). The road winds as the valley closes in and, at a *cingle* where a gravel road loops off to the left, pick up a footpath leading down to a lovely spot on the river. Follow this around the spur, back up to the road, then continue on.

Walk through a long tunnel, being wary of traffic, and immediately veer right on a track signed to the castle of **Tournel**. This winds up through a pretty hamlet and then to the dramatic ruins that reward inspection. Beyond the main ruins, a path continues to ruins of the old village, then back down to the road.

Turn right onto the road and pass a schist quarry, then take a track left to a suspension footbridge over the Lot. Cross this and follow green waymarks and then signs to St-Julien. These lead up to the hamlet of **Freissinet**. At a junction beyond this, turn left (rather than descending to St-Julien). At the next junction, by a menhir, turn right and then left along a lane, marked red-and-white. This rejoins the road and descends to the pretty village of **Orcières**. Cross the river and pick up the path to Le Bleymard, crossing pasture and passing a cottage. After an easy ascent the path descends, crosses a minor road and enters Le Bleymard at its south end. *Allow 5-6 hours.*

Around Florac

The tourist office at Florac has an excellent leaflet that outlines various circular walks or *petit randonnées* nearby. These include a climb onto the **Causse Méjean** and walks around **Puecheral** and the **Can de Tardonnenche**.

Château du Tournel

Tarn Gorges

The River Tarn rises in the granite uplands of Mont Lozère and tumbles down the Cévennes. At Florac it reaches limestone country where, working over time along fissures in the soft rock, it has created deep canyons that separate raised *causses* or plateaux. In places the gorges are sheer and narrow; elsewhere, the limestone mixed with marl has created fertile scree slopes. The riverside villages are unexpected gems. This all makes for some of the most spectacular gorge walking in France and, fortunately for walkers, a footpath – the *Sentier des Gorges du Tarn* – threads its way along the car-free side of the river.

Habitation here is sparse, as the river is prone to flash flooding when in spate. The occasional village – such as La Malène – became a trade centre for passing herders. Sainte-Énimie served likewise for pilgrims. These communities once cultivated the terraced sides of the valley, sending grapes, almonds and walnuts up and down the river on barges until the road between Sainte-Énimie and Le Rozier was opened in 1905.

A major exodus from the area occurred following WWII and today, only the wider sections of the valley are still under cultivation. Many hamlets, particularly those accessed only by footpath or river, stand abandoned, though some are now being reclaimed and restored as holiday cottages. The river is a popular summer holiday destination for French families and several activity centres here take groups canoeing, caving and rock-climbing. In other seasons you'll find it very quiet.

This encroachment by humans into the river valley makes the Tarn gorges more intimate than those of the Verdon, but they are far from tame. Bizarre rock formations loom over the river, encircled by vultures that nest high up on the *causse*. Beavers have colonised the river banks; you may see signs of their presence. Side streams gush from the rock as resurgent springs either right on the river's edge or a few metres away from it.

The walk starts from Ispagnac, set among orchards, and follows the path all the way to Le Rozier, crossing the river at the end of each day to find a bed in the gorges' isolated medieval villages. It is fairly easy walking; perhaps the hardest part will be getting to the start and away from the finish. We added this onto the Cévennes walk described in the previous chapter, and then departed Le Rozier on the school bus at some horrible hour of the morning.

NOTES
Type: a 4-day walk - 56 km (35 miles)
Difficulty: easy
Start: Ispagnac (bus from Alès to Florac then taxi, or see previous chapter)
Finish: Le Rozier (bus to Millau)
Tourist Office: 48210 Sainte-Enimie
☏ 0466485344 Fax: 0466484770
E: otsi-gorgesdutarn@wanadoo.fr
www.causses-cevennes.com
Map: IGN 1:25000 Gorges du Tarn
Best timing: Apr-Jun; Sep-Nov

A tranquil section of the Tarn

< The isolated hamlet of Hauterives

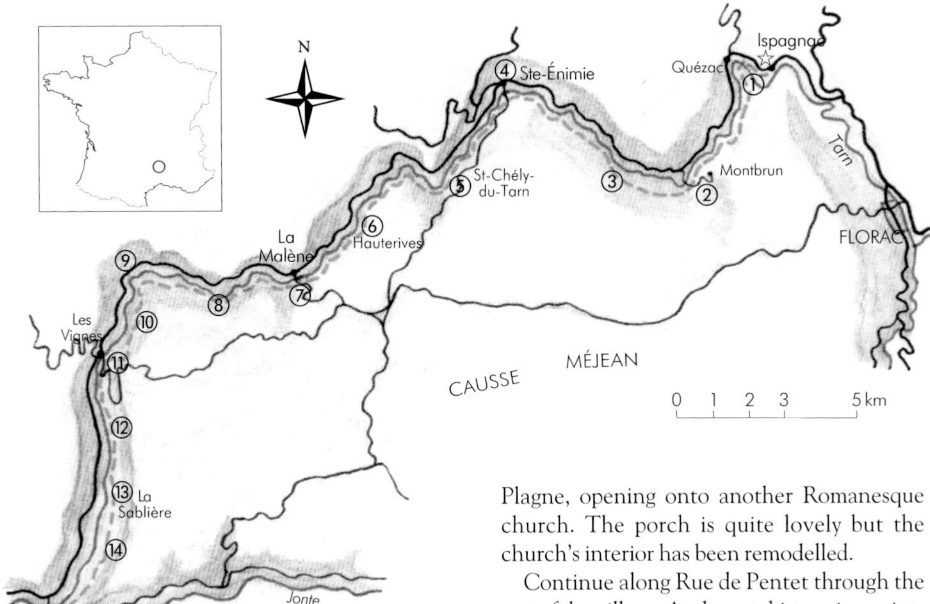

DAY 1: ISPAGNAC to SAINTE-ÉNIMIE

On this, the longest day, the Tarn river wends gently past charming villages to the medieval gem of Sainte-Énimie.

Distance	18 km (11 miles)
Time	6 hours
Notes	take lunch

Before you leave Ispagnac, stock up on lunch supplies from the supermarket on the main street. Also, be sure to visit the 11-12th-century church, a wonderful example of Romanesque design; inside, a button sets off a clever narration, music and light show.

From the church, walk down Rue de Barry, the medieval high street cobbled with limestone. Turn left at a cross, following yellow PR waymarks, to pass the camping ground and walk along the Tarn river. Cross on the Gothic ① **Pont de Quézac**, built originally at the request of Pope Urban V for pilgrims to reach the sanctuary he founded nearby. It was rebuilt in the 17th century, after the Wars of Religion.

Follow the road into the elongated village of **Quézac**, lined with three-storey houses, some built into the hillside. Several façades retain old pulleys at the top. You reach Place Auguste Plagne, opening onto another Romanesque church. The porch is quite lovely but the church's interior has been remodelled.

Continue along Rue de Pentet through the rest of the village. At the outskirts a sign points you along the river to Ste-Énimie. Soon, you pass the pretty hamlet of **Le Buisson** on the other bank. The paved road turns to gravel at a lovely cottage, Le Pentet. Here, pick up the green-and-yellow waymarks of the *Sentier des Gorges du Tarn*, which you follow throughout this four-day walk.

The grassy track becomes a stony footpath at a cottage and winds through woodland. After a short, steep ascent, reach a clearing with views across river of the Causse Sauveterre and behind of Causse Méjean. The path descends to river level, broadens, and passes a camping ground. You can soon see, up to the left, the hamlet of ② **Montbrun**, nestled in a side valley halfway up the causse. Keep on along the river, past a bridge and a right-forking road to the 16th-century château of Charbonnières. The village of Blajoux appears across river and then you reach the pleasant hamlet of **La Chadenede**. More road walking, with good views, brings you to the hamlet of ③ **Castelbouc** or 'goat's castle', nestled beneath its ruined castle. The houses are wrapped around the cliffs of the Causse Méjean, the rock providing a wall for many of them. Take the footpath through the hamlet, passing a poignant war memorial and cross the footbridge over a resurgent spring that gushes out of the limestone *causse*.

Ispagnac's church

The path descends to river level and enters forest. Shortly, the 13th-century fortress of **Prades** comes into view on the opposite bank, then the path veers left uphill. After a climb, it levels and follows a dry-stone wall through oak forest. Presently, the path descends to a minor resurgent spring gushing from below a rock. To cross, you need to climb the rock or wade through. Further on, you pass a weathered rock with deep caves above you.

The path undulates and becomes a dirt lane, then you divert right on a stony path passing a *Centre de Plein Air* and arriving at a low concrete bridge over the Tarn. Keep on along a wide track and then veer right on a footpath. The path is squeezed between the Roch des Egoutals and river, then broadens and climbs to a clearing to gain views of this day's destination. Cross the 17th-century bridge to enter the lovely village of

④ **Sainte-Énimie**. A monastery was built here in the 6th century to honour Énimie, a Merovingian princess who lived in a cave in the cliffs nearby after she was cured of leprosy. Pilgrims visited her relics and the village thrived from trade until the Revolution. Tourists now come to climb its steep, cobbled streets and stay in its various hotels. Inside the 12th-century church, the water stoup marks the height the Tarn has reached in spate. A footpath behind the Gîtes St-Vincent leads to Ste-Énimie's cave-hermitage, a return walk of 45 minutes.

DAY 2: SAINTE-ÉNIMIE to La MALÈNE

The gorges of the Tarn become more rugged and its villages, including the unspoilt St-Chély-du-Tarn, more isolated.

Distance	14 km (9 miles)
Time	5 hours
Notes	carry lunch supplies

Return across the bridge and follow green-and-yellow waymarks signed to St-Chély-du-Tarn. This route joins the D986 for a short distance and then veers off right on a stony path signed *Camin Ferrat*; the Camin Ferrat was used by pilgrims en route to Santiago de Compostela and, after 1 km, it splits off to the left to cross the Causse Méjean. Instead, keep right on the path to Hauterives.

This well-graded track reaches a small clearing and diverts up left to follow a high dry-stone wall, a reminder that the river valley was once

< Sainte-Énimie

A pigeonnière, Ste-Énimie

carefully terraced and cultivated. Now narrow, the path undulates through light forest, with signs of wild boar activity and frequent views: across the gorge, cliff walls feature rich mineral colours. You climb behind rock formations before making a steep, stony descent to

⑤ **St-Chély-du-Tarn**. You will want to linger here, for though small, the village is quite exquisite. The view from its high bridge is dramatic, and you should inspect the communal bread-oven and the Romanesque church with a square belfry. Most surprising of all are the two springs that pour into the Tarn here. One emerges from the Cénaret cave, at the mouth of which stands a 12th-century chapel.

Return to the back of the village and follow the minor road uphill; it becomes a stony path and, at a junction, take the lower path right, looping away from the river to cross the ravine below the Cirque de St-Chély. Soon, you gain an amazing view of St-Chély, with its spring cascading into the Tarn. After woodland, there is a view across river, of the hamlet of Pougnadoires, with its houses embedded in the rock. The cliffs behind are known as the **Cirque de Pougnadoires**, red-hued from the presence of dolomite.

The path now levels along the river before ascending, at times quite steeply to round the spur of Moulhoc. Just after an initial view of the 15th-century Château de la Caze on the opposite bank, the path switches back steeply down through mossy woods beneath otherwise impassable rocks. The path climbs once more, passing below the crags of La Taouille, then descends to the well-restored houses of

⑥ **Hauterives**. This quiet hamlet is accessible only on foot or by boat; supplies are ferried across the river by a cable. Above the houses are the ruins of the **Château de Haute-Rive** or 'high bank'.

From Hauterives, the path initially climbs and then levels to reach a rocky outcrop with a good view back to the ruined château. After this, the path descends steeply to the river to pass rock outcrops: sections are slippery and difficult to negotiate. From here the path hugs the riverbank, squeezed by cliffs and rocks; watch out for signs of beavers, reintroduced in the region. This section is subject to erosion and a resurgent spring, gushing from under a rock, is another obstacle: you may have to remove boots and wade. Fortunately, a larger stream is crossed by a concrete bridge. Soon after, you gain sight of a 17th-century château

La Malène

and you cross the Tarn to enter

⑦ **La Malène**. This village was a natural rest stop for shepherds and flocks during the *transhumance* (change of pasture). The barons of Montesquieu resided here until revolutionary persecution forced them into nearby caves. In 1793, troops set fire to La Malène, leaving a smoky mark on the Barre cliff. The château is now a hotel with an excellent restaurant. Below the cliff are fine old houses. Before the riverside road opened in 1905, trade relied on the village's skilled boatmen; today they do a good trade ferrying people to view the gorges close up.

DAY 3: La MALÈNE to Les VIGNES

Today's route covers the most dramatic section as the river tumbles through several rapids and vultures circle the clifftops overhead.

Distance	12.5 km (8 miles)
Time	5 hours 30
Notes	buy lunch supplies in La Malène

Cross back over the bridge and turn right onto a broad, level farm track that runs for several kilometres, passing by the ruins of a château on the other bank. Waymarks direct you left up onto a stony track, signed to Les Vignes and Le Rozier. The path climbs steeply to a junction. (A detour left will bring you, after a height gain of 430 m and a level walk for 750 m, to the Roc des Hourtous, a wonderful viewpoint over the Détroits; return by the same route, allowing several hours for the return trip.)

Continue straight on through mossy woods and, after 15 minutes or so, gain glimpses of

⑧ **Les Détroits**, where the Tarn is squeezed between sheer cliffs, up to 400 m in height. Admittedly, this section is best seen by boat, from where you can also see the Grotte de la Momie or 'mummy's cave'.

The forest path undulates for a while before reaching a diversion to a small outcrop, giving great views across to the Clapas de la Truque and up river. A steep descent brings you down to a forest glade, from where a short riverside detour through vegetation will give you filtered views at river level back to the Détroits.

From the glade, take the waymarked path up left. This climbs to skirt a property at La Croze and then continues up, giving views of

St-Chély-du-Tarn

⑨ **the Cirque des Baumes**, across the river. *Baumes* means caves and the multicoloured rock walls are pocked with them. The views become even more dramatic; look up left for strange rock formations on the Causse Méjean.

The forest thins, giving views back up river and down to the Pas de Soucy and the two rocks on either side of it: Roque Sourd and the dramatic Roc Aiguille. The path traverses several ravines, the vegetation changing as it does so. A side path to La Claze comes in, but you keep slightly downhill, passing a sign for a gîte. At a sharp bend, a detour right leads to the large outcrop of

⑩ **Roque Sourde**, providing a superb panorama, and a vulture's view down to the **Pas de Souci**. This jumble of boulders in the river landed there in two rockfalls or *soussitch*, the last during an earthquake in 580. Legend says that Ste Énimie called for the rocks to help her chase away the devil and, during the resulting rock slide, Roque Sourde hurled itself at the devil, forcing him to return to hell through a crack in the river bed.

The path now descends to several buildings at Le Ménial and becomes a paved lane, passing above a Romanesque church in the hamlet of

A vulture soars above the *causse*

St-Préjet, before crossing the bridge to
⑪ **Les Vignes**. Set in a broad river valley, this quiet village catches any available sun and is named for the vines cultivated nearby. It is less visited by tourists but has at least one hotel.

DAY 4: Les VIGNES to Le ROZIER

Today's path hugs the cliff face before the Tarn valley widens and you reach the twin towns of Le Rozier and Peyreleau.

Distance	12 km (7.5 miles)
Time	4 hours
Notes	take lunch

Cross the bridge and turn right onto the D16. Some 10 minutes on, after a small vineyard, follow the farm track veering down right and pass through a gate. The farm track provides beautiful views up left to rock formations and continues for some time before becoming a path through pasture. Near a sign saying '*chasse interdit 2.5 km*', watch carefully for
⑫ **a path junction** where green-and-yellow waymarks direct you left onto a narrow footpath. This passes through a gate (an old bedstead) and climbs steeply above crags then levels, passing wonderful overhangs and offering good views up and down the river.

After a time, the valley opens out and the path continues close by the river, passing several minor rapids. Ahead on the left looms the rocky outcrop known as **Cinglegros** (see one of the walks at the end of this chapter). Eventually, you pass through donkey pasture and follow signs to skirt the buildings of
⑬ **La Sablière**. This pretty hamlet is linked to the other bank by a cable, but is a long way from car access. The *sentier* has been rerouted around cottages and is not as per the map.

Beyond the hamlet, the route follows an old track that, after an easy 2 km, passes through
⑭ **Plaisance**. This abandoned hamlet gives you the opportunity to peer into several

Autumn colours near La Sablière

buildings, including the ruined oven. About 2.5 km further on, the track passes above the ruins of an old bridge and descends to the D996 road just beyond the new one. Turn left and enter the village of

⑮ **Le Rozier**. This has an amazing position, at the confluence of the Jonte and Tarn rivers and below the limestone *causses* of the Sauveterre, Méjean and Noir. Just south across the Jonte and up a steep hill is the village of Peyreleau, dominated by its château.

LONG DISTANCE STAGES

km	time	location	acc
		Ispagnac	H C
1.5	0h30	Quézac	C
4.5	1h15	Montbrun	C
5.5	2h	Castelbouc	G
7	2h15	Sainte-Énimie	H C
5	1h45	St-Chély-du-Tarn	H
5.5	2h	Hautèrives	G
3.5	1h15	La Malène	H G C
12.5	5h30	Les Vignes	H
12	4h	Le Rozier	H G

The Tarn from Causse Méjean >

Vase de Sèvres, above Le Rozier >

OTHER WALKS ALONG THE WAY

From Florac to Ispagnac

If you arrive early in Florac you might opt to walk along the river to our starting point in Ispagnac, following the green-and-yellow waymarks of the *Sentier des Gorges du Tarn.*

Take Ave. du 8 Mai 1945 past the Protestant cemetery to the district of Le Jouquet, then keep straight along the river to the hamlet of Salièges. Fork right at the fire station to walk through woods to Le Fayer, on a bend in the Tarn. A track heads west and crosses several gullies above the river. Before the hamlet of Biesses, turn left on a track that heads NW to buildings of Biessette. The track continues due north and then contours west around the spur, to cross the Tarn on a picturesque bridge. Turn left and follow the D907 a short distance into the centre of Ispagnac. *Allow 2 hours 30.*

Corniches du Causse Méjean

This strenuous circuit from Le Rozier up onto the Causse Méjean gives stunning views over the gorges of both the Tarn and Jonte rivers. It can be cut short by omitting the loop to Cinglegros, a section only suitable for the agile. Take food and water for the day.

Start at the GR sign on the road between Le Rozier's church and the bridge over the Tarn. The footpath, signed GR6a, climbs steeply, passing a hairpin bend and continuing straight up. At a communications tower, take a broad track up to the pretty hamlet of **Capluc**. A path to the left climbs the Rocher de Capluc, surmounted by a cross, but we continue on the GR, passing a communal oven.

Soon, take steps up left marked with a fading red 'Brunet', leaving the GR for the *Sentier Jacques Brunet*. Follow old red spots and newer orange ones up over rough ground; you soon gain a view over Peyreleau. A demanding scramble over rocks leads to the base of a massive rock, the **Enclume** or *anvil*. The path now heads through light forest and veers to give a good view up the Tarn valley, with the abandoned buildings of Plaisance below and Cinglegros in the distance.

The path winds and then rejoins the GR by a CAF monument; this marks the Col de Francbouteille. Keep left at the junction. The prow-shaped **Rocher de Francbouteille** looms on the right; across the gorge are the troglodyte houses of **Eglazines**. At a junction directly above Plaisance, turn left on the *Sentier Martel*, part of the GR6. (Note: For the short version, turn right here and then right at the second junction onto the GRP; see *.)

Some 10 to 15 minutes further on, a shelf offers a view of another troglodyte ruin, **St-Marcellin**, across valley. At a path junction, turn left on the *Pas des Trois Fondus* that descends steeply and then climbs the **Rocher de Cinglegros** using metal ladders and cramp-irons fixed into the rockface. The effort is well rewarded by the dizzying panorama from the rocky outcrop, particularly north up the Tarn.

Return to the junction and follow GR6a uphill. Follow yellow stripe waymarks along a broad track that winds and veers away from the Tarn to a junction by a power pole; here, turn right on GR6 signed to Cassagnes. An easy but relatively dull pine forest walk brings you to a junction near the farming hamlet of **Cassagnes**. Turn right to follow a damaged stone wall. At a junction, turn left onto a GRP*, waymarked red-and-yellow. These marks lead you along a broad track that suddenly narrows as it reaches the Jonte gorge where views open up. The GRP then weaves around the spectacular Corniches du Causse Mejean, passing the panoramic **Balcon du Vertige** and amazing rock formations, including the **Vase de Chine** and the **Vase de Sèvres**.

At a junction turn left, now following the GR6/6a down through the Ravin des Echos. This winds down below L'Enclume, returning to Capluc and then Le Rozier. *Allow 8 hours.*

Avignon

Every town has its own story and character, but Avignon's is quite different to that of any other in France. As the one-time headquarters of the papacy it drew large numbers of court officials, poets and artists, changing the shape of the town and making it a hub of artistic activity that continued after the popes had departed. Fortified to protect the papal wealth, Avignon today can appear a little intimidating and severe. Its setting, by a rocky spur or *rocher* near the confluence of the Rhône and Durance rivers, adds to this impression but there is much here to fascinate and delight.

Archaeological evidence suggests that this location, on a trade route between Italy and Spain, has been occupied for thousands of years. The Romans developed the site but it did not have the importance for them of Arles or Aix-en-Provence. Things changed somewhat in the 12th century when a bridge was built over the Rhône – the furthest south that the wide river could be crossed – and Avignon prospered as a trading centre. The building of the bridge was considered a miraculous feat and the 'Pont d'Avignon' later appeared in a children's song.

View across the Rhône to Avignon

NOTES

Getting there: rail from Paris, Lyon and Marseille

Tourist Office: 41 Cours Jean Jaurès, 84000 Avignon ☏ 0432743274
Fax: 0490829503
E: information@ot-avignon.fr
www.ot-avignon.fr

Markets: Tue-Sun, Place Pie

At the beginning of the 14th century, Pope Clement V sojourned in Avignon to avoid the turmoil of Rome. Successive popes stayed on and Avignon became the home of the papacy and the centre of Christendom until the Great Schism of 1378-1417, during which rival popes were based in Rome and Avignon. The power struggle was finally resolved, the papacy returned to Rome and Avignon slipped back out of the political limelight.

The legacy of that period of prominence is proudly on display in Avignon today, after being given the full restoration treatment by Viollet-le-Duc in the 19th century. The walled city is filled with two palaces and copious mansions and small museums. It draws many visitors, especially so in late July and early August when it hosts a festival of music and drama. Founded in 1947, this event is now the most lavish in the French arts calendar.

Summer can also bring a stifling heat to the streets of Avignon, while in spring and winter the mistral wind can be fierce. Indeed, the name Avignon is said to derive from the Celtic word *avenio*, which means either 'town of the violent wind' or 'town by the river'. Just across the bridge and well worth a visit, is neighbouring Villeneuve-lès-Avignon which is officially in Languedoc. Avignon, however, is definitely a city of Provence, a fact confirmed by stalls overflowing with chirruping cicada magnets and bolts of calico printed with bright Provençal designs.

Roofscape of the Palais des Papes >

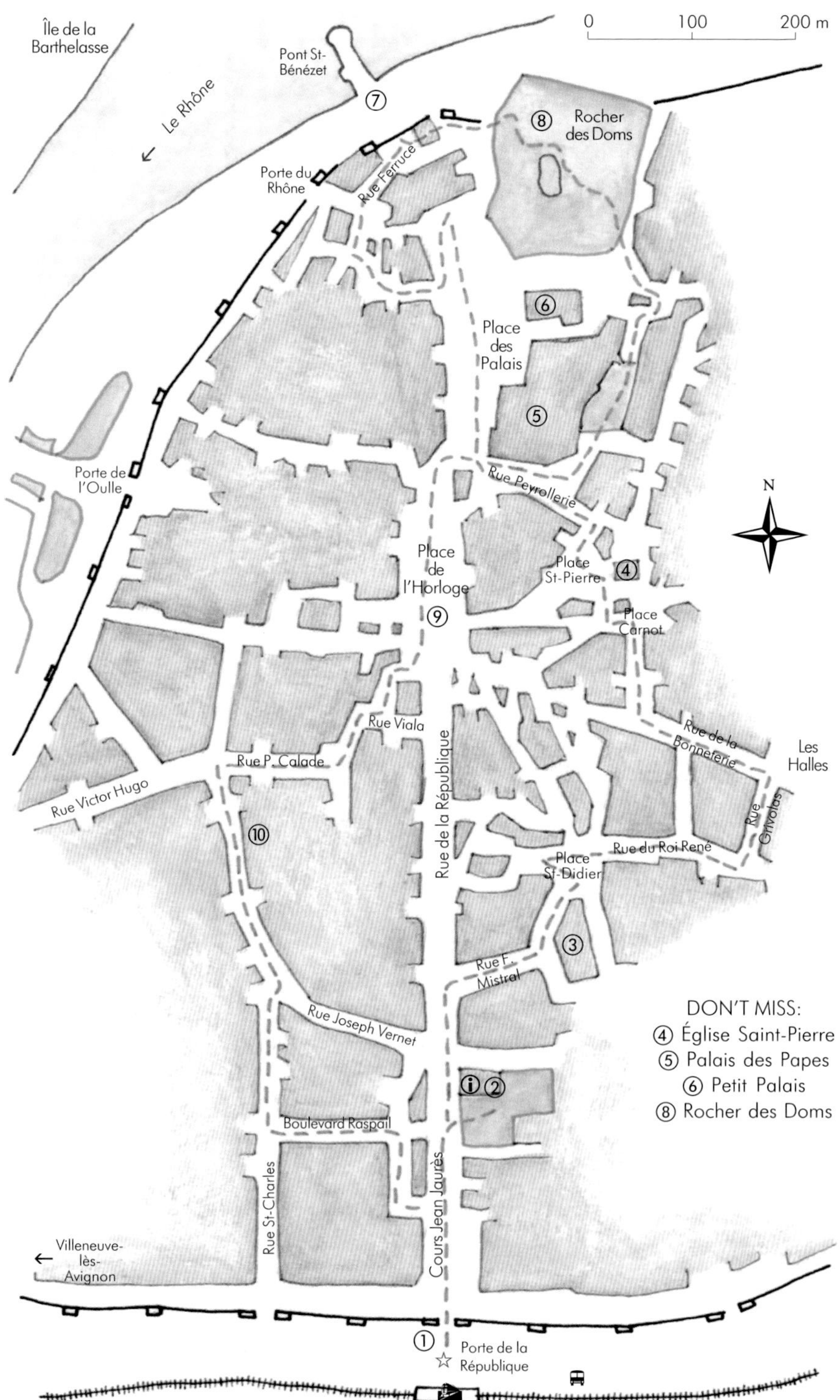

DON'T MISS:
④ Église Saint-Pierre
⑤ Palais des Papes
⑥ Petit Palais
⑧ Rocher des Doms

A WALK IN AVIGNON

A figure-eight loop takes you from Avignon's southern entrance to the Rocher des Doms and back, via all the major sites.

Avignon's bus and rail stations lie just south of the walled town. The arrival of the railway called for a new breach in the ramparts, the ① **Porte de la République**, created by Viollet-le-Duc. Sections of the walls encircling the city date to the 13th century, but most are 14th-century and were once girded with a moat.

Walk down the main thoroughfare, Cours Jean Jaurès for 250 m, to a park on the right, where you'll find the graceful buttresses of the ② **Église Saint-Martial**, part of a late 14th-century Benedictine monastery. The entrance to the church is in Rue Henri-Fabre. The tourist office now occupies the monastery buildings, entered from Cours Jean Jaurès.

Further along this road is the **Musée Lapidaire**, displaying Gallo-Roman sculptures in an old Jesuit chapel. Just before it, turn right into Rue Frédéric Mistral; the Provençal writer attended school in this street. At the end is the ③ **Musée Angladon**, an excellent fine arts collection from the 19th and 20th centuries, housed in a furnished mansion.

Opposite the museum is the 1340 **Livrée Ceccano**; a *livrée* is a cardinal's palace. This well-preserved mansion is open to the public as it now contains the municipal library, with its wealth of religious manuscripts.

A short way north along Rue Laboreur is **Église St-Didier**, built in 1359; the main entrance is through a passage on the left. From Place St-Didier, head west on Rue du Roi René, lined with 17th-century mansions. Note the sculpted masks on Hôtel de Crillon (no.7).

Turn left into Rue Grivolas and reach the indoor markets of **Les Halles**, worth a visit for provisions or just a look. Turn left along Rue de la Bonneterie, entering the pedestrian zone of the old town, a warren of old houses and tempting shops. Turn right into Rue des Fourbisseurs to reach Place Carnot. A short detour left leads to the **Synagogue**, standing in what was the 13th-century Jewish ghetto.

From Place Carnot, turn left into Rue des Marchands, passing a corbelled, half-timbered house dating back to the 15th century. Turn

Église St-Didier

right into Rue St-Pierre, which crosses a car-laden street to reach the striking ④ **Église St-Pierre**. A church has reputedly stood on this site since the 7th century; this one is mostly Renaissance, with doors that were skillfully sculpted in 1551.

Leave Place Saint-Pierre at the far end and turn left along Rue Peyrolerie, a curious passageway cut into the rock and spanned by a buttress of the palace. You emerge at the breathtaking Place du Palais, a space created in 1404. It is, of course, dominated by the ⑤ **Palais des Papes**, the largest Gothic palace in existence. The massive fortifications lend it an austere appearance but some of the popes who resided here lived in immense luxury. The palace was stripped after the Revolution of 1789. Allow plenty of time to wander through the numerous halls, chapels, towers, and chambers, not to mention the roof terraces.

Just next door is the once-Romanesque cathedral of **Notre-Dame-des-Doms**, dating back to the 12th century. It has suffered much heavy-handed reworking over the centuries, including the addition of a gilded virgin on its bell tower. At the northern end of the open space is the Renaissance façade of the ⑥ **Petit Palais**, 'small' only by comparison with the Palais des Papes. Built about 1320 for a cardinal, it was badly damaged during the

Pont St-Bénézet

Great Schism when it served as a citadel. Since 1976 it has been a museum and contains the finest collection of Italian paintings from the 13th to 15th century outside of Italy.

Take steps on the west of Place du Palais, known as the Pente Rapide, and descend to a passageway, passing souvenir shops. Turn right into Rue de la Grande Fusterie and then left into Rue Ferruce to reach, by the ramparts, the entrance to the half span of

⑦ **Pont St-Bénézet** or the Pont d'Avignon, as it is known in the famous song. This marvel of engineering was built in the 12th century, initiated, it is said, by a young shepherd named Bénézet, inspired by God. It suffered damage during the Albigensian wars (when Avignon was besieged) and was rebuilt soon after, with 22 arches and a span of 900 m. It had to be repaired frequently following floods and was finally abandoned in 1668; only four arches now remain, making it a picturesque ruin.

Climb up through the nearby **Tour des Chiens**, named for the dog pound it once held. You gain excellent views over the bridge and across to Villeneuve as you scale the

⑧ **Rocher des Doms**. This site of first settlement was fortified during the Roman and Medieval periods. It catches any breeze and was a popular location for windmills and those seeking fresh air during the plague years. It was turned into parkland in the 19th century and offers a wonderful view of the Rhône valley. Take the Sainte-Anne steps down and turn right to walk through a former military storehouse (now a cultural space) and discover the orchard of Urban V with an amazing view of the Palais' eastern face, bristling with towers.

Turn right into Rue du Vice Légat and walk again through Rue Peyrolerie. This time, leave Place du Palais by its southwest corner, near the sculpted Hôtel de Monnaies (1619), now the music conservatorium named in honour of Olivier Messiaen, a native of Avignon. This brings you to the café-lined

Place du Palais >

Fort St-André

⑨ **Place de l'Horloge**, location of the town hall, opéra and, of course, the clock tower. At the southwest corner, a brief detour west leads to the 14th-century Gothic **St-Agricole**, dedicated to one of the city's patron saints.

Further along is Place Louis le Cardonnel, marked by a bust of Mistral. Turn right to pass the 15th-century **Palais du Roure**, now a centre of Provençal culture. Rue College du Roure curves left and you then turn right into Rue Viala, then left into Rue Bouquerie. Veer right through the pretty Plan du Lunel and walk down Rue de la Petite Calade.

Turn left along Rue Joseph Vernet, where you'll find the excellent

⑩ **Musée Calvet**, a wide-ranging collection of art housed in an 18th-century mansion. Just next door is the **Musée Requien**, a natural history museum. Continue on and then veer right into Rue St-Charles. Vestiges of 13th-century ramparts can be seen hereabouts. Rue Violette on the left leads to the entrance of the Lambert Collection of modern art, but the next left (Boulevard Raspail) offers a good view of its building, the Hôtel de Galeans-Gadagne.

A dogleg right brings you past the entrance of the lovely **Cloître St-Louis**; the adjoining hospice is now an upmarket hotel. Another turn and you are back near your starting point.

VILLENEUVE-LÈS-AVIGNON

This outlying town lies on the west bank of the Rhône; it originated as a frontier post for the French kingdom but grew as a refuge for the Avignon clergy; it is quietly fascinating.

From Avignon's *gare* SNCF, catch a #10 bus to Villeneuve's Place Charles-David. From Rue des Recollets, climb Rue Pente-Rapide and then Montée du Fort to the massive **Fort St-André**, enclosing medieval houses and a former abbey and offering wonderful views.

A path winds around to the Carthusian monastery of **Val de Benediction**, founded in the 14th century. A little way south is the collegiate church of **Notre-Dame**. At the foot of Montée de la Tour stands **Tour Philippe-le-Bel**, built to guard the French end of the Avignon bridge. Return to Avignon by crossing Pont Daladier. *Allow at least 5 hours.*

OPENING HOURS

Musée Angladon	open Wed-Sun 1-6
Palais des Papes	daily 9-7 Apr-Jun, Oct; 9-9 July; 9-8 Aug-Sep; 9.30-5.45 Nov-Mar
Musée du Petit Palais	open Wed-Mon 9.30-1, 2-5.30 Oct-May; 10-1, 2-6 Jun-Sep
Pont St-Bénézet	daily 9-7 April-Sep; 9.30-5.30 Oct-March
Musée Calvet	open Wed-Mon 10-1, 2-6

The Luberon

Directly north of Marseille, in the Parc Naturel Régional du Luberon, is a land that is quintessentially Provençal. Here are villages that seem to tumble down the rocky hillside, separated dry plateaux, rough gullies, vines and the occasional field of lavender, all lit by a wonderful sunshine that has inspired artists for centuries.

Though now quiet, the Luberon hasn't always been so. Many a small village here began as an *oppidum*, a prehistoric fortified settlement. The region has often harboured people seeking refuge from persecution. In the Dark Ages, it was a haunt for druids and hermits and there is still a strong culture of superstition among today's inhabitants. In the 14th century, the Vaudois – followers of a fundamentalist Christian sect – settled here with Protestants. In the mid-16th century the Catholic church launched a bloody attack on these heretics and whole villages were massacred and destroyed.

The landscape is dotted with *bories*, dry-stone dwellings that look akin to a beehive or an igloo. These may have been primitive dwellings for shepherds or were perhaps used by people trying to escape epidemics of the plague. Some were inhabited until the early 20th century. More luxurious dwellings are now appearing as city-dwellers and foreigners build or restore holiday homes. Visitors too are increasing in number; there's a strange sense of sweaty achievement to arrive on foot and pass a crowd of leisurely tourists. Despite the fact that summer is when lavender is in bloom, the great heat of these months makes it less suitable for walking. Much of the rougher ground is covered with *garrigue* – a mixture of oaks, broom and gorse – but there are surprisingly shady pockets of vegetation along the narrower river valleys.

Our walk begins at Apt, a market town between the limestone mountains of the Luberon and those of the Vaucluse. The route takes quiet lanes and waymarked paths to contour the lower slopes of the Grand Luberon and then the Petit Luberon. It then crosses the broad, fertile valley of the Calavon river and climbs into the lower hills of the Vaucluse. Along the way, we visit picturesque hilltowns – Bonnieux, Lacoste, Goult, Roussillon, Gordes – and ancient sites. The destination is Fontaine-de-Vaucluse, where the Sorgue springs out of the limestone *causse* or plateau.

NOTES
Type: 5-day walk of 69 km (43 miles)
Difficulty: easy, with short stages
Start: Apt (bus from Avignon or Aix)
Finish: Fontaine-de-Vaucluse (bus to Avignon via L'Isle-sur-la-Sorgue)
Tourist Office: 20 Avenue P. de Girard, 84400 Apt, ☎ 0490740318
Fax: 0490046430
E: tourisme.apt@pacwan.fr
www.provenceguide.com
Map: Didier Richard *Luberon* 1:50000
Best timing: avoid July-August

Looking towards the Luberon range

The quiet village of Lacoste >

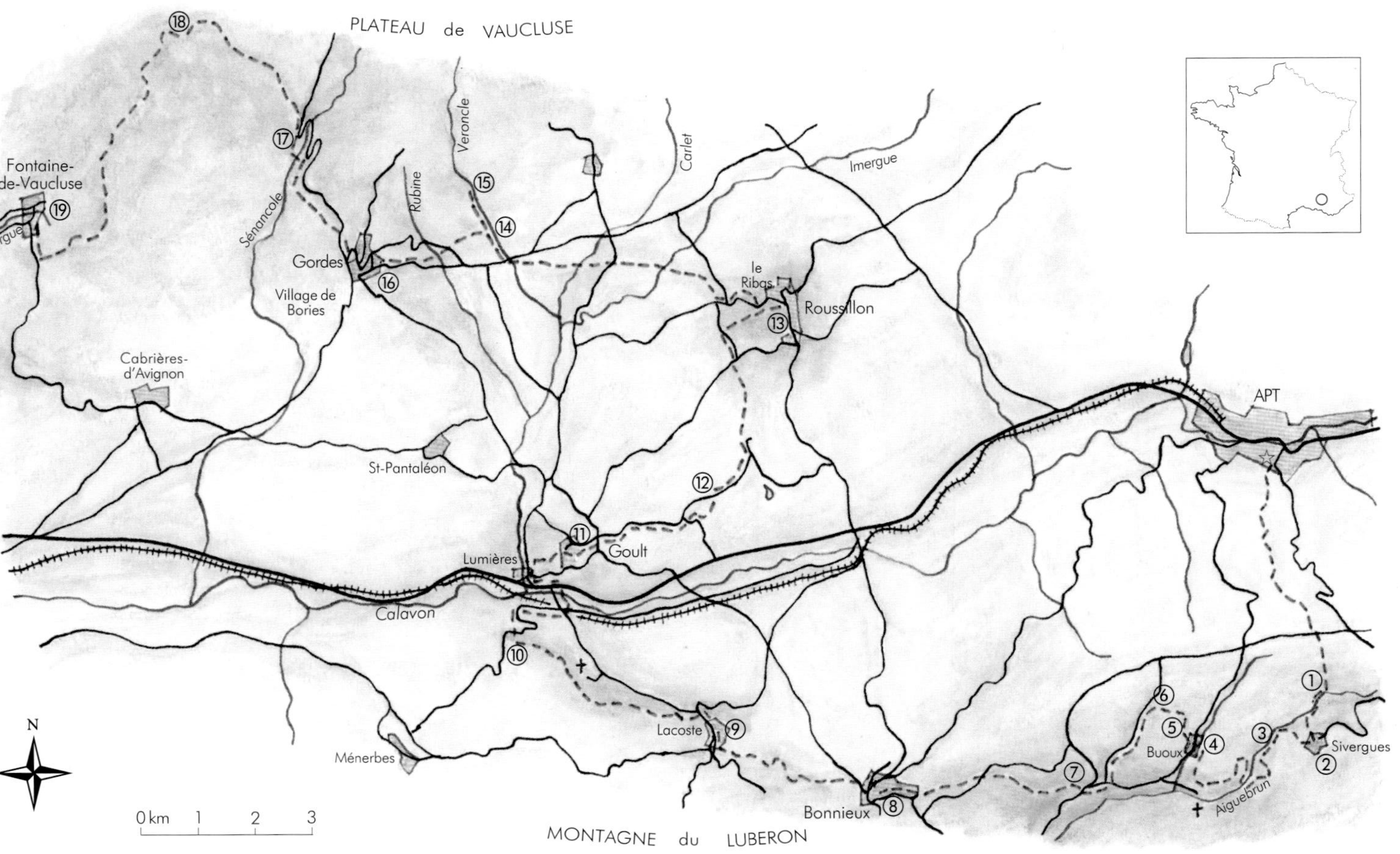
PLATEAU de VAUCLUSE
MONTAGNE du LUBERON
Fontaine-de-Vaucluse
Sorgue
Sénancole
Gordes
Village de Bories
Rubine
Veroncle
Carlet
Imergue
Cabrières-d'Avignon
St-Pantaléon
le Ribas
Roussillon
APT
Lumières
Goult
Calavon
Lacoste
Ménerbes
Bonnieux
Buoux
Sivergues
Aiguebrun
N
0 km 1 2 3

A house in Buoux

DAY 1: APT to BUOUX

A climb out of Apt is followed by a meander through the surprisingly verdant valley of the Aiguebrun, the site of prehistoric settlement and now a haven for rock climbers.

Distance	12 km (7.5 miles)
Time	4 hours 30
Notes	take lunch; there is limited accommodation in Buoux

From Place de la Bouquerie, by the Cavalon river, walk on through Place Gabriel Peri and up Bd. Mal Foch, passing the *mairie* and a war memorial. The road curves as Bd. Nationale and you turn right into Ave. des Druides, then right into Rue des Bassins, following GRP waymarks (red and yellow stripes) and a sign to Sivergues.

About 200 m uphill, turn left into Chemin de Saint Vincent and, after a crossroads, veer right uphill on a stony path which soon rejoins the road. Up left are great views of Saignon, on its rocky promontory. Further on, fork right up onto a stony track that follows a dry-stone wall in the shade of oaks. Shortly, turn left onto a broader track and then immediately right to reach the **Saint Vincent** junction; continue on towards Sivergues. Waymarks direct you to fork right onto a footpath, soon passing a lavender field on your right.

At the signpost on **the Claparèdes plateau** keep straight ahead for Sivergues. Pass another signpost, cross a road, and continue ahead on a gravel track. At the Barbe Blanche signpost, take the footpath left, passing blackberries, a small *borie* and a field of daisies to reach the edge of the narrow

① **Vallon de l'Aiguebrun.** Follow the path waymarked as a GRP that weaves down the hillside between crags to cross the gully floor and climb up through woodland. This mule track brings you to the small

② **village of Sivergues,** where you will find little more than a chapel and a few dwellings. Once this was a stronghold of the Vaudois movement; today it is very quiet. After a rest, walk down in front of the 16th-century church and past the communal oven to drop to a house built against the rock ledge.

Cross the paved road and pick up the PR path, signed to Les Seguins. The path winds down, then forks left and continues up the Aiguebrun valley through lush vegetation and past trees espaliered onto the rock face. The

PR follows the stream, with good views of the crags opposite, and then rises to a signpost at **Ravin de l'Enfer**; take the path right, signed to Buoux. Another signpost soon directs you right. However, an interesting detour could be made here to the **Fort de Buoux**, some 1.5 km from this junction. This 13th-century fort was built on the site of a Celto-Ligurian *oppidum* and occupied by the Vardois until they were driven out (entrance fee; open all year).

Otherwise, cross the stream and join the GR9, following another signpost right to Buoux. Zigzag up the hill with a view across valley of three strange *bories*, and then of
③ **a troglodyte settlement** a little further back up the valley. The path follows along the natural balcony with some good viewpoints, then suddenly veers right and up to Les Ramades; from where you take the path to Buoux. This contours around a spur to join a road and cross a bridge over the Loube river. Take the track straight uphill to a signpost, where you turn right to gain the centre of
④ **Buoux**. During the second half of the 17th century, those who had lived in the shelter of the Fort de Buoux settled here. The village has an 18th-century church with an ancient altar and there is a gîte d'étape and a hotel.

Chapelle Ste-Marie

DAY 2: BUOUX to LACOSTE

A lovely chapel and several old bories *are passed en route to picturesque Bonnieux, then backroads between vineyards lead to a superb perched village.*

Distance	12 km (7.5 miles)
Time	3 hours 45
Notes	could visit Fort de Buoux first

Leave Buoux by taking the path signed to Bonnieux and Chapelle Ste-Marie from the town hall. The road winds uphill to the walled
⑤ **Sainte-Marie**, a 13th-century Romanesque church with a unique nave and a pretty setting.

From here, pick up the GRP footpath, signed to Bonnieux. This path descends, then a signpost directs you right to
⑥ **Châteaux du Buoux**. This walled estate is the property of the Luberon nature park. At the gate, waymarks direct you left on a track which joins the road; keep left, signed to St-Symphorien and Grotte des Brigandes. The paved road gently descends a pleasant valley for 1.5 km and then reaches another road. Turn right and cross the nearby bridge. Hereabouts you could detour to see the ruined priory.

Otherwise, the road climbs past another signpost to Bonnieux, then joins the D943 road. Turn right, then pick up a footpath on the left, signed to Bonnieux and Baume d'Estellan. This

< St-Symphorien in the Aiguebrun valley

Bonnieux

path soon offers a good view SE to the priory of ⑦ **St-Symphorien** in the Aiguebrun valley below. The course of the river south of this point is known as the Combe de Lourmarin and it marks the division between the Petit Luberon and the Grand Luberon.

The path continues uphill by a dry-stone wall. At a junction of many paths, keep straight ahead on the GRP track uphill. A signpost at a cross points you to Bonnieux and Les Blayons. Cross the D232 road and pick up a footpath along a dry-stone wall. Keep straight ahead, passing an intact *borie* on the left, then a yellow house on the right. The footpath becomes a track then a paved road into the upper level of

⑧ **Bonnieux**. This village, perched on the north face of the Luberon, has wonderful views towards the Vaucluse. It began as an *oppidum* and prospered in Roman times due to its position along the road from Cadiz to Milan. It served as a centre for the Knights Templar in the Middle Ages and much of its fortifications remains intact. There is also a museum of bread-making and a lovely upper church.

From the new church at the foot of the village, take the main road left downhill. At a pottery, take the left-forking road called Chemin de la Gardiole, signed to Lacoste and Le Petit Moulin. In less than 1 km, follow a track to La Beguine. Turn left onto a road; fork off right onto a path, picking up another road. Continue straight on to climb the hill to

⑨ **Lacoste**, a quiet, gated hilltown with a hotel/gîte d'étape. It is crowned by the remains of a château that belonged to the de Sade family; the infamous Marquis de Sade lived here when ostracised from Paris. After the Revolution, the château was partly dismantled for its stone and today it is an evocative ruin.

DAY 3: LACOSTE to ROUSSILLON

Woodland paths lead you down from the Luberon hills to cross the Calavon valley, before a scramble up to pretty Goult and a walk through undulating farmland to the remarkable village of Roussillon.

Distance	17 km (10.5 miles)
Time	5 hours 30
Notes	lunch available in Goult

From Lacoste's post office, take the lane that passes below both it and the bell tower. At a cross, fork left onto a white gravel track marked as a PR; it becomes a grassy track between two

Lavender near Lacoste

dry-stone walls. Turn left onto the D106 road for a short distance, then left onto a paved lane called the Chemin de Font Pourquière, following waymarks.

The lane leads along pleasant vineyards to an attractive

⑩ ***lavoire*** or public wash house. Keep straight on a grassy, limestone track, then ascend on a footpath straight ahead into woodland. The PR waymarks direct you to fork right into more scrubby *garrigues* and then descend gently. Continue past a large dry-stone building and down a vehicular track, then fork right into more scrub, passing a ruin and descending.

The view opens up to reveal Goult and you soon reach the road at Les Artèmes. Look for a PR footpath between the white gravel track and the descending road and take this downhill through overgrown woodland. When you reach a driveway, take it straight ahead and then continue straight on along the road.

The road curves, passing pumpkin fields and then shaded by trees on one side. Turn left, signed to Lumières and Goult. Cross the Calavon river and the N100, then take the road towards Lumières. Before you reach this unremarkable hamlet, turn right, then soon left on the D60 to Gordes. In 20 m or so, take the steps on the right up to an overgrown PR footpath. This climbs steeply, past elaborate terracing to reach a district known as Jerusalem. Turn left, passing a large windmill and entering ⑪ **Goult**, a pleasant village where you can try a Côte du Luberon at a wine cellar.

After exploring Goult, make your way down to the main square, Place de la Liberation. Take Rue de Republique and soon turn left into Avenue Ducroit, passing the *lavoire* and the *boulodrome*, where locals gather to play petanque or boules. The road curves right, passing a restored lavoire. At a cross 150 m on, fork right onto a road uphill, waymarked as a PR.

This pleasant country road ascends steeply and then passes an old ochre quarry; for the rest of the day you will see numerous colour changes in the soil. Further along, you pass the vineyards and buildings of

⑫ **La Verrière**. Descend past an abandoned building and cross over a bridge. The PR marks direct you left onto a white gravel track, then, some 15 m on, right onto a footpath which climbs up a red ochre bank and then veers left. The route skirts vines and then crosses a road

Vines in the Calavon valley >

junction, following PR marks. You soon cross a stream by a large tree and turn left onto the Chemin de Marsellais, marked with PR stripes and orange spots. This eventually reaches a track; turn right, then left onto a paved road signed Chemin des Medons, which descends.

Turn right onto the Cabiscol track and keep straight on as the PR becomes a grassy track, then turn sharp right over an old footbridge and up on a rough path that merges with a track and then the road to reach a car park. Here you'll find steps leading to the centre of ⑬ **Roussillon**, classified as one of France's most beautiful villages. The whole village is dressed in the red and orange hues that come from one of the world's largest veins of ochre, mined here until the mid-20th century. Make sure you walk the *Sentier des Ocres* which, for a small fee, takes you through a bizarre landscape of pillars and other formations shaped by mining, erosion and the wind.

DAY 4: ROUSSILLON to GORDES

Today's short journey allows time for extra excursions: a stroll through Roussillon's ochre quarries, a detour up the gorges of the Véroncle to the ruins of an ancient mill, or a visit to the Village des Bories.

Distance	13 km (8.1 miles)
Time	3 hours 30
Notes	includes Véroncle Gorges detour

Ochre at Roussillon

Leave Roussillon along the D102, following waymarks for the GR6/97; with the exception of the Véroncle detour, today's route is entirely along the GR6. After 15 minutes, branch left on the D169, signed to Taillon and Lumières. After only a few minutes, follow the GR right onto a minor road signed Le Colombier. This narrow, paved road descends for 15 minutes before the surface changes and you soon fork right on a grassy path with a hand-painted sign to Gordes.

The footpath broadens and becomes a level farm lane, with good views opening up W to Gordes and NW to Joucas. The track merges with a paved lane and continues very straight. Cross the D60 and continue ahead, passing a somewhat desultory horse farm on the left (marked on some maps as a gîte d'étape). After a slight rise, turn left onto the busy D2 for 200 m or so before turning right onto an unpaved road signed to Gorges de Véroncle. After 500 m, you reach ⑭ **Les Grailles**, where a signboard indicates the start of a 1.5 km circular 1-hour walk up the fascinating Combe de Véroncle. The yellow-

< A windmill at Goult

Gordes in the late evening

waymarked path takes you above the right bank of the gorge and then zigzags downhill to the ruins of

⑮ **the Cabrier mill**, one of many grain mills built along the gorges in the 16th century; the elaborate hydraulic system which fed this one is still visible. A short way up the gorge (reached by use of chains and ladders) you reach the dam wall and the gorge narrows intriguingly. This is a good point to turn back, though there are two more well-preserved mill sites between here and Murs. The route back is along the floor of the former river.

Back at the noticeboard, pick up the GR by going left on a level lane past a holiday village. Cross the D102 and go straight ahead on a gravel lane, with lovely views of Gordes up ahead. At the St Eyriès junction, continue straight ahead on the GR via Le Turon. After 5 minutes, turn right uphill on the busy D2 for 150 m then fork right uphill on a paved road, soon passing a lavoire in the base of a stone building. From here, follow the GR signs to climb steadily up to

⑯ **Gordes**, one of Provence's most spectacular *villages perchés*. Its natural defensive site made it important to the Romans and it was a stronghold for Protestants during the Wars of Religion and for the Resistance movement in WWII. The village is dominated by a solid château begun in 1025 and rebuilt in 1525.

If you have time to spare after exploring, you might consider taking a 3 km petite randonnée to the Village des Bories, a museum/village of dry-stone houses SW of Gordes.

< One of many dry-stone walls

DAY 5: GORDES to FONTAINE

This most remote day's walk takes you past the fascinating abbey of Sénanque and over the secluded Vaucluse hills to the emerald-green waters of Fontaine-de-Vaucluse.

Distance	15 km (9.3 miles)
Time	4 hours 30
Notes	take lunch supplies

Leave the Place de Château by the Rue de la Gendarmerie, picking up GR waymarks; we follow the GR6 for most of today's walk. Just after a hairpin bend, the GR forks right up a path by a Calvary cross. (For a wonderful view of Gordes spilling down the hillside, detour further along the road for 100 m.)

The uphill GR path soon reaches the D177

Abbaye de Sénanque

where you turn right. After a few minutes, you veer down left on a minor road. Almost immediately, a junction signpost points you towards Sénanque. Follow a broad mule path along dry-stone walls. Look out for a *borie* on the right; a gap in the wall allows you a closer look. Follow GR waymarks through a track junction. The path broadens and climbs to reach the road at the Côte de Sénancole signpost. There are good views from here down into the Sénancole gorge. Continue along the road for 50 m and then fork left downhill onto a woodland path. There are glimpses of the abbey below, before you cross a service road and descend to the car park of the

⑰ **Abbaye de Sénanque**, a lovely example of Cistercian architecture and the order's preference for seclusion. Founded in 1148, it took about a hundred years to complete the complex, most of which is open for your investigation following payment of an entry fee, despite the fact that a small number of monks still live here.

The GR6 continues to the right of the carpark and then joins the road. Follow this and then turn left onto the D177. After 30 m or so, turn right on the GR footpath uphill. It crosses the switchback in the D177 and then climbs

Limestone bluffs near Fontaine

relentlessly up valley, above a dry riverbed. The path eventually levels when a ridge is reached, with a view down left over another valley.

A more gentle ascent along the ridge brings you to a gravel track; turn left and continue uphill for a few minutes before veering right onto a stony path. A lengthy walk through the forest of **Pouraque** brings you eventually to a path junction at la Plaine, where GR waymarks direct you up left on a broad track. 100 m on, a signpost at la Plaine Est directs you right on a farm track signed to Fontaine. After 10 minutes or so, turn left at an unsigned junction where there is sporadic waymarking. You soon reach the Lauzas Nord junction, where you turn right.

After several kilometres of hard walking on a stony downhill track, you arrive at a giant underground cistern and a large cave overhang. This is the

⑱ **Fontaine de l'Oule**, a sometime spring, set in a rocky amphitheatre among beautiful trees. From here the path becomes more scenic, as the forest gives way to limestone rock formations: first a dramatic cirque, then cliffs and huge, weathered outliers. The path continues down the limestone gorge to reach a gate. Shortly after, take the middle of three paths; it is waymarked but with no sign.

Soon, you reach the D25a, where you part company with the GR6 by turning right and following the road for 1 km into the popular

⑲ **Fontaine-de-Vaucluse**. This village nestles where the river Sorgue pours out from its subterranean course into an emerald pond over 300m deep: how strong the spring is depends on the season. It is overlooked by the Vache d'Or, a rocky outcrop that vaguely resembles a cow.

The setting was sufficiently beautiful to have attracted the Italian poet Petrarch, who lived here from 1337 to 1353 and whose inspiration was Laura, the wife of Hugues de Sade. There is a museum dedicated to the poet; others focus on the Resistance, speleology and papermaking, for which the village was once renowned.

OTHER WALKS IN THE REGION

Fôret des Cèdres

If you can get transport along a forest road south-west of Bonnieux, you'll find a marked path through the forest of cedars planted in 1861 with seeds brought from the Atlas mountains in Morocco. There are plenty of viewpoints and information boards on the Luberon vegetation. *Allow 2.5 hours.*

Terraces of Goult

A waymarked path leads you around the ancient terraces of the village of Goult. *Allow 2 hours.*

LONG DISTANCE STAGES

km	time	location	acc
		Apt	H,G,C
6.5	2h30	Sivergues	C
5.5	2h00	Buoux	H,G
7.5	2h30	Bonnieux	H,G,C
4.7	1h15	Lacoste	H/G,C
8.5	2h30	Goult	H/G,C
8.5	3h00	Roussillon	H,C
9	2h30	Gordes	H,G,C
15	4h30	Fontaine	H,G,C,A

Arles

If, for some unfortunate reason, you only had the opportunity to visit one town in Provence, your destination should be Arles. It is layered in history, has charm in abundance and Provençal character to spare. Moreover, it is an ideal size to assay on foot. Despite all this, it escapes the sense of being a stage set for tourists and retains the spirit of a healthy provincial centre.

Arles lies on the Grand Rhône, just south of where the Petit Rhône branches off. The Greeks settled here before the Romans arrived around 125 BC. Once a canal to Fos on the coast was built, the city grew rapidly. It supported Julius Caesar in his victorious campaign against Marseille and was then favoured over the rival port and given most of its wealth. Constantine made Arles the capital of Gaul and built a palace here.

The city flourished as a trade centre until the empire crumbled. Following occupation by the Goths, Franks and Saracens, Arles was rebuilt in the 12th century. It served as an alternative port at times when Marseille was blockaded but it otherwise lay isolated between the Rhône and the Camargue marshlands, a factor in its state of preservation. By the time Van Gogh arrived in 1888 the town was in decline. He stayed for a year, living in Place Lamartine and depicting many of Arles' locations in his paintings. Arles' other famous resident is the poet Frédéric Mistral, who used his Nobel prize money of 1905 to set up a local museum of all things connected to Provençal life.

The walls of the Arena

NOTES

Getting there: rail from Marseille or Avignon

Tourist Office: Blvd des Lices, 13200
☎ 0490184120 Fax: 0490184129
E: ot-arles@visitprovence.com
www.arles.org

Markets: Wed and Sat

Note: a monuments pass is available

You can see a contemporary slice of this at Arles' Saturday market. For a larger serving, you could attend a session of *tauromachie* at the arena. Bullfighting takes two forms here: there is the traditional Spanish *corrida* in which the bull is taunted and then killed, and there is the *courses camarguaises* in which *razeteurs* attempt to pluck ribbons from the bulls' horns. These festivals of the bull are held between Easter and All Saints.

The bulls and horses that feature in these contests are reared in the protected delta flatland south of Arles, the Camargue. It is also home to a rich variety of birds and other wildlife, including biting insects. There are several walking trails but you do need to be well prepared.

Back in Arles, it's worth buying a pass that allows you entry into the town's many monuments and museums. The town becomes particularly lively during the arts festival known as Fêtes d'Arles (late June) and the Festival Mosaïque Gitane (mid-July), celebrating Gypsy culture.

A scene along the waterfront >

A WALK IN ARLES

The pedestrian has the advantage in Arles; this route leads along steep and winding alleys to visit its grand monuments and some quieter spots along the way.

Some 600 m south of the rail station, beyond the shady Place Voltaire, is the focal point of Arles, its Roman amhitheatre ① **Les Arènes**. Built around 90 AD, this massive arena consists of two storeys of sixty arcades each. It holds up to 20,000 spectators who once came to watch gladiators fight against

Arles' magnificent amphitheatre

each other or wild animals; today they watch bullfights. In the Middle Ages, the arena served as a citadel, further fortified with the addition of the three towers that still stand. Some 200 houses and several churches clustered within the walls until the resulting slum was cleared in the early 19th century.

Exit the amphitheatre turning right and ascend the steps nearby to **Place de la Major**; the church of Notre-Dame-de-la-Major is where *gardiens* or cowboys of the Camargue celebrate the feast day of their patron saint. On the balcony to the left is an observation board and a stunning view north to the ruined abbey of Montmajour and, on a clear day, Mont Ventoux. Descend to the back of the amphitheatre and walk through Place Bornier to the entrance of the

② **Théâtre Antique**. Built near the end of the 1st century BC, this was once a major monument, seating an audience of around 10,000. The back of the stage was adorned with numerous columns and statues. Sadly, the theatre was used as a quarry during the Middle Ages; what little remains is used as a venue for summer festivals.

Continue down the hill, along Rue de la Calade and turn left to enter the **Place de la République**, containing the 17th-century town hall and a granite obelisk that once stood in the Circus, Arles' Roman racetrack. What draws the eye here though is the amazing porch of the 12th-century

③ **Cathédrale Saint-Trophime**, a masterpiece of Romanesque art. St Trophimus was a late-2nd or early-3rd century bishop of Arles, who is said to have brought Christianity to the region. One tale has him arriving in Arles in time to prevent the sacrifice of three youths to a pagan divinity. The high-vaulted interior of the church, with its Gothic additions, is sparsely decorated. To the right of the church's façade is a lane that climbs to the **Clôitre Saint-Trophime**. These beautiful cloisters, created in the 12th to 14th centuries, contain more medieval carvings and the setting is quite serene.

Cross the square and walk along the traffic-free Rue de la République. On the right is **Musée Arlaten**, exhibiting all things unique to Provençal life. Turn right just after it and then right again, along Rue Balze. In the 17th-century Jesuit chapel, you'll find the access to the slightly unnerving

④ **Cryptoportiques du Forum**. These huge

Ruins of the ancient theatre

subterranean galleries were carved out between 30 and 20 BC, possibly for food storage or for housing public slaves. It also provided the foundations for the Gallo-Roman forum.

Continue along Rue Balze then turn left and walk through the lively **Place du Forum**, edged with restaurants. Pillars of an ancient temple can be seen in the corner of the Nord-Pinus hotel. Ahead, on the crooked Rue du Sauvage, stands the charming **Hôtel d'Arlatan**, built onto the walls of the Imperial Palace, Constantine's residence. Keep on in the same general direction, along Rue D. Maisto to the entrance of the
⑤ **Thermes de Constantin**, all that really remains of the emperor's palace that once stretched along the waterfront. These extensive thermal baths hint at the opulence of the palace.

At the bottom of the street, turn right and note the elaborate entrance of the 15-16th century Commanderie de Sainte-Luce on your right. Facing this is the
⑥ **Musée Réattu**, housed in a 15th-century priory. Jacques Réattu (1760-1833) was a local artist and his works are displayed here. There are some excellent modern pieces, including a series of sketches made in Arles by Picasso.

Beside the museum you can climb up the embankment of the Rhône and look upstream to see the vestiges of the old Roman bridge. Van Gogh used to walk here at night wearing candles on his hat, their reflection inspiring him to paint *The Starry Night*. The walk downstream along the embankment is very pleasant, passing the back of the church of the Frères Prêcheurs, fragments of medieval walls, and old warehouses in a district that was once a bustling quayside.

As you near the major road over the Rhône, you'll see the **Tour de l'Ecorchoir**. About 400 m directly downstream, on the site of the old Circus, and well worth the detour, is the ⑦ **Musée de l'Arles Antique**. This must be one of the best museums dedicated to Gallo-Roman history; its extensive collection is wonderfully arranged and explained, and it includes many beautifully-preserved mosaics.

Back at the tower, head southeast and then turn left up Rue Raillon, through Place Genive and up Rue de la Roquette, passing the church of St-Césaire. At the end of the traffic-free Rue des Procelets, you can turn right onto Rue

Cathédrale Saint-Trophime >

Mosaic, Musée de l'Arles Antique >

Gambetta to visit the ⑧ **Espace Van Gogh**. Following an argument with his friend Gauguin, Van Gogh sliced off his own ear and was dispatched to the Hotel-Dieu hospital for treatment. This has been turned into a cultural centre and its courtyard is planted according to Van Gogh's painting and description.

Courtyard of Musée Reattu

LES ALYSCAMPS

Southeast of the town centre is the charming Les Alyscamps, possibly a corruption of Elysian Fields. This ancient burial ground served as a meeting place for early Christians and was revered as the site of miracles; it was supposedly consecrated by an appearance of Christ himself. It became a prestigious place to be buried and was in use until the 12th century. Despite the fact that the most elaborate sarcophagi were removed or given away centuries ago, the place is still evocative, especially so in the late afternoon. The scene was painted by both Van Gogh and Gauguin.

From the tourist office, walk along Boulevard des Lices then turn right to follow Avenue des Alyscamps as it bends to cross the rail line. This leads to what remains of the necropolis and, at the end of the tree-lined avenue, the Romanesque Église Saint-Honorat. *Allow 1.5 hours return.*

OPENING HOURS	May-Sep	Oct	Nov-Feb	Mar-Apr
Les Arènes	9-7*	9-6*	10-5*	9-5.30
Théâtre Antique	9-1*,2-6*	9-12*	10-12*,2-5*	9-1*,2-6*
Clôitre St-Trophime	9-7*	9-6*	10-5*	9-5.30
Cryptoportiques	9-12.30,2-5.30	9-12*	10-12*,2-5*	9-1*,2-6*
Thermes de Constantin	9-12.30,2-5.30	9-12*	10-12*,2-5*	9-1*,2-6*
Les Alyscamps	9-12.30,2-5.30	9-12*	10-12*,2-5*	9-1*,2-6*
Musée Réattu	10-12.30*,2-7* May-Sep (until 6* Mar-Oct); 1-5.30* Nov-Feb			
Musée Arles Antique	9-7 Mar-Oct; 10-5 Nov to Feb			

* last permitted entry is half an hour before this time

Verdon Gorges

Far inland from the touristed Côte d'Azur, Haute Provence is a realm of wild limestone *préalpes* or Alpine foothills. One such range, the Préalpes de Castellane, has been eroded along a geological fault line by the river Verdon to form a gorge over 700 m deep in parts of its 21-km length. This awesome gorge was an all but impenetrable barrier between north and south before the capricious Verdon was tamed for hydro-electric power. It was only fully explored in 1905 by speleologist Edouard Martel and the vertiginous north-bank road was not completed until 1973. Now known as a paradise for outdoor enthusiasts, the spectacular Grand Canyon du Verdon justly attracts climbers, canyonists, rafters and kayakers alike during summer. For the walker, its beauty can be enjoyed on waymarked paths that descend to the river on both sides of the gorge. Far less frequented is the wild mountain scenery in the remote country to the east of the Verdon, between the towns of Entrevaux and Castellane. This is a depopulated area where, sadly, walkers' refuges have closed in recent years for lack of patronage.

NOTES
Type: a 5-day walk - 93 km (58 miles)
Difficulty: strenuous with one long day
Start: Entrevaux (rail from Nice)
Finish: Moustiers-Ste-Marie (bus or taxi to Castellane, then bus to Nice)
Tourist Office: 04120 Castellane, ☏ 0492836114 Fax: 0492837689 E: office@castellane.org www.beyond.fr
Map: D&R 1:50000 *#19 En Haute Provence* or IGN 1:100000 *#61*
Best timing: Mar-Jun, Sep-Nov

Pic de Taloire

The walk begins at medieval Entrevaux, a 90-minute journey from Nice on the wonderful Train des Pignes. Travelling on this narrow-gauge railway line is a scenic expedition in itself, superb mountain vistas opening up as it wends its way through the valley of the river Var.

The route follows a section of the 1100-km-long GR4, one of France's first and longest *grandes randonnées* and provides some of the most singular walking in the south of France. The walk reaches some of Provence's most remote and photogenic *villages perchées* and lovely Moustiers-St-Marie provides a fitting finale.

Though not technically difficult, this walk is nonetheless challenging. A long first day, involving much height gain and a detour off the GR4 to tiny Soleilhas is made necessary by the lack of accommodation on the GR between Entrevaux and Castellane. Subsequent days, though shorter, also involve considerable height variations and the walk along the Sentier Martel negotiates several long tunnels (carry a torch) and metal ladders. These rigours are a small price to pay for the chance to encounter such magnificent scenery.

At river level, along the *Sentier Martel* >

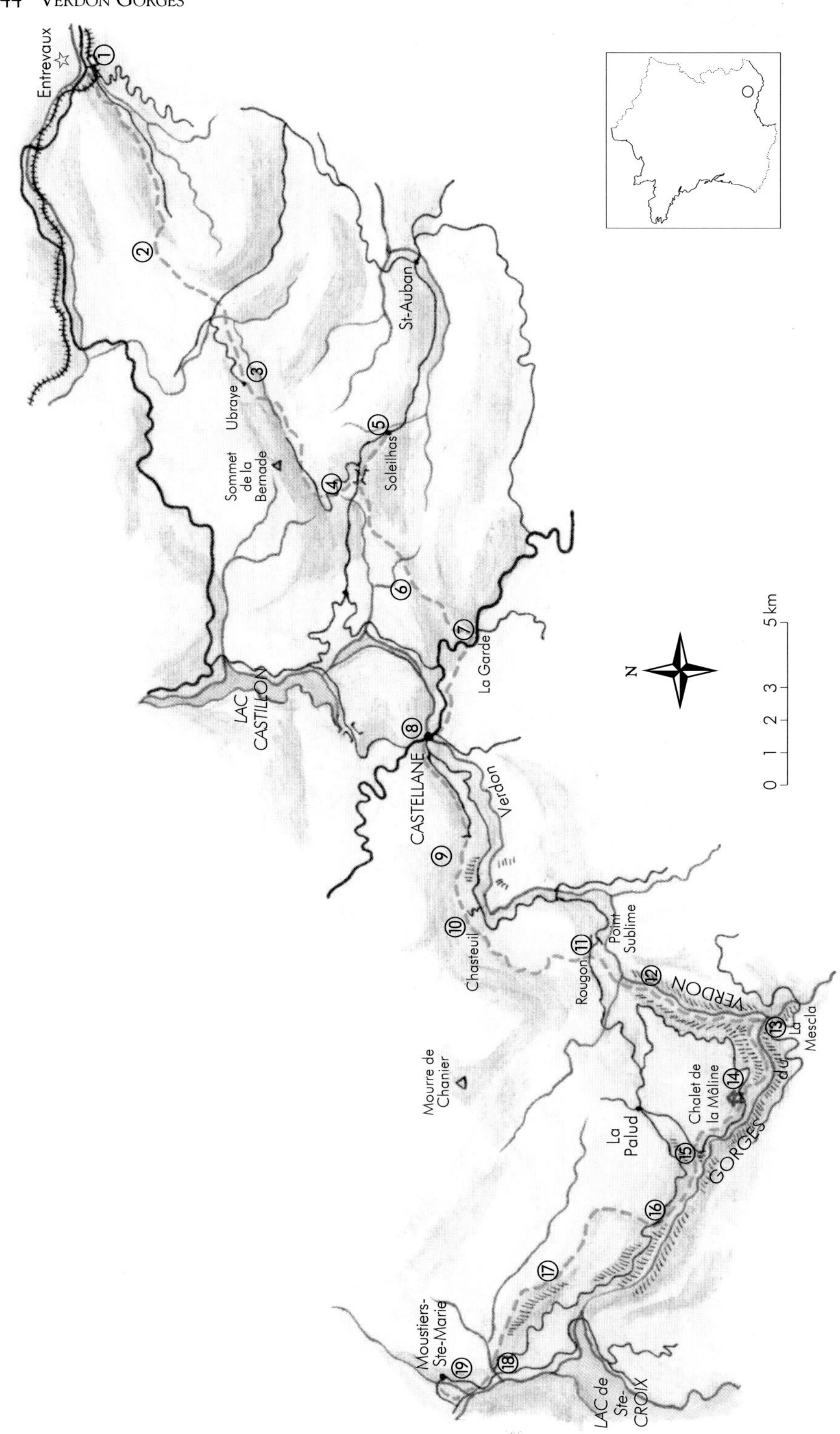
Entrevaux
Sommet de la Bernade
Ubraye
Soleilhas
St-Auban
LAC CASTILLON
La Garde
CASTELLANE
Verdon
Chasteuil
Rougon
Point Sublime
VERDON
La Mescla
Chalet de la Mâline
GORGES
La Palud
Mourre de Chanier
Moustiers-Ste-Marie
LAC de Ste-CROIX
N
0 1 2 3 5 km

DAY 1: ENTREVAUX to SOLEILHAS

From a fortified village you climb to a ridge, traversing the wooded hills between the rivers Var and Verdon. The hamlets en route serve as a reminder of the local population decline.

Distance 25.5 km (16 miles)
Time 9 hours
Notes leave early; take food and water

Our starting point is
① **Entrevaux**, set astride the Var beneath a spur of rock upon which perches its citadel. Once a frontier outpost on the old border between French Provence and the Duchy of Savoie, it was fortified by the military engineer Vauban in 1690 against invasion by the Duke. Vauban connected the citadel with the town via a walled walkway that zigzags up through twenty gateways. He also erected the town walls, entered through a gated drawbridge.

Leave Entrevaux on the D610 road to Bay and soon turn right on a tiled path. Note that the red-and-white GR waymarkings are poor until Bay. Keep straight on; do not cross a boardwalk over a gully. Cross a minor road and then another, continuing up. Turn right on a road then right onto a track up past a Spanish-style house. When the track deteriorates, take a path forking left, climbing above a ruin to turn right onto the road. Soon turn right off the road then quickly left on a poorly marked path (also a trail marked with a peak on a white disc) that zigzags uphill before entering oak woods. Join a broad track and, where it curves soon after, take a footpath (easily missed) right uphill. Reach a paved road and turn right uphill, turning off right onto a footpath at a house. Soon rejoin the road and follow it into **Bay**.

Entrevaux, on the Var river

Continue to the chapel of St Claude and, after 1 km on the paved road, turn right uphill on a stony path. The climb continues through oak wood to the ridge top (the Travers du Content) before dropping through coppiced beech woods to a clearing and shrine at the
② **Col de St-Jeannet**. Turn left, descending less steeply; to the right are fine views of mountains and, soon, of the **Chapelle de St-Jean du Desert**. Walk past a small spring, the first water supply since Entrevaux, and over a landslide to a signpost where you turn sharp left, signed GR4 to Ubraye. This skirts left of a ravine and reaches a shrine at the **Col de St-Jean** where you turn left downhill. At a fork, keep right and look for waymarks, descending a pretty valley to reach the Chapelle Notre-Dame de la Riviere and cross

< The remote village of Ubraye

The descent to Soleilhas

a stone bridge over a stream. Turn right on the D10; after 0.5 km, cross a bridge and take the second path left. This climbs to ③ **Ubraye**, passing the village's old communal oven. After five hours of walking, the water pump at Ubraye makes a scenic spot for a late and well-deserved lunch.

Leave on the road, passing the church. Before the sign that marks the village limits, turn left along a car track and take the gravel track right at a cross. Head towards buildings and climb on a path up to the le Touyet road, with a view of Ubraye behind you. Follow the road briefly left before again leaving it left at a hairpin to climb steeply. The path eventually levels to skirt a mountain then climbs again to a cross from where Le Touyet can be seen. Keep on, contouring the hillside, and turn left at the road. The GR4 follows the road through tiny **Le Touyet** (where there's a public phone) and turns left onto a broad track. Pass a shrine, continuing uphill until a hairpin (25 minutes from Le Touyet) where you take a footpath left at a GR4 sign to descend a picturesque gully. Cross a stream and climb steeply to level ground beneath the peak of Picogu. The mountain scenery is dramatic, with the peaks of Bernade and Gourre and their connecting ridge standing imposingly to the right.

The path becomes indistinct (look for waymarks on rocks) as it climbs gradually through treeless meadows to the broad ④ **Col de Vauplane**, at 1650 m the highest point reached on this walk. Head for the ski complex and reach the road, following it down until it starts to zigzag. Watch for a poorly signed path off right and immediately fork left down into a ravine. Care is required navigating here; yellow and blue waymarks are also encountered. Presently you reach **Chapelle de St Barnabe** nestled in beautiful surrounds. Just below the chapel, the GR path diverts on a grassy track to the right but to detour to Soleilhas you continue on an unsurfaced track straight ahead, crossing the Soleilhas road (D102) at a metal cross. Keep downhill on a fairly steep, stony path (marked with orange dots) through beautiful mountain scenery, for 2 km to reach ⑤ **Soleilhas**. Soleilhas offers one hotel-restaurant (open all year) and a gîte d'étape.

DAY 2: SOLEILHAS to CASTELLANE

A short walk as you descend easily to the aqua Verdon river, leaving you time to explore the thriving town of Castellane and surrounds.

Distance 15 km (9.5 miles)
Time 4 hours 30

Leave Soleilhas by retracing your steps up the path to the junction with the D102; follow this towards Castellane for 750 m to where the GR4 comes in right from the Chapelle de St Barnabe. At a sign, take the waymarked track, veering left and initially following the line of the road. Follow this level forest track for several km as it contours around the Crête du Teillon, gaining good views of Demandolx village across a ravine. Later there are views of the dams of Chaudanne and Castillon, two of the artificial lakes harnessing the Verdon for water and hydroelectricity, and superb views of the mountains beyond. Leave the track on a downhill section, veering left onto a footpath through bushes. Cross a stream and return to the track, following it to emerge at ⑥ the **Clot d'Agnon** ruins at a pylon. Care is required to navigate here; at the second pylon (where cables change direction), a shorter GR4 variant descends to Castellane. The main GR4 route via La Garde continues ahead, less steep and narrowing to a footpath. This descends through woods to reach the N85 (Route Napoleon) at

⑦ **La Garde**. This tiny village, dating from the 12th century, was once guarded by a château from which it derives its name. The church of Notre-Dame des Ormeaux was built on the château's ruins. Take time to explore the buildings to the south of the N85.

The GR4 follows the main road out of La Garde and forks left off the road soon after a chapel. A path descends to a track where you turn left, descending the Ravin de Destourbes and crossing a stream to join a minor road. Continue for 2 km, then turn left onto the N85 for a 1.5 km road walk. Leave the N85 to cross the Verdon on the 15th-century footbridge, skirting the base of a cliff to enter

⑧ **Castellane**. Though Castellane itself is invisible from a distance, you will have seen the extraordinary limestone outcrop that overlooks it, known simply as Le Roc (see the end of this chapter). Castellane teems with tourists and lovers of the outdoors in summer. There's a tourist office here, along with banks, hotels and other facilities.

Cadières de Brandis

Castellane's medieval bridge

DAY 3: CASTELLANE to Pt. SUBLIME

Magnificent walking, traversing twisted limestone formations north of the river and ancient perched villages on a Roman road.

Distance	18 km (11 miles)
Time	5 hours 30
Notes	take lunch supplies

From the main bridge, take the road along the Verdon's north bank. Turn right at a T-junction and left onto the D952, soon veering right on the minor C8 road to Villars-Brandis. It's worth turning to admire the receding views of Castellane and Le Roc. Near the end of the hamlet of La Colle the GR4 leaves the C8 left over a bridge on a track. This contours around a mountain, providing striking views of the river below. The GR4 route now passes beneath the hamlet of Villars and the ruins of Brandis (it once climbed to visit them). The path contours beneath dramatic terrain, most strikingly, the serrated pinnacles of

⑨ the **Cadières de Brandis** silhouetted against the horizon. Hardy hikers with 6 hours to spare could make an ascent of the Cadières (*chairs* in Provençal) by detouring to Villars. Also on view here are two imposing peaks that

The village of Chasteuil

squeeze the Verdon through its first gorge: the Pic de Taloire with its summit chapel on the opposite bank and an unnamed peak on which the Chapelle St-Jean is visible. It can be reached in a 10-minute detour left about 0.5 km after the Villars-Brandis junction.

The GR4 continues past a right-forking path to Blieux and a water source to reach the tiny perched village of
⑩ **Chasteuil**, a cluster of golden buildings set amidst mountain scenery. It has a *buvette* and a *crêperie* (both open only in summer) and chambres d'hôtes with meals. From here, the path climbs gradually through forest to the Col de Coron, passing left of the Rocher de Baux. At a ruin, a signpost directs you to veer left for Rougon. Gradually the scenery alters; you are now on the **Plateau de Suech**, a lonely moor, denuded of trees, where sheep are grazed. At the far edge of the plateau is another junction: keep straight on towards pylons. Descend on a broad, stony path, contouring right of the Barre de Catalan. You soon glimpse the perched village of
⑪ **Rougon**, standing sentinel over the entrance to the Grand Canyon. At a shrine a path diverts left steeply down to the village. Overlooked by medieval ruins, Rougon is extremely photogenic in late afternoon sun. It has the only shop before La Mâline. It's a steep 15-minute descent from Rougon to the D952 where you turn left to reach the Auberge du Point Sublime, the only hotel in the vicinity.

DAY 4: POINT SUBLIME to LA MÂLINE

An amazing day's walk through the gorges on the famous Sentier Martel, a footpath hewn out of the rock face in a triumph of engineering.

Distance	12 km (7.5 miles)
Time	7 hours
Notes	take lunch and water

Today, the GR4 follows the course of the **Sentier Martel**, the classic walk through the Grand Canyon du Verdon and named after the speleologist who explored it. A picnic lunch may be ordered the night before if staying at the auberge. River water should be purified and you will need a torch. Walkers should check weather conditions and river flow before setting out. Before commencing, it is well worth crossing the fissured limestone sheets of the Plateau des Lauves to the Point Sublime Belvédère for a splendid view of the ⑫ **Couloir Samson**, a *couloir* or corridor at

Rougon, perched above the gorge

The Verdon cuts through the gorges

the mouth of the Grand Canyon 190 m below.

From the auberge, walk along the D952 towards Castellane. After 50 m the GR4 path veers sharply right downhill. Soon the GR49 forks left; continue right beneath the cliffline down to a car park. Detour briefly from here through a rock tunnel to view the torrent of Le Baou as it cascades into the Verdon. Steps from the car park lead across a footbridge over the Baou. After climbing more steps you reach the entrance to the **Tunnel du Baou**, 670 m long and 3 m in diameter, that cuts through the narrows of the Couloir Samson. Several 'windows' in the left wall let you see the river below. After 400 m, a steep stairway leads down to the river at the mouth of the **Baume aux Pigeons**, a cave at the foot of a 350-m cliff through which the river flows. The tunnel ends about 250 m after this detour and is soon followed by the much shorter Tunnel de Trescaire. After this you bypass a third tunnel and for the next few hours remain within earshot and often in sight of the river. Watch for rock formations known as the **Tours de Trescaire** on the other bank.

The path descends to a pebbly beach, an idyllic spot for lunch. After this it soon begins a steep switchback climb to bypass a rockface, reaching 200 m above river level before descending beneath impressive overhangs. The path again climbs to reach a series of metal ladders ascending the **Brèche Imbert**, a narrow cleft between rockface and crag. At the top, there is a wonderful viewpoint to the left. The path begins another descent and soon reaches a sign indicating the halfway point of the Sentier Martel. Below here the Verdon changes direction sharply at
⑬ **La Mescla** (*mixing* in Provençal), the confluence with the river Artuby. A side path takes you down to this beautiful spot (20 minutes return). Further on, the main path descends to the river and ascends steeply once more (via fixed cable and short ladders) and continues up and down for some time before starting the final ascent out of the gorge.

Before this ascent, a junction indicates the beginning of the GR99 that descends to the river. The **Passerelle de l'Estelliér**, a footbridge over the Verdon on the GR99, was washed away in 1994 but has now been rebuilt: you might consider a detour here along the south bank on the **Sentier d'Imbut** (see notes at the end of this chapter). The GR4 climbs steeply away from the river, winding up to another ladder and then to the cliff top.

A farm building

⑭ **Chalet de la Mâline** (☏ 0492773805) comes into sight as the path contours the hillside. The chalet is superbly positioned on the rim of the gorge with breathtaking views from its terrace. If the walkers' chalet is full, you can telephone for a taxi for the 8 km along the D23 road to La Palud, a village catering to adventure enthusiasts.

DAY 5: LA MÂLINE to MOUSTIERS

After a balcony path, we climb to gain more views of the gorges and of the lake into which the Verdon flows. The destination is Moustiers-Sainte-Marie, a golden village backed by cliffs.

Distance	22 km (13.7 miles)
Time	8 hours
Notes	take lunch and water

Take the D23 left from the chalet to walk along the Route des Crêtes, passing the ⑮ **Belvédères d'Imbut**, where the gorge narrows and the Verdon disappears beneath a chaos of fallen rocks, **du Maugue** and **du Baucher**. After 4.5 km of road walking, at the Ravin de Mainmort, turn left onto the **Sentier du Bastidon** (white stripe waymarks). This descends in steep switchbacks and then becomes a lovely balcony trail, passing below brown zebra-striped cliffs. The path continues for 5 km, offering magnificent canyon vistas.

After reaching the ⑯ **Ravin de Ferné**, begin a zigzagging climb to reach the D952 at a bend by the Belvédère de Maireste car park. Take the right fork of the road and, at the next hairpin, leave the road up left on a steep path following the Ravin du Busc. After 500 m you reach a path fork; the left fork is the quicker way to rejoin the GR4, meeting it at a forest road. Follow this left and, at a junction, take the GR4 straight ahead over the Plain de Barbin to eventually reach the Col de Plein Voir (or go left over the Crêtes de Plein Voir on a longer but more scenic waymarked route to the *col*). A little way on, near the first of two pylons, is ⑰ **an excellent viewpoint** of the Lac de Sainte-Croix. The path now descends under the second pylon and reaches the Col de l'Ane, 'the pass of the donkey'. Ignore side paths, remaining on the ridge to climb the Signal de l'Ourbes, the highest point of the day's walk from which there are further splendid views. Descend to a plateau at the end of which begins the long descent of the Crêtes de l'Ourbes to the D952. The winding route is spectacular, offering close views of rock pinnacles and more distant views of the lake and the Valensole with possible glimpses of the Luberon and Lure mountains. The path crosses the D952 several times as it winds

The Maire valley below Moustiers

The Styx, on the Sentier d'Imbut >

downhill, eventually following the road right for 500 m towards Moustiers, passing the ⑱ **Chapelle St-Pierre**. Turn left onto the Chemin de Peyrengue and, soon after crossing a stream, turn right at a T-junction onto a gravel road through a meadow. The contrast between this gentle countryside and the limestone mountains just traversed is intense. At a path junction the GR4 heads sharply left, bypassing Moustiers, but you cross the stream on concrete stepping stones to pick up a path marked with a yellow stripe; this soon becomes a minor road ascending to

⑲ **Moustiers-Sainte-Marie**. This lovely and lively town is a fitting end to the walk. It is an astonishing sight, overlooking a fertile valley yet backed up against twin limestone mountains. The waters of le Riou cascade down the ravine, bisecting the village. High up on a ledge is the restored chapel of **Notre-Dame de Beauvoir**, a pilgrimage place since medieval times and built on a site of a 5th-century chapel. It is reached on a steep path with stations of the cross and defensive doorways, and the view over the roofscape to the Maire valley is magnificent. Above the chapel a gilded star hangs from a 227-metre iron chain fastened to the rock on either side of the Riou gorge. This improbable feat was first performed by a knight to fulfil a vow on his safe return from the crusades. The centrepiece of the village is the 12th-century Notre-Dame church with its three-storey bell-tower in Lombard Romanesque style. During summer, tourists come here to buy blue-glazed *faience* pottery, made in *ateliers* or workshops.

LONG DISTANCE STAGES

km	time	location	acc
		Entrevaux	H G
25.5	9h	Soleilhas	H G
11	3h	La Garde	H G
4.5	1h30	Castellane	H G
10.3	3h30	Chasteuil	C
7.3	1h45	Rougon	G (summer)
0.3	0h15	Point Sublime	H
12	7h	La Maline	R
(8)		(La Palud)	H G A
22	8h	Moustiers	H G

SIDE WALKS ALONG THE WAY

Le Roc above Castellane

While in Castellane, it's almost obligatory to climb up Le Roc, the limestone outcrop rearing up behind the town. It bears the 18th-century chapel of Notre-Dame-du-Roc where once there was a Roman fort. A steep path to the chapel, starting behind the Romanesque church of St-Victor, is lined with stations of the cross and offers wonderful views. It passes above the Tour Pentagonale and a section of ruined 14th-century fortifications, built when the inhabitants of Castellane moved down off the rock into the valley. *Allow 1 hour.*

Sentier d'Imbut

Stay an extra night at La Mâline chalet-refuge to take this most beautiful path into the canyon. Retrace your step on the last part of Day 4, descending the gorge to reach the GR99 junction. Contine descending to cross the Verdon on the new Estelliér bridge, turning right to follow the river downstream on the Sentier d'Imbut. After an hour of riverside walking, you reach the rocky chaos of the Styx, and about 25 minutes later, l'Imbut or 'funnel'. A climb over boulders brings you to Baou Béni, the 'blessed rock'. Return by the same route. *Allow 6 hours.*

— THE MERCANTOUR —

The Parc National du Mercantour is full of breathtaking mountain scenery. Here is a landscape dotted with glacial lakes, rugged granite peaks, high meadows and deep valleys that carve the park into distinctive areas. The mountains that help form the Italian frontier and the Mercantour massif, while not high by Alpine standards, provide challenging mountain walking.

The park was created in 1979, its unpopulated central zone lying high in the Alpes-Maritimes, the southernmost massif of the French Alps. Its enjoys long hours of sunshine and the combination of Alpine and Mediterranean climate makes for an exceptional richness of flora and fauna. Indeed, the park contains some 2,000 plant species, almost half of France's total. The park's emblem is the rare *Saxifraga Florulenta* with its striking spikes of pinkish flowers. Wildlife abounds: chamois, marmots and reintroduced ibex above the treeline; stags, roe deer and wild boar in the woodlands. Wolves have recently returned to the area from Italy! The skies are dominated by the golden eagle and bearded vulture or lammergeier, another successful reintroduction.

Chamois near Refuge de Nice

NOTES
Type: A 5-day walk - 48 km (30 miles)
Difficulty: medium-strenuous; steep inclines
Start: Le Boréon (buses from Nice)
Finish: La Bollène-Vésubie (bus to Nice)
Park Office: 23 Rue d'Italie, 06006 Nice
☏ 0493167888 Fax: 0493887905
E: mercantour@wanadoo.fr
www.parc-mercantour.fr
Maps: IGN 1:25000 #3741OT & 3841OT
Best timing: Jun-Oct

The park is crossed by long-distance paths: the GR5 as it heads for Nice, the GR52 and the GR52A or *Panoramique du Mercantour*. Our five-day walk in the park's east combines sections of the latter two GRs to form a near-circular, high-level route connecting the upper valleys of the Vésubie, Boréon, Madone de Fenestre, Gordolasque, Valmasque and the Vallée des Merveilles. None of the stages is over long and some could be combined by the energetic to free up extra days for side trips, of which two are described, both starting from refuges.

The walk starts at bucolic Le Boréon, 8 km up valley from St-Martin-Vésubie. Getting there involves a twice-daily bus #730 from Nice to St-Martin, followed by a pleasant road walk or taxi trip. After Le Boréon, all accommodation is in mountain refuges. The isolated Refuge de Nice has a shorter season than the others; if it is closed, Days 2 and 3 could be combined into one long day, increasing the level of difficulty.

Walking mostly above the tree line, you will encounter the desolate beauty of these mountains, particularly around the Nice refuge and in the Vallée des Merveilles. This long and isolated valley is now a protected site, its 'marvels' consisting of over 36,000 rock engravings, carved around 3,500 years ago by early Bronze Age peoples. Many engravings may only be viewed with an official guide but exploring this valley will be a highlight of your walk.

Vallée des Merveilles >

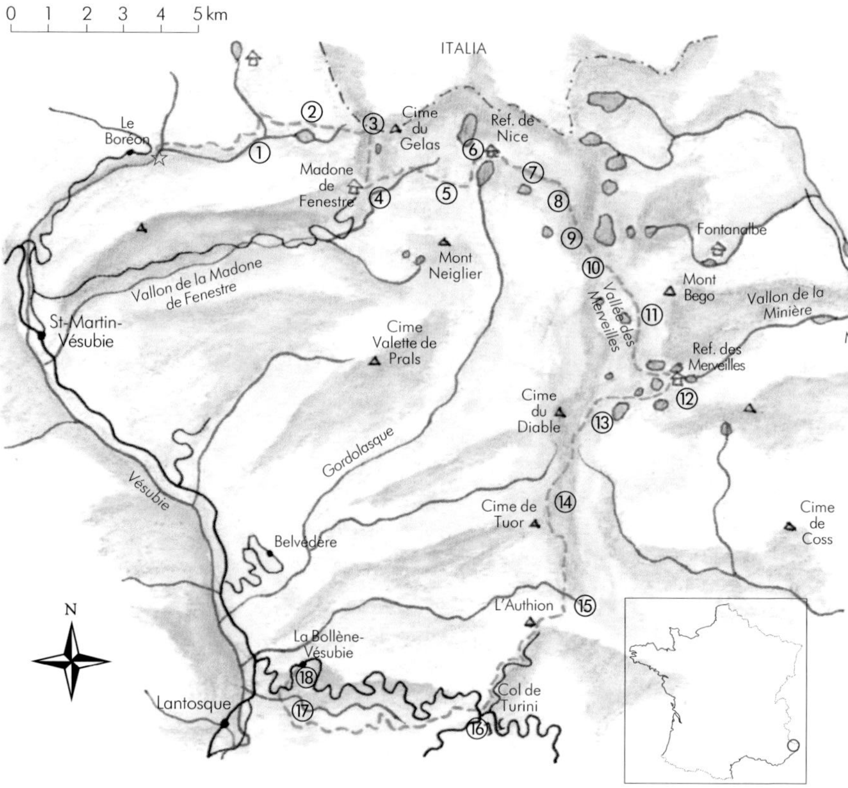

DAY 1: Le BORÉON to M.de FENESTRE

This day offers a wonderful introduction to the Mercantour, with pretty woodland, alpine lakes and dramatic mountain scenery.

Distance	8.5 km (5.25 miles)
Time	5 hours 45
Notes	take lunch supplies or detour to Refuge de Cougourde

Pick up the GR52 path (marked red-and-white) just above the gîte d'étape at Le Boréon. This climbs steeply to a junction at *balise* (signpost) #371. Turn right and keep uphill into pine woods. The path crosses two streams and traverses the northern slope of the valley to reach, after an hour, a junction near the Vacherie de Boréon.

Follow the path signed to Lac de Trécolpas and keep left, heading uphill. During a climb, a footpad right offers a short detour to view the

< Autumnal myrtille

① **Peïrastrèche cascade**, a name derived from the Provençal words meaning 'narrow rocks'. Climb steeply past the falls and then past a footbridge, where a balise points straight on. The valley opens up as you cross rock-strewn pasture, with views up the narrow valleys of Sangué and Haut Boréon and of the surrounding mountains, including the dramatic Tête de Trécolpas.

At signpost #425, a left turn would lead to the Refuge de Cougourde (so-called because the nearby peak of Cougourde is shaped like a marrow); we continue on the GR52 heading right, crossing the Boréon torrent on a footbridge. On the ridge looming ahead is the pass you will cross. First though, enjoy a rest by the enchanting

② **Lac de Trécolpas**, a jewel of a lake set in a hanging cirque, frequented by chamois, marmots and deer.

The path skirts the northern edge of the lake and heads for a dip in the skyline, climbing steeply via a series of switchbacks where snow sometimes lingers. At the Pas de Ladres sign #428, take the path left, signed to Col de Fenestre. (If you want to reach the night's destination more quickly, continue on the more direct GR52.) A half hour's walk along this balcony path brings you to signpost #369, from where you should make the short detour up to the dramatic

The stream of the Boréon

③ **Col de Fenestre** (2474 m) on the Italian border. This is one of the great passes of the Alps, used by the Romans and those that followed as a trade route between Piemonte and Provence. Today it is the route of the long-distance Via Alpina. The nearby blockhouse and ruined fortifications are used by ibex or *bouquetin* for shelter. On clear days, you can see north to Monte Rosa in Switzerland.

Return to the signpost and take the path steeply downhill to pass **Lac de Fenestre** on a well-laid track, and descend the grassy slopes below the needles of Caire de la Madone. After crossing the Magnin spring, rejoin the GR52 at junction #368 and continue down to reach the CAF refuge (☏ 0493028319) at

④ **Madone de Fenestre**. This tiny hamlet was once the site of a Roman temple to Jupiter. A sighting of the Virgin Mary prompted the rebuilding of a chapel here and a statue of the Virgin said to have been made by St Luke was treasured within. Although the chapel was burnt

< Lac de Trécolpas

Lac Niré

during the French Revolution, the statue survived. A pilgrimage procession now takes the statue for safe-keeping in St-Martin-Vésubie each September and returns it in May.

If you have extra time available, you might want to spend a day walking the Lacs de Prals circuit described at the end of this chapter.

DAY 2: MADONE de FENESTRE to REFUGE de NICE

A short walk takes you over the rugged Pas du Mont Colomb and down to a lakeside refuge where chamois are often to be seen.

Distance 5 km (3 miles)
Time 3 hours 30

Between the chapel and the Hôtel de Pélerins, follow the signpost to cross the river by the *vacherie* (cowshed), then turn left at signpost #359. Some ten minutes further on, #367 directs you left, along the GR52, and you head back up the valley, over grassy pasture dotted with larches. The massif of Gélas dominates the skyline to the northeast. The path veers east at a spur and you climb across the base of Caire de la Madone and then up the Vallon du Mont-Colomb.

Refuge de Nice

Pass the small lake and continue on, climbing steeply up over scree, with the narrow pass in view. About two hours' walking brings you to the dramatic

⑤ **Pas du Mont Colomb**, a 2548-m-high gap between the peaks of Colomb and Ponset. Pause for breath before descending the gully over the pass: it is very steep and rocky and requires more scrambling than walking.

At the bottom, you reach balise #416. This is a possible departure point for a short detour down the Vallon de la Gordolasque to the cascade of L'Estrech, or for a longer detour down valley and then up to Lac Autier. Whatever your choice, return to this junction and follow the GR52 towards Refuge de Nice.

The route ascends past the *barrage*, a dam wall which has created the artificial Lac de la Fous. The path stays on the western bank, crosses several streams draining into it and climbs to the small

⑥ **Refuge de Nice**, set on a knoll on the southwestern spur of Mont Clapier. The CAF refuge (☏ 0493046274) is in a good location for an afternoon of leisurely animal-and-mountain watching.

DAY 3: REFUGE de NICE to REFUGE des MERVEILLES

This day's walk entails ascents over two high passes, amply rewarded by stunning mountain lakes and ancient engravings.

Distance	8.5 km (5.25 miles)
Time	5 hours
Notes	take lunch supplies

From the signpost #417 by the refuge, take the path signed to Baisse du Basto which climbs up to the high pasture of Clos de Roquebilière. From here you climb up into the Vallon du Niré and, after half an hour from the refuge, you reach the banks of

⑦ **Lac Niré**, a deep, circular pool at 2253 m. This is the first of a string of lakes that you follow up valley, below the Tête du Lac Autier looming to the south.

The path veers southeast to cross the stream and waymarks guide you up a long and arduous climb, zigzagging past large boulders, with no clear destination to beckon you on. After several

Lac des Merveilles

stony gullies, you finally gain

⑧ **Baisse du Basto**, at 2693 m, the highest point on this adventure.

Continue over the pass, directed towards Baisse de Valmasque, which you can see on the southeast horizon. Waymarks lead past a small,

⑨ **hidden lake**, tucked away to the left. The next section of the route is over large rocks with few waymarks; aim for a large one painted on a vertical rockface on the right-hand side of the valley.

From here you skirt above the southern end of the long Lac du Basto and then zigzag up the inevitable ascent to the

⑩ **Baisse de Valmasque** (2549 m), with Mont Bego looming to the southeast and a long view down the Vallée des Merveilles.

After a rest, follow the GR52 as the good path zigzags steeply downhill and then continues to descend more gently. A signboard alerts you to look out for engravings along the path. You pass intermittent upper lakes and then arrive at the delightful

⑪ **Lac des Merveilles**, at 2294 m. Beyond this, the path reaches a huge rockface bearing an 1829 bandit's signature, amongst many

Morning mist below Pas du Diable

others. Some rocks along the path have a wonderful green hue due to their mineral composition. The GR has been rerouted to stay west of Lac Long Superieur, passing path junction #93 and bringing you to

⑫ **Refuge des Merveilles**, a large and popular CAF refuge (☏ 0493046464) where you will likely meet fellow walkers from various countries. If you have extra time available, you might want to add the two-day Fontenalbe circuit described at the end of this chapter.

DAY 4: REFUGE des MERVEILLES to COL de TURINI

A string of lakes leads you up to the eerily-named Pas du Diable, from where you gently descend along a ridgeline, eventually leaving the GR52 for accommodation.

Distance	15 km (9.3 miles)
Time	5 hours
Notes	carry lunch; you could start early and reach La Bollène-Vésubie

From the refuge, climb up past the boulders to signpost #92 and follow the GR52 signed to Lac du Diable. You ascend past a series of dammed lakes – Fourca, du Trem and then de la Muta – as you head southwest. Near the top of the valley are the small Lacs du Diable, one of which is sometimes dry.

At #404, the GR veers left, signed to Col de Raus. Pass over the rounded

⑬ **Pas du Diable** at balise #405 (2430 m or 2440 m, depending on which sign you trust). From here you descend, at first via hairpin bends and then gently traversing grassy slopes to reach Baisse Cavaline.

The path veers southwest to traverse the slope of Cime de Raus and arrive at

⑭ **Col de Raus**, balise #406, below a gun emplacement. Continue on, below the Cime de Tuor, to reach a grassy ridge known as the Crête de l'Ortiguie. Follow this down to another saddle, Baisse de St-Véran, below more fortifications. Looking west, down into the Vallon de Caïros, you can see a grass-roofed *vacherie* on a spur just below you. From here the path drops just off the ridgeline and traverses its western flank to reach

⑮ **Pointe des Trois Communes**, where you leave the GR52. Head 500 m west to the main peak of l'Authion where there is a ruined fort, the site of heavy fighting in April 1945.

< Monte Bego

Continue southwest along the ridgeline to reach an orientation table at the end of the D68 road. Follow this down to the

⑯ **Col de Turini**, a base for skiers and cyclists, where there are three hotels, including Les Chamois (☏ 0493915831).

DAY 5: COL de TURINI to La BOLLÈNE-VÉSUBIE

A short walk through the forest of Turini brings you down into the Vesubie valley, where you can end your journey at La Bollène-Vésubie or the larger town of Lantosque.

Distance 10.5 km (6.5 miles)
Time 2hours 45

From the Col, pick up the GR52A path, waymarked red-and-white, to follow a forest track heading west. It traverses a steep, north-facing slope, covered with spruce and fir of the Forêt de Turini.

Follow the track for about 7 km to the Cime de l'Escaletta. On the spur, you come to a

⑰ **junction of paths**, where you have a choice. The 52A-variant leads south then west down to the town of Lantosque, on the main Vésubie valley road. The GR52A descends north and then west in hairpin bends, crosses a stream and then climbs to the village of

⑱ **La Bollène-Vésubie**, where there is accommodation and a bus stop. Beyond this, should you wish to add another day-and-a-half of walking, the GR52A continues up the side of the Vésubie valley, through the village of Bélvèdere and then on to St-Martin-Vésubie, near your starting point.

LONG DISTANCE STAGES

km	time	location	acc
		Le Boréon	G,H
8.5	5h45	Madone de Fenestre	R
5	3h30	Refuge de Nice	R
8.5	5h	Refuge des Merveilles	R
15	5h	Col de Turini	C,H
10.5	2h45	La Bollène-Vésubie	C,H

A stone building down valley

OTHER WALKS ALONG THE WAY

Lacs de Prals

This circuit walk from Madone de Fenestre takes you up through charming *mélézin* or larch forests and over high pasture to a string of tiny lakes, then up to a grassy peak and back down via another pass. As part of the route is outside of the national park, note that hunting is allowed September-October. You'll need lunch supplies.

Between the chapel and Hôtel de Pélerins, follow the sign to cross the river by the *vacherie* (cowshed) and turn left at balise#359, on the path to Baisse de Cinq Lacs. Ten minutes on, balise#367 directs you right, leaving the GR52.

Climb on a stony footpath, following cairns up past ancient larches to reach a grassy *plan* (flat) high in the Vallon du Ponset. Mont Caval looms on your right. Cross the boggy plateau and climb to a large cairn at the Baisse de Cinq Lacs (2335 m), from where you can see several of the lakes in question.

The path drops down to the lakes: a wonderful place to swim on a hot day or just to enjoy the reflections. Cows and marmots are likely to be found nearby. The path continues on, marked by cairns, and descends below a spur. Watch out for a footpad forking left that traverses the slope; if you miss it, descend to a national park sign and reascend on the path to Baisse de Prals. Pick up the path marked by yellow stripes; it zigzags up to a junction with a view down into the Gordolasque valley.

Fork right, signed to Cime Valette di Prals and climb the ridgeline to the summit at 2496 m, marked by a cairn and a large metal cross. Enjoy the panorama, which extends over the Gordolasque, the high Vésubie and, on a clear day, as far as the sea.

Continue ahead, following the yellow stripes to drop slightly and traverse the sheltered side of the ridgeline. This passes below a cairn marking the Tête de la Lave to reach junction #298. Turn sharply left downhill towards Baisse de Férisson, dropping below a spur and gaining a view down valley.

The path drops to an unsigned junction; turn right to continue in the same direction, crossing a grassy slope dotted with *alpenrose*. Reach Baisse de Férisson (*balise* #297), marked by a large wooden cross, from where there's a view over the Madone to the cirque of Gélas. Turn sharp right and descend a steep slope clothed in *myrtilles*, alpenrose and larches.

Keep straight on at signpost #354. At #362 you re-enter the national park by crossing a footbridge on the path to Madone de Fenestre. At #361 this reaches the road; turn right and follow it uphill. Just before the bridge, turn right onto a gravel track, passing the *vacherie* and returning to the refuge. *Allow 6-7 hours.*

A Bronze Age sun

Lacs de Prals

Fontanalbe

A visit to Fontanalbe valley, rich in prehistoric engravings, could be made on a two-day loop from Refuge des Merveilles. Alternatively, you could use this route to exit the Mercantour at St-Dalmas-de-Tende, on the rail line.

From Refuge des Merveilles, walk back up the valley, pausing to inspect engravings, to Baisse de Valmasque then descend towards Lac du Basto. Fork right before the lake and then right again to climb to the Baisse de Fontanalbe. Descend to the lovely **Lac Vert** and then continue on to visit the Lacs Jumeaux before reaching the privately operated Refuge de Fontanalbe (☎ 0493048919). *Allow 5-6 hours.*

On the second day, return towards Lac Vert but fork left to climb to Baisse de Vallaurette. Descend to Gias de Vallaurette; here you can turn right on a path leading up Val d'Enfer to Refuge des Merveilles (or turn left to descend along Vallon de la Minière to Lac des Mesches and then by road for 8 km to St-Dalmas). *Allow 3 hr 30; allow 5 hrs to St-Dalmas-de-Tende.*

Marseille & the Calanques

Unlike many of the towns and cities along the Côte d'Azur, Marseille has an immense amount of character. Some think it has a little too much character – the high rate of poverty here leads to some petty theft – but this city is also full of history, fine weather, friendly people and excellent seafood: good reasons to come and spend your money here. It is also kissed by some of France's most stunning coastline.

Greeks from Phocaea settled here in around 600 BC, calling their colony Massilia. After backing the ill-fated Pompey, it was seized by Caesar's forces in 49 BC and lost most of its fleet and trade as punishment, eventually falling into decline. Its fortunes recovered somewhat in the 10th century and it played an active role in the Crusades. It was ransacked by the Aragonese in 1423 and was passed onto the kingdom of France along with the rest of Provence in 1481. The Marseillais, however, were a rebellious lot and resisited French rule until Louis XIV imposed it more firmly in 1660, building fortifications to control them.

Greater tragedy overtook the city in 1720 when the plague, brought by boat from the Levant, killed half of its population. It was followed by a series of severe winters that ruined the harvests and led to starvation for the poor. The Revolution had great support from Marseille: its 500 or so volunteers who marched to Paris singing the battle song of the army of the Rhine gave France its national anthem.

NOTES

Getting there: rail from Avignon or Nice; shuttle from airport 20 km NW

Tourist Office: 4 La Canebiere, 13001
☏ 0491138900 Fax: 0491138920
E: info@marseille-tourisme.com
www.marseille-tourisme.com

Markets: Place des Capucins M-Sat 8-7; seafood: Quai des Belges M-Sat 8-1

The 19th century brought a long-overdue period of peace for Marseille and trade boomed, assisted by the opening of the Suez Canal in 1869. The city was caught up in turmoil once more during WWII when it was bombarded first by the Germans and Italians and later by the Allies. Today Marseille has an exotic air, due in no small part to its history of migrants from Mediterranean, Arab and African lands.

Astoundingly close to the bustle of Marseille are a limestone massif and strip of coastline known as Les Calanques: the Provençal word *calanque* refers to a steep, narrow inlet and there are many of these cutting into the white cliffs. Here sparkling, emerald seas lap against narrow beaches backed by towering white rock formations and the combination is sublime.

The area is protected, with limited road access, but a GR footpath traverses the Calanques, requiring two days to walk from the point south of Marseille west to the charming port of Cassis. As there is no accommodation along the way, you'll need to make transport plans, but the determined will be well rewarded for their efforts.

< Marseille's Vieux Port

Calanque de la Mounine >

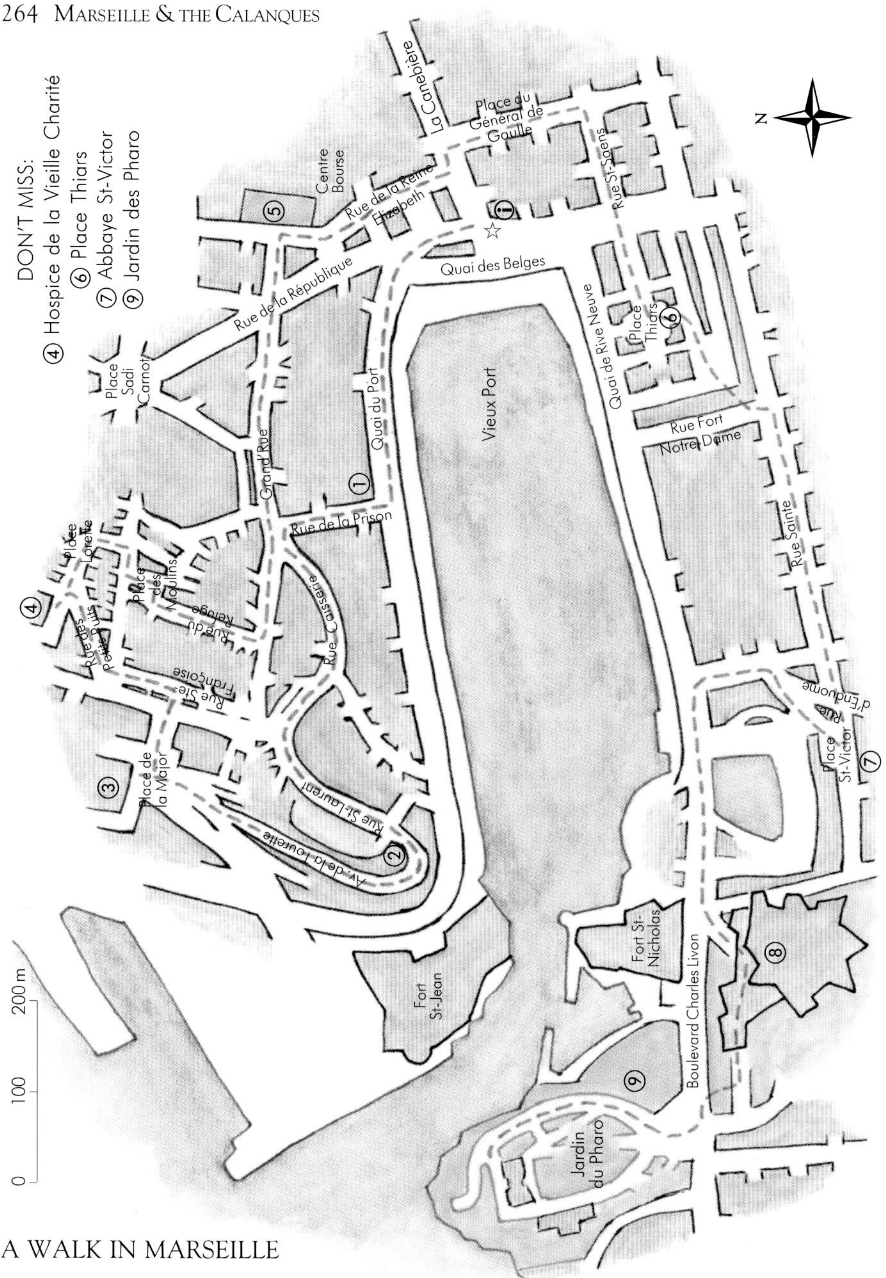

A WALK IN MARSEILLE

This walk around the Vieux Port covers two walks established by the city's tourist office; watch for a red line marked on the ground.

The tourist office is located at the head of the Vieux Port, in La Canebière, the main artery of Marseille. Follow Quai du Port around the ancient harbour to reach the 17th-century

① **Hôtel de Ville**. This was one of three buildings spared by the Nazis in 1943 when they dynamited the Panier quarter, which had become a refuge for the Resistance. In the post-war rubble, archaeologists uncovered a Roman warehouse; it can be seen at the nearby **Musée des Docks Romains** in Place Vivaux, off to the left as you walk up Rue de la Prison. As you climb this street you pass **Maison Diamantée**, built in 1570, another structure spared from the massive demolition.

At **Place Daviel**, named for the man who conducted the world's first cataract operation nearby in 1745, turn left onto Rue Caisserie. Follow this past Place de la Lenche, site of the Greek marketplace, and continue along Rue St-Laurent to

② **Église St-Laurent**. This pink sandstone church was built in Provençal-Romanesque style in the 12th century on the site of a temple dedicated to Apollo. It commands a fine view of the the nearby **Fort St-Jean**, raised in the 15th century when Marseille was a republic.

Now follow Avenue de la Tourette as it sweeps north to the grandiose, Neo-Byzantine

③ **Cathédrale Major**, constructed in the 19th century with profits from military conquest. It is also known as the 'new' cathedral, in contrast to the 11th-century ruins that stand, dwarfed, beside it.

Leave Place de la Major heading east, turn left into Rue Ste-Françoise, then veer right along Rue des Petit Puits, to arrive near

④ **Hospice de la Vieille Charité**. This workhouse, commissioned in 1670, has been restored to house two museums and temporary exhibitions. It is hard to imagine its now quiet arcades overflowing with destitute families.

Turn left out of the centre to reach Place Lorette, then walk down Rue Fontaine Neuve and then right into Rue du Panier. A left turn brings you to the pleasant **Place des Moulins**, named for the mills that once stood here.

Now walk down the Rue du Refuge and turn into Montée des Accoules. The **Préau des Accoules** at no.29 was once a Jesuit college. Descend the steps, past tall, narrow houses and walk back through Place Daviel and then along Grand' Rue, following the original Greek road. On the corner of this and Rue Bonneterie stands the 1535 **Hôtel de Cabre**, one of the city's oldest residences; it was the third of the trio unscathed in 1943, although it was later raised and rotated 90° to suit the new street plan.

Cross the busy Rue de la République and continue on, passing an excellent pâtisserie, to reach the edge of

⑤ **Jardin des Vestiges**, a collection of Greek and Roman remains jumbled amid plants favoured by the Greeks. This and the linked **Musée d'Histoire de Marseille** can be entered, somewhat absurdly, through the modern shopping complex, Centre Bourse.

Fort St-Jean and the cathedral

The original **Bourse** or stock exchange is now a maritime museum and you pass it on Rue de la Reine Elizabeth. Cross La Canebière and walk through Place du Général de Gaulle, where more digging a decade ago revealed a medieval suburb, along with 175 amphorae from the 5th or 4th century BC.

Turn right into Rue St-Saens, passing the neo-classical **Opéra**, opened in 1787. The interior was destroyed by a fire in 1919 and was rebuilt in art deco style. Walk through

⑥ **Place Thiars**, a lively restaurant-filled square. This lies in the heart of the former Arsenal that, in the 17th century held thousands of galley slaves in terrible conditions.

Leave the square and cut through to Rue Fort Notre-Dame and then turn into Rue Sainte, lined with soap factories during the 16th century. On the corner of this and Rue d'Enduome is Marseille's oldest bakery, the Four des Navettes: *navettes* are boat-shaped biscuits that celebrate the legendary arrival of

Vieille Charité

Mary Magdalene on the shores of Provence.

Walk through to Place St-Victor to visit ⑦ **Abbaye St-Victor**, built during the 5th century on the site of martyrs' graves. From the 11th century it was enlarged and fortified, as it stood outside the city walls: some of its walls are three metres thick.

Descend from the abbey and follow Quai de Rive Neuve along to the entrance of ⑧ **Fort St-Nicholas**, built by Louis XIV in 1660 to control the rebellious citizens. During the Revolution, townspeople took the chance to start dismantling this symbol of oppression but were ordered to cease by the National Assembly. The two sections of the fort were split in 1862 by the Boulevard Charles Livon.

Leave the high fort by its western end and cross the boulevard to enter the ⑨ **Jardin des Pharo**. This park, sitting high above the water, offers breathtaking views of the old port and is a popular spot for locals in the late afternoon. It contains Napoléon III's Palais des Pharo and a merry-go-round in tribute to victims of the sea. By now you might prefer to catch bus 83 back to the city centre.

OTHER EXCURSIONS

Notre-Dame de la Garde

For sweeping views over Marseille, make a visit to this Second Empire basilica, high atop a hill south of the old port. You might catch a bus (#60) there and stroll back down the hill.

Château d'If

This well preserved 16th-century prison was made famous by Dumas in *The Count of Monte Cristo*. Boats for the island of If leave regularly from the Quai des Belges.

A square in old Marseille

OPENING HOURS

Musée des Docks Romains	daily except Mon; 10-5 in winter; 11-6 in summer
Cathédrale Major	daily except Mon; 9-12, 2.30-5.30
Musée d'Histoire de Marseille	daily except Mon; 10-5 in winter; 11-6 in summer
Abbaye St-Victor	daily 8.30-6.30

N
Marseille
Massif de Marseilleveyre
Les Baumettes
Mont Puget
0 km 5 10
① ② ③ ④ ⑤ ⑥ ⑦ ⑧ ⑨ ⑩
Sormiou
Morgiou
Cassis
MER MÉDITERRANÉE

THE CALANQUES

This is a thrilling coastal walk for those who have no fear of heights and are nimble of foot. There is no accommodation en route (unless you're prepared to camp out), necessitating a detour mid-way to Les Baumettes for a bus to Marseille or Cassis for the night. On a positive note, this allows you to travel light.

Type: A 2-day walk - 33 km (20.5 miles)
Difficulty: medium-strenuous; steep inclines
Start: Callelongue (buses from Marseille)
Finish: Cassis (train to Marseille or Nice)
Map: IGN 1:15000 Les Calanques 3615
Timing: From July to mid-Sept, path access is restricted due to fire risk; these months are too hot for walking in any case!

DAY 1: CALLELONGUE to MORGIOU

GR waymarks lead over white limestone slabs, through occasional tunnels of green pine and past an azure Mediterranean dotted with islands.

Distance	12 km (7.5 miles) + 3 km to Les Baumettes
Time	6 hrs
Notes	take lunch, sunscreen and a hat!

From Castellane *métro* station in Marseille, take bus #19 to La Madrague de Montredon and then transfer to connecting bus #20 that shuttles along the coast road to Callelongue. This quaint fishing village, set in a narrow calanque, features a bar/restaurant.

Pick up GR 98-51 red-and-white waymarks on a corner to climb east out of the village. You are also following the black stripes of *Sentier de la Douane*, or Customs Path, a reminder that smugglers were active here. The path swings south, giving fine views back to Île Maire and ahead to Île Jaïre and, beyond it, Île Riou.

You soon head east, passing above the ① **Calanque de la Mounine**. Each time the path passes a calanque, you must cross the gully behind it; there's usually a footpad detouring down to the water. Tempting though it is, you won't have time to swim at them all!

The stony path stays close to the sea. At times, the limestone is quite slippery so take care. Pass ruins of 'le théâtre' and skirt behind shacks at Calanque de Marseilleveyre. After 600 m a footpad leads down through pines to ② **Calanque des Queyrons**, a lovely inlet and an ideal swimming spot.

The path traverses the slope, with minor changes in height, limestone formations gleaming white above. It heads inland near

Limestone pillars along the path

Morgiou harbour

Cirque des Walkyries, then climbs out of the gully and continues east for a scramble up to ③ **Col de Cortiou** and, soon after, the Col de Sormiou. Here the seascapes are exchanged briefly for a view up valley as far as the high-rise of Marseille. The road to Sormiou snakes below: this road is closed to traffic in summer.

Descend and cross the road, then follow a track across the back of the Sormiou valley to Col des Baumettes. The GR now descends below rocky spurs to the popular beach at ④ **Sormiou**, where there is a bar/restaurant. In 1991 a local diver, Henri Cosquer, found a cave decorated with prehistoric paintings deep in the cliffs of Sormiou, accessed by a passage some 36 m underwater. The depictions of land and sea animals, some only known previously from fossils, are well over 25,000 years old. While you can't see them, it's thrilling to know that Grotte Cosquer exists.

The GR path wends around to the left of the beach, past a tiny harbour (that was concealed until now) and around weekenders, before it starts a punishing climb, punctuated by a short level section. This brings you to le Carrefour, with panoramic views. The next section of the path is very dramatic, but if you are short of time, you could descend more quickly to Morgiou via footpath #5.

The GR path leads along the ridgeline of Crête de Morgiou, giving a view over Cap Morgiou. It descends sharply and forks left to traverse the wall of the calanque and drop into ⑤ **Morgiou**. This charming harbour has a bar where you can enjoy a well-earned drink.

When you're ready, follow the road up the valley and pick up path #6 that follows on or near the narrrow road. At the top of the valley, it shortcuts the road to climb straight ahead, over Col de Morgiou, and descend along Vallon des Escampons to meet the road again very close to a bus-stop. Bus #22 runs frequently, passing the prison of Baumettes, to reach the *métro* at Rond-Point du Prado in Marseille.

DAY 2: MORGIOU to CASSIS

From Morgiou, the coastline becomes more rugged, leading to the lovely calanques of Cassis, and finally to their picturesque port.

Distance	15 km (9.5 miles) + 3 km from Les Baumettes
Time	7 hrs
Notes	start early; take lunch

Return to Morgiou by catching bus #22 from Rond-Point du Prado to the Les Baumettes-Morgiou stop and then walking on path #6 to the Calanque de Morgiou.

The GR 98-51 path leaves the port east and climbs to the base of a rockface that it follows towards Cap Sugiton. Descend by ladder to the Calanque de Sugiton, after which the route climbs north and then leads below Falaise des Toits to climb a rock chimney. On the ridge above, you meet a track (where you could turn right and follow path #6 close to the sea and regain the GR at Cheminée du Diable).

The GR crosses the track and ascends around a spur, then climbs another level. The path now levels, winds around spurs then climbs to ⑥ **Col de la Candelle**, where it veers north and then southeast as it contours around the Vallon de la Candelle. It then skirts the Devil's Chimney or Cheminée du Diable and descends to the cliff-top of Falaise du Devenson. The views along this section are wonderful: southeast to the Cap Morgiou and then southwest to the pink Cap Canaille, beyond Cassis. A scramble downhill leads to a particularly good ⑦ **viewpoint** for the Aiguille de l'Eissadon.

Calanque d'En Vau

After a further descent, the GR leads up a narrow valley to the dry wells of Puits de l'Oule and then ascends to a cistern at Col de l'Oule. Follow a track downhill to the floor of the Vallon d'En Vau and then veer south along this gully, which becomes increasingly dramatic. Watch out for climbers on the numerous limestone pinnacles as you near the beach at

⑧ **Calanque d'En Vau**. It's a spectacular place, popular with tourists who can reach it by boat, and you should join them for a rest or swim here before the challenging next stage.

The GR route now climbs the steep wall on the eastern end of the beach. (If you don't feel up to this, return 750 m up the gorge and pick up path #8 that climbs the less exposed Portalet d'En Vau and descends to the next calanque.) The GR ascends very steeply to give amazing views over the long channel of the calanque.

Waymarks lead gently down the spur to the ⑨ **Calanque de Port-Pin**, which, although less dramatic than En Vau, catches more sun in the late afternoon.

The well-trodden path crosses the isthmus of Pointe Cacau and hugs the water's edge then passes the Carrières Solvay, where limestone was quarried until 1981. Parallel paths along this section converge at the end of the Calanque de Port-Miou, a harbour for small boats. Turn right onto the road and follow this uphill as it crosses the point of Port-Miou. Turn left into Traverse du Soleil and left again into Av. de l'Admiral Ganteaume which leads past Plage du Bestuoan and into the port area of

⑩ **Cassis**. This charming town, set between the limestone of the calanques and the pink sandstone cliffs of Cap Canaille, is justifiably popular. It has plenty of hotels and restaurants should you choose to stay a night and enjoy a boat ride to view the calanques from the sea. If you need a bus for Marseille, ask at the tourist office on the quay for times.

Calanque de Port-Pin and Cap Canaille >

Corsica

The island of Corsica, in French hands since 1769, adds a whole new dimension to France. Its Mediterranean flavour and strong cultural identity, hewn from a turbulent history of occupation by various powers, make it a fascinating place for the traveller. Despite surface similarities, Corsica is unlike mainland France, surprisingly and even confrontingly so. Outside its few cities, the population is sparse and infrastructure minimal. In the hinterland you will discover farmers battling a harsh terrain to make a subsistence living.

Of course, many people visit Corsica purely for its sun-drenched beaches, and they are well catered for in resorts along the coast. But Corsica is also a paradise for walkers, as the diversity of the island's environments and the number of footpaths criss-crossing the under-populated terrain offers a huge choice of adventures.

The hardiest walkers take on the challenge of France's toughest GR, the GR20, a high-level route that only passes through two remote villages in 15 days, but there are countless other routes for the less serious walker. Five other long-distance routes have been created, named with a confusing array of variations on *mare* (sea) and *monte* (mountains). We've created our own itinerary – one that combines sections of the *Mare e monti nord* and the *Mare a mare nord* – to include a taste of the dramatic western coastline with a crossing of Corsica's mountainous spine.

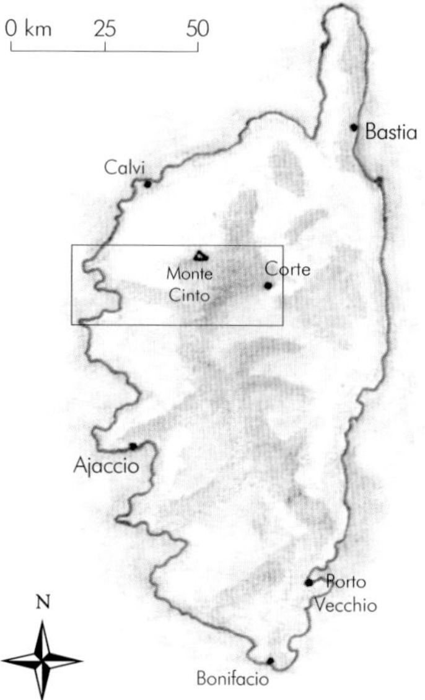

NOTES
Type: a 6-day walk - 84 km (52 miles)
Difficulty: medium-strenuous
Start: Girolata (boat from Calvi)
Finish: Corte (buses and rail line)
Tourist Office: La Citadelle, 20250 Corte
☎ 0495462670 Fax: 0495463405
E: corte.tourisme@wanadoo.fr
Park Office: www.parc-naturel-corse.com
Maps: IGN 1:25000 4150 & 4250
Best timing: May-Jun; Sep-Oct

Along the way you'll encounter a variety of landscapes: emerald-washed beaches, scrubby *maquis* (a mix of hardy shrubs), oak and chestnut woods, deep gorges and forests of beech and towering pines. You'll also visit a number of very Corsican settlements, starting with the fishing hamlet of Girolata, reached only by boat or by foot. Inland villages such as Serriera, Ota and Evisa offer a warm welcome to walkers. We also suggest stopovers in mountain gîtes and refuges, where you'll find *camaraderie* and a slightly less comfortable bed, before you reach the destination of Corte, a mountain town with a fascinating history and a strong Corsican identity.

Of course, you may wish to break up the itinerary differently to tailor it to your needs and preferences. Corsica's long hours of sunshine mean that you have plenty of hours in which to walk, but you might want to rest in the heat of the day. You should also carry plenty of water and snacks, as settlements are widely-spaced.

Cattle graze on the Bocca a l'Arinella >

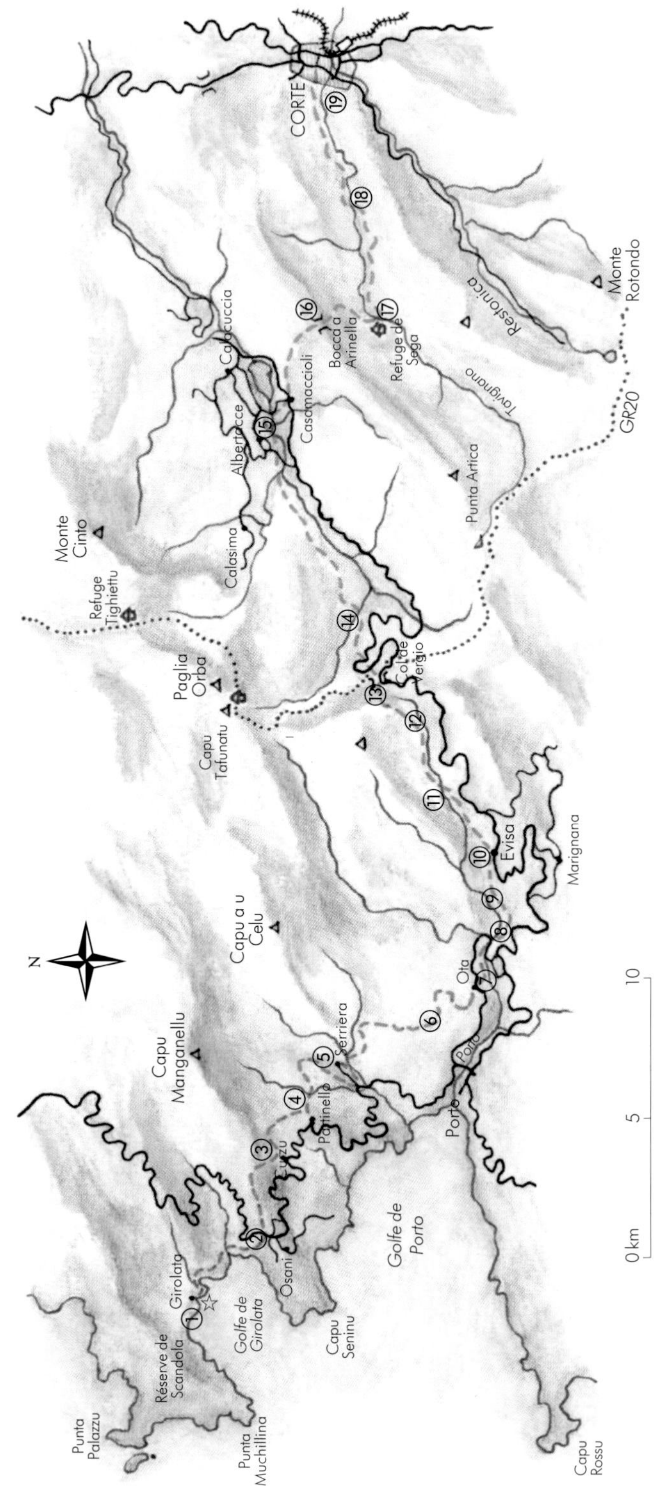

CORTE
Calacuccia
Albertacce
Casamaccioli
Bocca a Arinella
Refuge de Sega
Restonica
Monte Rotondo
Tavignano
GR20
Punta Artica
Monte Cinto
Refuge Tighiettu
Calasima
Paglia Orba
Capu Tafunatu
Col de Vergio
Evisa
Marignana
Capu a u Celu
N
Ota
Porto
Serriera
Partinello
Curzu
Capu Manganellu
Golfe de Porto
Osani
Girolata
Golfe de Girolata
Capu Seninu
Réserve de Scandola
Punta Palazzu
Punta Muchillina
Capu Rossu
0 km
5
10

Girolata, with Scandola beyond

DAY 1: GIROLATA to SERRIERA

At the isolated coastal village of Girolata, we take the 'Mare e monti nord' path to climb through maquis, with fine views back.

Distance	17.5 km (11 miles)
Time	8 hours 30
Notes	carry lunch and plenty of water

On the western coast of Corsica, south of Calvi, lies the nature reserve of Scandola, a wild area of cliffs and *calanques* or inlets, teeming with wildlife. Just outside the reserve is the hamlet of

① **Girolata**, with its Genoese fortress and two gîtes d'étape. To get there, you could take a boat trip from Calvi, Porto or Ajaccio and leave it at Girolata, having enjoyed the Scandola coastline. Alternatively, catch a bus from Porto and get dropped at Bocca a Croce, walking the first section below in reverse.

Leave Girolata along the beach and pick up the lower of the two variants of the *Mare e monti nord* path, which stays between the ridgeline and the coast. This route is sporadically marked with white splashes or red dots. You soon gain wonderful views back, over Girolata's castle, to the red rocks of Scandola.

Ascend on a footpath through open forest and scrub, passing *arbusier* shrubs that bear a cherry-sized fruit. At a cairn just above the beach of **Cala di Tuara** you join the main path, waymarked with an orange stripe. Cross the beach and follow the orange stripes to climb steeply on a clear, if somewhat eroded, path. Not long after you pass a trickling spring (top up your water!), you gain the road at

② **Bocca a Croce**, where a 10-minute detour along a signed footpath leads to an orientation table offering 360-degree views.

Return to the road and turn left to pick up a broad track climbing from across the road. This soon becomes a footpath which ascends steeply

< Arbusier fruit

A doorway in Curzu

to pass a communications tower. Keep ascending and take a much needed rest at the top of the spur. Follow the ridge line and, some 40 minutes further on, you reach the junction of your variant with the main track. The path left leads up to **Capu di Curzu** and another orientation table; your route veers right to descend and skirt above the village of

③ **Curzu**. Lower down in the village is a gîte d'étape, but little else. Continue on the path, signed to Partinello and Serriera. After 2.5 km, the footpath descends the hill of Sant'Angelu to meet a broader track where you have the option of a short-cut (3.25 km) to lower Serriera via Partinello (where there's a hotel); this is a good option when rivers are swollen or there's a risk of forest fire. The *Mare e monti nord*, however, turns left and soon leaves the track. The path descends for quite a distance to reach a trickling stream which then joins the

④ **Ruisseau de Vetricella**. Ford this and, on the other bank, ascend steeply to a ridge. Just below the top, the path branches right and leads downhill on a well-graded mule path. The *Mare e monti nord* has been rerouted to zigzag down the hillside to gain

⑤ **Serriera**. In the centre of the village are a bar and store selling basic provisions; some way down hill on the D524 are the gîte d'étape and a hotel with a restaurant.

DAY 2: SERRIERA to OTA

Today involves a steady climb of some 830 m to Capu San Petru and a descent via a porphyry ravine to the lovely perched village of Ota.

Distance	11 km (7 miles)
Time	6 hours
Notes	carry lunch and plenty of water

In the centre of Serriera, take the path below the church and walk down to cross the Santa Maria stream on a wooden footbridge. Climb briefly then turn left onto an unpaved forest road and follow this east for almost 2 km. At a sharp bend, by a rock daubed with an orange arrow, fork right up onto a rocky footpath, signed to Ota.

After over an hour of unrelenting uphill that includes a series of switchbacks, reach a false summit, at 755 m, where you can rest and enjoy the view over Serriera. After this, the path levels, undulates and then heads through pleasant forest before the final switchback assault on the main summit. This effort brings

The village of Ota

Ponte Vecchiu

you to the pass of **Bocca am Petru** where, by detouring right onto a level grassy path, you soon reach

⑥ **Capu San Petru**, at 914 m. The views take in the Gulf of Porto and, if the sun isn't too fierce, rocks around the ancient junipers offer a fine lunch spot.

Return to the shady path junction and continue on; the path stays level through woods of chestnut and pine for some 20 minutes. After passing to the left of a hut for chestnut drying, you reach the source of the Vitrone where a trickle of water emerges from a spring. The path now veers SW and leads you in switchbacks steeply down the southern side of a ravine, with a dramatic red porphyry rockface opposite. You now cross the ravine twice and, on the second occasion, tucked off the track by the stream is a shady grove where you can cool down.

From here, the path negotiates a route between rock outcrops, and then contours a series of spurs to gain an enticing view of your destination, nestled on the hillside with the imposing rock of Capu d'Ota perched high above. The lovely mountain village of

⑦ **Ota** offers a shop and a choice of two gîtes d'étape, gardens of citrus and bougainvillea and balconies set high above the Porto river.

DAY 3: OTA to COL de VERGIO

A magical day, starting with the Spelunca gorges, a climb to Evisa where we change course to follow the 'Mare a mare nord', via the pools of Aïtone, to cross the Col de Vergio.

Distance	19 km (12 miles)
Time	8 hours
Notes	food available midway

The orange waymarked footpath leaves Ota by the lower road behind the church; it becomes an old mule track that descends between road and river to cross the restored

⑧ **Ponte Vecchiu**, a particularly graceful 15th-century bridge built by the Genoese. The path continues along the other bank, rising to cross the road at the modern bridge at the confluence of the Lonca and Aïtone rivers, and then follows the latter upstream into the **Gorges de Spelunca**. About 1.5 km on, in a shady side gully, cross the Tavulella on the

⑨ **Pont de Zaglia**, another Genoese bridge. On a hot day, this is a wonderful place for a refreshing dip.

The footpath now climbs more steeply, via a series of beautifully engineered switchbacks, past a spring and up through ilex and then pines. You are rewarded with glimpses back over the gorges before you gain the road, which you then follow uphill for ten minutes into

⑩ **Evisa**. This relatively bustling town offers a gîte d'étape, hotel accommodation, several bars and a small supermarket.

At Evisa, our route leaves the *Mare e monti nord* path and picks up that of the *Mare a mare nord*. Opposite the bar/tabac, turn left into an alley signed to Col de Vergio to pass a *sechoir*, a hut for drying chestnuts. Follow the path known as 'Way of the Chestnuts' as it undulates through a beautiful chestnut plantation inhabited by roaming pigs.

< The view southwest from near Evisa

Just over 2 km from Evisa, the path touches the D84 road where a short detour to a lookout provides a stunning view down the gorges of the Aïtone river. Follow the road a short distance and then fork off left on a descending forest path; it soon forks again and you take the left fork gently downhill. Soon after, detour off the path for 50 m, down concrete steps, to reach the lovely

⑪ **Piscine d'Aïtone**, a series of natural pools on rock shelves. A recent sign advises against swimming here, but the temptation may be hard to resist. Treading carefully, detour along the left bank below the pools to view the Cascade de la Valla Scarpa.

Take care when leaving the pools, as forestry work has disturbed the waymarking (we found ourselves walking through the holiday village on an old route). The correct route crosses a tributary and then the Aïtone stream to follow it upstream (with it on your right) with orange waymarks to guide you. The path switches back to climb around an outcrop and then contours several gullies before dropping back to the stream at a footbridge. Stay on the same bank and follow the orange waymarks uphill on a broad, stony track.

A *sechoir* in Evisa

After a short, steep climb, reach a concrete road where you turn right downhill to cross the Casterica stream on the

⑫ **Pont de Casterica**, where a sign 'Col de Vergio - 1 hr' points ahead. Immediately, you branch left onto a level forest track and then fork left over a rocky slope onto a gravel path uphill. This forest track stays level through beautiful beech forest, ascends a little, then levels through more beech and pine trees.

At a small reservoir, fork up left, following orange waymarks and cairns on a steep footpad. After a long climb, the path veers right and levels out to reach the D84 at the

⑬ **Col de Vergio**, where a giant statue marks the traditional border between Haute-Corse and Corse-du-Sud. The hôtel/gîte of Castel di Vergio is 1.5 km down the D84 over the pass.

DAY 4: COL de VERGIO to REFUGE de la SEGA

An easy descent into the Golo valley is followed by a demanding climb to cross into the next valley where the Refuge de la Sega nestles in a magnificent river setting.

Distance	23.5 km (14.5 miles)
Time	8 hours
Notes	food available midway

< Piscine d'Aïtone

Calacuccia & snowcapped Monte Cinto

From the hôtel/gîte, take the D84 road back up towards Col de Vergio and, after 200 m or so, fork right at a sign to Refuge Ciuttulu di i Mori and follow the GR20 path (marked red-and-white) down through a forest of Lariccio pines. After 20 minutes, you reach a path junction. * For a taste of the demanding GR20 you could diverge at this point; see the notes at the end of this chapter.

Otherwise, turn right to rejoin the route of the *Mare a mare nord* that leads downhill to cross the winding D84 twice and pass the Ciattarinu military camp. Leave the road below the camp on a track that becomes a footpath, leading down through the forest of Valdu Niellu. Turn left onto a forest track and cross the Golo river on the

⑭ **Pont San Rimeriu** to reach the Bergerie de Tillerga; a *bergerie* is a shepherd's hut, used in summer months. The waymarked path soon climbs a little, crosses the plateau of Vinacce, and then contours the hillside, crossing several streams, including the Castellu and the Alzetu. Some 1.5 km from the latter, a track comes in from the left (from the village of Calasima) and you continue NE to cross a saddle and descend steeply to cross the Viru on the Pont de Muricciolu by a mill. At the oratory, the route veers right and contours to reach the road at the edge of

⑮ **Albertacce**; there is a bar and a gîte d'étape should you wish to linger here. Across the road, the path continues down to skirt the head of the dammed Calacuccia lake and down to the D218 road. Here, the waymarks direct you to turn right to the village of **Casamaccioli**, where there is a gîte d'étape. The *Mare a mare nord* continues beyond the village, forking right off the D218b road to pass the Funtana d'Erbaghiolo and then cross the Lavertacce stream. It then starts to climb, crossing a winding road several times. Keep uphill, following signs to Refuge Sega. The climb becomes increasingly steep, but you gain increasingly wonderful views looking back over the lake and to the mountains beyond.

The footpath climbs in a series of switchbacks, passes between rocky outcrops, and eventually gains the high ground of the

⑯ **Bocca a l'Arinella** where you can recover and enjoy the inspiring view back. Directly NW across the lake is the peak of Monte Cinto, Corsica's highest at 2706 m. To its left are the spiky fingers of Cinque Frati, sometimes called Cinq Moines or 'five monks'. Left of this is the distinctive peak of the Paglia Orba, Corsica's third highest mountain at 2525 m.

Descend briefly on the other side of the pass to a memorial by the road. Turn left and soon follow the sign to Refuge Sega on a path to the right that descends past the Bergerie de Boniacce and then down through pasture, offering a superb view of the Tavignano valley below. The path drops through a delightful woodland and crosses a small stream by a pretty cascade.

It levels through a chestnut grove and then ascends gently upstream for 5 minutes to reach the modern and inviting

⑰ **Refuge de la Sega** in a spectacular position on the bank of the Tavignano river.

The Tavignano valley

DAY 5: REFUGE de la SEGA to CORTE

An easy but thrilling walk along the remote Tavignano gorges brings you to the historic bastion of Corte.

Distance	13 km (8 miles)
Time	5 hours
Notes	carry lunch supplies

From the refuge, cross the wooden footbridge and walk down the right bank. A beautifully graded footpath leads you through forest of magnificent Lariccio pines with the river tumbling along below you. After 40 minutes or so the scenery opens up and, after an hour, you reach a spur from where you glimpse a dramatic view of Corte, way down valley.

Corte's Citadelle

Cross the gully of the Castagnolu stream and gain views back across the Tavignano valley of Fughiccia and, later on, of Capo Aleri. A switchback soon after offers good views both up and down valley, making a good rest point.

The path becomes steeper as you make a switchback descent to cross the recently rebuilt ⑱ **suspension footbridge**, high above the river. On the other side, the path undulates around several side gullies, now through *maquis* vegetation. As you near Corte, you can see its citadel on this side of the town, but you also gain good views of the rolling hills beyond.

Finally, the mule track descends to the western outskirts of the town and, by following the Rue Saint-Joseph and descending Rampe Ste-Croix, you very soon find yourself in the main street of

⑲ **Corte**. Founded in 1419, Corte is the only fortified town in central Corsica. It was the scene of fierce fighting during battles against

A street scene in Corte

the Genoese and it was Pascal Paoli's capital when he founded the first independent Corsican government in 1755. In 1765, Corsica's only university was established and its students inject a lively, untouristy feel to the town. When the French took possession of Corsica in 1793, they made Corte a garrison town, but it remains a stronghold of Corsican culture.

The small town is dominated by the Citadelle and château, built in 1419 and extended by the French in the 18th and 19th centuries. Inside the ramparts is a museum of all things Corsican.

LONG DISTANCE STAGES

km	time	location	acc
		Girolata	G
10	5h30	Curzu	G
3	1h+	Partinello	H
4.5	2h00	Serriera	G, H
11	6h00	Ota	G
7	3h00	Evisa	G, H
12	5h00	Castellu di Vergio	G-H
13	3h00	Albertacce	G
3	1h00	Casamaccioli	G
7.5	4h00	Refuge de la Sega	R
13	5h00	Corte	G, H

OTHER WALKS IN THE REGION

A Taste of the GR20

The GR20 is a very challenging route that runs roughly north to south along the mountainous spine of Corsica. It involves 15 or so days of strenuous walking and those who undertake it need to carry food supplies for several days at a time, a sleeping bag and, in case the mountain refuges are full, a tent. If this sounds a little beyond your level of endurance, you might like to sample a section of the GR20 mid-way along the walk outlined in this chapter. This two-day route takes you up the pretty Vallée du Golo and over a pass to the Refuge de Tighiettu, then back to rejoin the route at Albertacce, essentailly adding a day to the intinerary. The terrain and altitudes reached make this section unsuitable in bad weather or in winter.

DAY 1: From the hôtel/gîte at Castel de Vergio (see Day 4), follow the GR20, marked with red-and-white stripes, to the point marked *. From here, continue straight ahead on the GR20 through the beech forest of Valdu Niellu to another junction; keep straight on to the **Bergeries de Radule**. Below the huts is a delightful cascade, worth a short diversion.

Below Bocca di Foggiale on the GR20

Peaks high in the Restonica valley

From here the GR20 climbs alongside the Golo river on an ancient drove route. By the ruined Bergeries de Tula, the path veers left and climbs steeply along the slopes of the Paglia Orba to gain the Refuge de Ciuttulu di i Mori (1991 m) offering a bunk. The route descends gently to a dramatic pass, **Bocca di Foggiale**, where you sight the distinctive profile of Cinque Frati, and further away, the lake of Calacuccia. The route now descends very steeply over rocks and then veers north to contour the slope, crossing streams as you walk through pine forest. At the **Bergeries de Ballone** (serving meals when open in summer), the valley starts to narrow as you ascend beside the Stranciacone stream. The route crosses it and climbs steeply on rough ground to reach **Refuge Tighiuttu**, where you can get a basic meal and a bunk bed. Blankets are not supplied; you'll need warm sleepwear. *Distance of 14 km; allow 8 hours.*

DAY 2: Those who are very fit, might climb the 535 m behind the refuge to Bocca Minuta, for a look into the dramatic **Cirque de la Solitude**, a highlight of the whole GR20. Otherwise, return downhill on the GR20 to the Bergeries de Ballone. Here, cross the stream (which can become a torrent after heavy rain) and pick up a track that follows above the other bank, contouring the base of the jagged Cinque Frati. This becomes a road, passing a monument to firefighters who died in 1979. Past this is **Calasima** (Corsica's highest village at 1100 m) where there's a bar but little more. Some 5 km down the winding D318 road is **Albertacce**, where you can rejoin the *Mare a mare nord* route. *Distance of 13 km; allow 5 hours.*

La Vallée de la Restonica

This spectacular river valley runs parallel to that of the Tavignano, however this one is accessible by a narrow, winding road. In summer AC minibuses (☏ 04 95460212) run up the valley from Corte; out of season a taxi or hire car is your only official option. After a stunning drive, a carpark by the Bergeries de Grotelle (1370 m), at the end of the road, is the starting point of an excellent hike upstream.

From the carpark, the marked path follows the right bank of the Restonica. At a river crossing, you have the option of staying on the same bank for a more difficult ascent, but most cross to the left bank and climb, after an hour, to **Lac di Melu** at 1711 m.

A narrow path then skirts the northern edge of the lake and climbs amongst rocky spurs to the exquisite **Lac di Capitellu**, at 1930 m, reached after a further 45 minutes. At this point, you are very close to the route of the GR20 as it runs along the high ground. Take care on the descent as it can prove slippery. *Allow 4 hours return from Bergerie de Grotelle.*

GR paths are waymarked with a red-and-white parallel stripe. Crossed stripes indicate that you are going the wrong way.

GRANDES RANDONNÉES

Grandes Randonnées, created and maintained by the FFRP, criss-cross the whole of France. IGN publish an excellent map of France (#903) that indicates the routes of all current GR paths. Here is a list of the sections that we made use of for walks in this book.

No.	NAME	SECTION COVERED	CHAPTER
GR2	*Sentier de la Seine*	Pont de l'Arche to Giverny	Seine Valley
GR3	*Sentier de la Loire*	Angers to Chinon	Loire Valley
GR4	*Sentier Méditerranée-Océan*	Entrevaux to Moustiers Puy de Sancy circuit	Gorges du Verdon Monts-Dore
GR5	*Sentier Hollande-Méditerranée*	C.de Calvaire to Grand Ballon	Alsace & Vosges
GR5/55	*Tour de Vanoise*	L'Orgère to L'Arpont	The Vanoise
GR6	*Sentier Alpes-Océan*	Gordes to Fontaine-de-Vaucluse	The Luberon
GR10	*Sentier des Pyrénées*	Cauterets to Gavarnie	Pyrénées
GR20	*Sentier de la Corse*	Col de Vergio to Rif Tighiettu	Corsica
GR34	*Tour de Bretagne*	Cancale to Erquy	Coast of Brittany
GR46/652	-	Martel to Rocamadour	The Dordogne
GR52	*Tour du Mercantour*	Le Boréon to La Bollène-Vésubie	The Mercantour
GR65	*Sentier de St-Jacques-de-Compostelle*	Aumont-Aubrac to Conques Le Puy to Aumont-Aubrac	A Pilgrimage A Pilgrimage (end)
GR70	*Sentier Robert Louis Stevenson*	La Bastide-Puylaurent to Florac	The Cévennes
GR91	-	St-Nizier to Villard-de-Lans	Grenoble & Vercors
GR98	-	Marseille to Cassis	Marseille/Calanques

OTHER WALKING AREAS

France has many other country areas perfect for walking. Here are a few of them.

AROUND PARIS

There is good day-walking in the nearby forests that were once the hunting grounds of the Bourbon kings: Fontainebleau, Chantilly, Ermenonville, Halatte and Rambouillet. More good walking is to be had in the river valleys of the Chevreuse (near Cernay's ruined abbey) and the Marne (among vineyards). The GR1, the *Tour de l'Île-de-France*, encircles Paris.

BURGUNDY

Great food and wine combined with France's finest Romanesque architecture. An excellent three-day itinerary would leave from the walled hilltown of Avalon on the GR13 through the pilgrimage centre of Vezelay with its magnificent basilica. From here, walk north on the GR13 to Auxerre, rated by some as the prettiest town in France.

PARC NATIONAL DES ECRINS

This incorporates a high Alpine massif; the peak of Barre des Ecrins is at 4102 m. The park holds more than 2000 species of Alpine wildflowers and much wildlife, including ibex. The villages of La Bérade and La Grave are both good bases for day-walking. There is an excellent long-distance circular walk around the massif, the 183-km *Tour de l'Oisans*.

PARC NATUREL DU QUEYRAS

This is a smaller park than the Ecrins to its west; it includes some of the Franco-Italian border and most of its mountains range between 2000 and 3000 m in height. With three hundred sunny days per year, there is fine, uncrowded ridge and valley walking to be enjoyed. The best centres for day-walking are Saint-Véran, Guillestre (just outside the park), Aiguilles and Abriès. The GR58, *Tour du Queyras*, encircles the park.

CHAMONIX – ARVE VALLEY

This is a hugely popular Alpine walking destination, full of classic walks. It has hundreds of kilometres of waymarked trails and an excellent network of chairlifts. Chamonix is surrounded by magnificent mountains: Mont Blanc, the Grandes Jorasses and the Aiguilles Rouges, to name just three massifs. The *Grand Balcons Sud* and *Nord* are both superb balcony walks. There are walks to mountain tarns and glaciers as well as easy valley walking. The *Tour du Mont Blanc* is a classic challenge.

THE ARDÈCHE

Lying between the Rhône and the source of the Loire, the Ardèche is a wild area providing excellent walking off the beaten track. The Monts du Vivarais allow for wonderful, open hiking above the 1000-m mark. Alternatively, the gorges of the Ardèche river are among France's most spectacular. Good weather and the beauty of the landscape, particularly around the infant Loire, are both inducements to discover this area. Liamastre is a good centre for day-walking and several GRs pass through the region for long-distance walking.

NORMANDY'S CÔTE d'ALBÂTRE

In Haute Normandie, the chalk cliff coastline between Dieppe and Etrêtat, provides some spectacular walking along the GR21. The cliffs near Etrêtat are remarkable. Here are natural arches, *aiguilles* (rock spires or needles) and cliffs over 100 metres high, all viewed from dramatic clifftop paths.

INLAND BRITTANY

Brittany's interior, the Argoat (or 'country of wood'), is far less visited than its coastline. In the northeast, the magnificent fortresses of Vitré and Fougères must be seen. Fougères makes an excellent walking base, along with Liffré. To the west, the forest of Paimpont, once known as Brocéliande, is the place of Arthurian legend where Merlin's stone can be found. In the southern Morbihan department, the Nantes-Brest canal provides excellent towpath walking.

FURTHER READING

GENERAL WALKING BOOKS

The Independent Walker's Guide to France by Frank W. Booth (short walks)
Walking in France by Sandra Bardwell et al (more demanding walks)
Walking in France by Rob Hunter (an overview of walking areas and GRs; now out of print)

REGIONAL WALKING BOOKS

Topo guides by FFRP; each guide provides detailed notes on a GR (or the various PRs in a region) and includes topographic maps.
Footpaths of Europe series of selected topo-guides translated into English, published by Robertson McCarta but sadly out of print.
Walking in the French Gorges by Alan Castle
Walks in Volcano Country by Alan Castle
Walks & Climbs in the Pyrenees by Kev Reynolds
The Way of St James: GR65 by Hal Bishop
Tour of Mont Blanc by Andrew Harper
100 Hikes in the Alps by Ira Spring & Harvey Edwards (not just French Alps)

RELATED TOPICS

Wild France edited by Douglas Botting
Michelin Green Guides

USEFUL CONTACTS

La Maison de France (Tourist Office)
www.franceguide.com

Australia
25 Bligh St, Level 13, Sydney NSW 2000
☏ 02 92315244 Fax: 02 92218682
E: info.au@franceguide.com

Canada
1981 Ave McGill College, Montreal H3A 2W9
☏ 514 2882026 Fax: 514 8454868
E: canada@franceguide.com

Great Britain
178 Piccadilly, London W1J 9AL
☏ 09068 244123 (60p/min) Fax: 020 74936594
E: info.uk@franceguide.com

USA
444 Madison Avenue, New York NY 10022
☏ 410 2868310 Fax: 212 8387855
E: info.us@franceguide.com

FRENCH WALKING CLUB (FFRP)
14 Rue Riquet, 75019 Paris
☏ 0144899393; Fax: 0140358567
www.ffrp.asso.fr

CLUB ALPIN FRANÇAIS (CAF)
24 Ave de la Laumière, 75019 Paris
☏ 0153728700; Fax: 0142035560
www.clubalpin.com

MAP SUPPLIERS
Espace IGN, 107 Rue de la Boetie, Paris
☏ 0143988000; Fax: 0143988511
www.ign.fr

Au Vieux Campeur, 2 Rue de Latran, Paris
☏ 0153104848; Fax: 0146341416
www.auvieuxcampeur.fr

Internet map suppliers:
www.stanfords.co.uk
www.mapworld.net.au
www.itmb.com
www.complete.traveller.com

< The authors

A path in the Lot valley >

GLOSSARY

FRENCH	ENGLISH
abbaye	abbey
abri	shelter
aiguille	needle (of rock)
alimentation	grocery
arête	narrow ridge
auberge	inn or hotel
" de jeunesse	youth hostel
balade	short walk
balise	waymark
bas	low
barrage	dam
bastide	fortified town
belvédère	viewpoint
bergerie	shepherd's hut
blockhaus	military hut
bois	woods
borie	stone shelter
boucle	loop
boulangerie	bakery
bouquetin	ibex
buron	shepherd's hut
CAF	Club Alpin Français
calanque	narrow inlet
calvaire	crucifix, cross
cap	headland
cascade	waterfall
cathédrale	cathedral
car	coach
carrefour	crossroads
carte	map; menu
causse	limestone plateau
cave	wine cellar
chambre d'hôte	bed-&-breakfast
chapelle	chapel
charcuterie	delicatessen
château	mansion, castle
château d'eau	water tower
château fort	fortified castle
chemin	path
cime	mountain peak
cirque	corrie
clôitre	cloister
col	mountain pass
combe	wooded gully
commune	district
couloir	ravine
corniche	cliff road
côte	coast
cour	courtyard
crête	narrow ridge
demi-pension	half board
departément	administrative sub-region
doline	dip, depression
donjon	castle keep
draille	sheep road
eau potable	drinkable water
éboulis	scree
église	church
épicerie	small grocery
étang	pond
falaise	cliff
fermé(e)	closed
ferme-auberge	farm-inn
FFRP	French walking federation
fontaine	fountain, spring
fôret	forest
gare	rail station
gare routière	bus station
gîte d'étape	walkers' hostel
grande randonnée	long-distance path
GR	see above
GRP	long circuit path
grotte	cave
hameau	hamlet
haut (e)	high
haute chaume	high pasture
hôtel	mansion or hotel
hôtel de ville	town hall
hôtel particulier	private mansion
hourquette	steep pass
île	island
jas	sheep pen
jardin	garden
lac	lake
mairie	town hall
maison	house
maison du parc	park office
maquis	scrub
marché	market
mas	farmhouses
menu	fixed-price meal
moulin à vent	windmill
névé	frozen snow
ouvert(e)	open
palais	palace
pâtisserie	cake shop
phare	lighthouse
piste	ski trail or slope
plage	beach
pont	bridge
porte	gateway
PR	short walk
presqu'île	peninsula
puits	well for water
puy	volcanic plug
refuge	mountain hostel
rivière	river
rue	street
ruisseau	stream
sentier	path
SNCF	rail system
supermarché	supermarket
syndicat d'initiative	tourist office
téléphérique	cable car
télésiège	chair lift
torrent	river
vallée	valley
vieux ville	historic centre
ville	town

DIRECTIONS

à droite	turn right
à l'est	east
à l'ouest	west
à gauche	turn left
au nord	north
au sud	south
derrière	behind
devant	in front of
direction	direction
loin d'ici	far away
près d'ici	near here
tout droit	straight on

ASKING FOR HELP

au secours!	help!
pharmacie	chemist
médecin	doctor
urgence	emergency
trousse	first aid kit
blessure	wounded
carte	map
à pied	on foot
le temps	weather
mauvais temps	bad weather
la neige	snow

CONVERTING DISTANCES

1 metre	1.09 yards
1 metre	3.28 feet
1 kilometre	0.621 miles

INDEX

INDEX...